Writings of
German Composers

The German Library: Volume 51

Volkmar Sander, General Editor

WRITINGS OF GERMAN COMPOSERS

Edited by Jost Hermand
and James Steakley

CONTINUUM · NEW YORK

1984

The Continuum Publishing Company
370 Lexington Avenue, New York, NY 10017

Library of Congress Cataloging in Publication Data

Main entry under title:

Writings of German composers.

(The German library ; v. 51)
1. Musicians as authors. 2. Composers—Germany.
3. Composers—Austria. I. Hermand, Jost. II. Steakley,
James D.
ML90.W75 1984   780   84-16999
ISBN 0-8264-0292-5
ISBN 0-8264-0293-3 (pbk.)

Contents

Contents · vii

viii · *Contents*

Contents · ix

Introduction

Many people think that we should not read about music but simply listen to it. For them, music—in contrast to all the other arts—has an immediacy that speaks directly to our innermost feelings. The creation of literature and painting, so we are frequently told, is based primarily on a thorough knowledge of events and facts of the outer world as manifested in history, society, and nature. Music, on the other hand, is supposed to originate in the realm of the emotions and find expression in melodies capable of stirring us on a much deeper level than any merely intellectual or visual impression.

Since the days of pagan antiquity, there have been legends about especially gifted composers, such as the singer Orpheus, able to move not only men and women but also animals and even the inorganic world of stones. During the Middle Ages, this concept of the power of music was transformed and elevated into the celestial realm of God's creation. Various medieval theoreticians came to regard music as an almost transcendental force, emanating from the constant movement of those crystalline spheres that—according to Ptolemy—create the spherical sound of perfect harmony, based on the cosmic rules of their creator. There were also angels, praising in endless seraphic song the wonderful work of God, who had created the world so perfectly. Music thus played a central part in the religious ceremonies of the Middle Ages, from Gregorian chant up to the works of the Flemish masters and the masses of Palestrina. Because of its transcendentalism, music was considered by some the highest of all the arts.

At the onset of the Renaissance and with its turn to the here and now, to the sufferings and glory of humankind, the concept of the celestial power of music became increasingly outmoded. What had been divine became quite worldly in the course of the following centuries. But other forces were at work too, and not just in the realm of sacred music, which continued within the older traditions. Even among composers of secular music, a new longing developed for a music higher, more absolute, more heavenly, than all the courtly pomp and circumstance connected with creating operas, ballets, orchestral suites, fireworks- and water-music. Especially in the field of bourgeois music in the second half of the eighteenth century, from so-called Sentimentalism up to Romanticism, music was once more elevated into the pietistic, the soulful, the absolute. This is particularly true of those composers who, living in the highly fragmented society of Germany, were not so closely allied with a broad bourgeois audience as their counterparts in France or England. For the Germans, soulfulness—in an emotional, subjective sense of the word—came to occupy the center of musical theory. Thus it is scarcely surprising that some of the theoreticians of Sentimentalism and Romanticism once again regarded music as the most perfect example of the sublime, of the deepest emotional forces. Only the representatives of the German Enlightenment, who were a minority in any case, spoke out in favor of the "realistic" character of literature and painting, and therefore tended to downgrade music—especially instrumental music—as something useless, incapable of bringing about any betterment of the world. Meanwhile, those theoreticians who sided with the Sentimental, Storm and Stress, and Romantic movements not only upgraded the status of music but again elevated it to the highest form of artistically creative expression. They regarded music as the one and only art that can dispense with any clearly recognizable content, any purpose, any message at all, because music has the capacity—through its harmonious and melodic sounds—to ennoble people more profoundly than the message of any novel or painting.

Since that time, Germany has been home to the Romantic cliché that music is a form of art surpassing reason, created in the innermost depths of the soul, expressing the otherwise unspeakable, that it is the voice of the soul, the voice of the universe, and thus ultimately the voice of a divine power. For many people who have embraced such concepts as these down to the present day, music remains the highest expression of the ineffable, which should not be mediated or watered down by unnecessary explanations. They may therefore scorn any attempt to enhance musical appreciation through lectures or books, through radio announcements or record jacket blurbs and the like. As something that comes from the heart and should speak only to the heart, music does not need any verbal transmission. For these people, music is still something authentically subjective and needs to be preserved and defended against all the gibberish of academic rationalizations. Granted: many of the announcements we hear on the radio and many of the blurbs we read on record jackets are indeed gibberish of the worst sort. But that does not mean that any explanation of music has to be—by its very nature—superficial, dry, and meaningless. There is an abundance of incisive commentary that is extremely helpful for a deeper understanding not only of the formal aspects of music but also of the semiotics of the musical idiom itself, and it enables a careful listener to gain a deepened insight into the inner workings of musical pieces and their very specific content.

Among the written texts that are helpful in this manner, those written by composers themselves deserve a very special place. This is not because these texts necessarily offer the most authentic insight into the music of their creators but because they help us understand the political, social, financial, aesthetic, and personal milieus in which these composers lived and created their music. By knowing more about these facts, our response to the music will be not diminished but elevated to a higher level of understanding. The key element is not the biographical information we glean from these texts, or what composers thought about each other. These texts can help us to see their authors as men—and they are all men—of their times, reacting in very different manners to the ever-changing political, social, and economic conditions of the eras they lived through.

And this is reflected in their music as well. If we see Schütz, Bach, and Händel as servants of their respective princes and kings, Mozart and Beethoven as rebellious citoyens of the new Enlightened age, Schumann and Mendelssohn as representatives of the Romantic internalization brought about by the political and economic stagnation of the German middle class, Mahler and Strauss as members of the apolitical secessionist movement around 1900, Weill and Krenek as composers of the Weimar Republic, and Henze and Stockhausen as spokesmen of two different schools of thought in today's Federal Republic of Germany—only then are we able to apprehend their music in the right spirit.* This sort of historical relativizing does not in any way detract from their greatness. On the contrary, by seeing these composers as struggling human beings— sometimes humiliated, sometimes victorious—a new dimension is added to their music. Beyond its emotional quality and artistic craftsmanship, it presents itself to historically informed listeners as a mirror of its time, reflecting not only the political and intellectual battles but also the emotional conflicts of a given era.

The music of these composers, who were all quite aware of what was going on in the fields of politics and ideas, is therefore a product of a specific time, not only in style, in genre, in the special forms of phrasing or embellishment, but also in content. Just as there is a history of ideas, there is also a history of feelings, and music is one of the finest seismographs registering changes in the emotional climate of a certain period. It responds almost instantly to new inner conflicts brought about by changes in the basis or superstructure of any society. In the same way that representative forms (such as the fugue, the sonata, the rhapsody) change from one period to another, so too the inner structure of realistically portrayed feeling takes on the form of new intonations, corresponding to the sounds of the progressive or reactionary forces in history. There is nothing static, eternal, or archetypal in any great music, for even one's "innermost feelings" do not originate in a psychic vacuum; they are part and parcel of a very specific political, social, and intellectual milieu that influences both the creative act of composing and the receptive act on the side of the audience. Far from existing in a vacuum, music—by virtue of its creation, performance, and appreciation—is always deeply embedded in the social situation.

German composers who worked for such institutions as the church or the courts never put this close interrelationship in question. The need to take a stand within this tangled network of political and social relationships is something that did not arise until about the middle of the eighteenth century, with the advent of the Enlightenment. Even composers, who in preceding centuries had worked more like craftsmen, now had to be intellectuals, to take a position, to side with certain movements or ideologies, and to

---

* All of the aforementioned are included in this volume except Karlheinz Stockhausen who declined permission to anthologize his writings.

reflect their stance in their works by using intonations that were in tune with the progressive or regressive forces of their times. Abstract or nonrepresentational music does not exist; there is only program music, if we stretch this term to its outermost limits. To compose the *Eroica,* Beethoven had to be a Jacobin and an admirer of the young rebellious Napoleon. To express his sufferings the way he did, Schubert had to live under the tremendous restrictions of the Metternich regime. To write a work of class compromise such as *Die Meistersinger von Nürnberg,* Wagner had to be a disillusioned Forty-Eighter. To become a propagator of totally hermetic and esoteric music, Schönberg had to be an Austrian secessionist and a monarchist. These composers were no longer just "products of their times," as had been many of the older composers. They had to take a stand on the political and social conflicts of their times—and most did not in the least hesitate to do so.

The more we know about these composers, the more we will know about the content of their music. A deeper knowledge of their convictions, their feelings, their political, moral, and religious views will certainly not diminish, dilute, or flatten our responses to their music—as certain existentialists have claimed. This knowledge can put us, as listeners, into a very intense dialectical relationship with what we hear, a relationship that might not otherwise develop. It will make us realize that there were many people before us who tried to cope very courageously with the inner conflicts of their times. Granted: the issues and problems of their periods differed from those of the present, and the ways of dealing with them were necessarily different too. But one thing has remained unchanged: overcoming the inner contradictions of a given time in a new synthesis requires mustering up all the inner strength at one's disposal. And in this struggle, many of the great German composers of the past are still exemplary. The intellectual effort and the emotional commitment they put into their works can also inspire us to rally our psychic energies for this ongoing challenge. If we do not hear their works in this manner, they will become museum pieces, nostalgic souvenirs, pure sound, or just entertainment. But if we hear them in a consciously historical way, their dynamic impact could be tremendous.

J.H. & J.S.

Johann Walther

Foreword to the Revised Edition of the *Wittenberg Hymnal* (1537)

No wonder that music is so utterly despised and rejected at this time, seeing that other arts, which after all we should and must possess, are so lamentably regarded by everyone as altogether worthless. But the Devil will have his way: now that, by the grace of God, we have overthrown against him the popish mass with all its trappings, he in turn throws to the ground, as best he can, all that God requires. Yet, in order that our fair art may not be thus wholly destroyed, I have—in God's praise and in pure defiance of the Devil and his contempt—brought out in print the spiritual songs formerly printed at Wittenberg, setting the greater part anew, insofar as God permitted me, carefully correcting and improving the rest, and further adding several little pieces for five and six voices. So I pray that every pious Christian may bear with this my insufficiency and do the same or better for the glory of God and the furtherance of the art. And although these my songs will have many critics, I readily concede to anyone the honor of being my judge, seeing that I perhaps am still a student in this art. With this I commend all pious Christians to almighty God; may He grant us all His grace. Amen.

Translated by Oliver Strunk

Heinrich Schütz

To Elector Johann Georg I of Saxony (1628)

Venice, November 3, 1628
of the new calendar

Most gracious and illustrious Elector:

My earnest wish, while offering Your Lordship my humble and obedient services to the utmost of my ability, is that God may grant you the greatest happiness of body and soul.

As is the bounden duty of a subject, most gracious Lord, I do not neglect to notify you hereby that after obtaining your kind permission, I left Dresden on my projected journey to Italy. Because of the blocked passes in Germany and especially along the Venetian border, however, I was unable to reach Venice until a few days ago. I entertain the confident hope, Your Lordship, that with the help of God this journey will widen my experience and help me in various ways in my humble profession.

Nonetheless it is my fervent desire and profound hope that Your Lordship will not regard my absence with disfavor, nor permit anyone to apply for or take the office that I have thus far filled to the best of my humble ability. I hope, on the contrary, that it will remain unfilled until my return, which will be started without delay obedient to my Lord's commands, except for an act of Providence.

Furthermore, my gracious Lord and Elector, I have every reason to express to you my humble gratitude for granting permission to continue my regular salary even in my absence. While I was able to start my journey with these means and to continue it thus far, it will be very difficult and arduous to carry this project further at my own expense, considering that the journey at present is in its tenth week and has already been rather costly.

Further resources will be needed also for the purchase of many new and beautiful musical works, for I feel that since I came here the first time, compositions have changed a great deal. The music suitable at court for dinner, ballets, comedies, and the like has improved and increased a great deal. Consequently I feel justified in humbly begging Your Lordship (blessed as you are by God's bounty, it would seem but a trifle) to permit me, Your Lordship's most humble and faithful servant, to have an additional grant and accordingly order it added to the draft.

May I assure Your Lordship again with due devotion that my task here aims at nothing but an increase in Your Lordship's fame, and to qualify myself the better to render you my most humble service. In future, so long as God grants me life, I shall show my gratitude more by deed and constant attention to your wishes than now by this flow of words. I shall always attest this by applying myself to the best of my ability. Commending myself (especially now, sojourning abroad) in this most important matter to my Lord's gracious and favorable consideration, and begging God's holy protection for Your Lordship and Electoral house, I remain Your Lordship's most humble and obedient servant,

Henrich Schütz

Translator anon.

Dedication of *Symphoniae sacrae* II (1647)

To the most serene all-powerful high-born Prince and Lord
Lord Christian V
Prince in Denmark, Norway, and of the Wends and Goths;
Duke of Schleswig, Holstein, Stormarn, and the Dithmarschen;
Count of Oldenburg and Delmenhorst, etc.;

My most gracious Prince and Lord.

Most serene and all-powerful Prince and gracious Lord: That, now two years ago in connection with my then most humbly rendered personal attendance in Copenhagen, Your Princely Serenity received and accepted with uncommon grace the present insignificant little musical work, composed by me and at that time extant only in manuscript copies; that, out of inborn princely inclination toward all praiseworthy arts and especially toward noble music, you caused the same to be used and performed on several occasions; and also that you gave me real and conspicuous assurance of your gracious satisfaction in that, my humble dedication; all this I call to mind in everlasting and most respectful recollection and, in consequence, find myself obliged in turn, out of bounden gratitude, to celebrate at all times and to the best of my ability your heroic nature and outstanding princely virtues and to consider at each and every opportunity how the great and unmerited favor shown to me may, through most bounden attendance, be to some extent repaid.

Moreover, since for various reasons (some of them hereinafter stated in my memorial to the reader) this little work, thoroughly revised and somewhat enlarged and improved, is now through publication to be brought to light, I have regarded it as in all respects my duty not to pass by Your Princely Serenity in silence but, with this now new and public edition, to renew my first and earlier humblest dedication, thereby above all demonstrating and reaffirming my unceasing and most bounden devotion.

May it thus please Your Princely Serenity now, with your gracious hands and eyes, to accept anew, as you did before, my repeatedly mentioned unworthy little work (which I herewith once more present to you in deepest humility) and, with princely indulgence and graciousness, to be further inclined, so always to remain, toward my insignificant person and toward the praiseworthy profession of music, which otherwise has thus far suffered during these tumultuous martial times great loss of its patrons.

May the All-Highest, whose honor, praise, and glory the heavenly hosts continually do sing, again lend unity and good harmony on all sides and to all stations and also long preserve in health and happiness, and in all prosperity pleasing to Him, Your Princely Serenity, together with Your Princely Spouse and the whole most praiseworthy crown of Denmark, to the honor of His holy name, to the improvement of the free arts and especially of beloved music, at present greatly deteriorated, and also to the advantage of my unworthy person in particular. I faithfully and humbly commend Your Princely Serenity to His fatherly care, and myself to your perpetual and gracious affection.

> Dresden, on the first day of the month of May in the year 1647.
> Your Princely Serenity's
>> Most dutiful and humble
>>> Servant,
>>>> Heinrich Schütz

Ad benevolum lectorem.

Dear gracious reader: How, in the year 1629, when I had come for the second time to Italy and had resided there a while, I composed in conformity with the insignificant talent God has lent me and, be it said without vanity, in a short time a little Latin work for one, two, and three vocal parts, with two subordinate violins or similar instruments, in the musical style I then met with there; and how I caused the same to be set up and printed in Venice under the title *Symphoniae sacrae;* none of this shall be concealed from you here.

Since, at that time, from copies of the work, some of which had been exported to Germany and had there fallen into the hands of musicians, there came to my ears a report that the work was there thought to be of real value, further, that it was being diligently performed in various distinguished places with German words in place of Latin adapted throughout; I regarded this as a special incentive to me to attempt another little work of the same sort in our German mother tongue; and, after a bold beginning, I accordingly finished the same at length, with God's help, together with other works of mine (such as are here included).

Since then, however, and up until the present, I have been no little dissuaded from giving these out in a public edition, not only by the wretched times which still continue unabated in our beloved fatherland, unfavorable no less to music than to the other free arts, but also, and indeed above all, by the modern Italian manner used therein, still unknown to the majority, both as regards the composition and the proper performance of it, by means of which (in the opinion of the keen-witted Signor Claudio Monteverdi in the foreword to the Eighth Book of his madrigals) music is thought to have at length attained its final perfection.

Indeed (to admit the truth here reluctantly), experience has thus far repeatedly shown that this same modern music, whether Italian or after the Italian manner, together with the measure proper for it and for the notes of lesser value therein introduced, will neither rightly adapt itself to most of us Germans on this side, as many of us as are not bred to it, nor yet becomingly depart from us; in that (doubtless even in those places where one has thought to have good music) things thus composed are often so abused, defamed, and as it were actually broken that to an intelligent ear they can occasion nothing less than disgust and annoyance, to the author and to the praiseworthy German nation a wholly unjustified disparagement, as though the latter were in fact unskilled in noble music (as indeed there is no lack of such accusations on the part of certain foreigners).

But inasmuch as this little work, completed some years ago, was at that time humbly presented as manuscript to the serene all-powerful Prince and Lord, Lord Christian V, Prince in Denmark, Norway, and of the Goths and Wends, etc., as is, with other matters, to be seen from the foregoing most humble dedication; and inasmuch as I have since learned how many pieces of my composition, carelessly and incorrectly copied, scattered far and wide (as is now usual), have come into the hands of distinguished musicians; I have been obliged, therefore, to take the same once more in hand myself, and, after carrying out a thorough revision, I communicate them herewith through publication to those who may seek pleasure in them.

Now, since I should needlessly address myself to competent musicians, trained in good schools, if I were to call to their attention the pains I have expended herein (and, after the glory of God, it is to please these alone that the present few copies are now come to light); and since the manner herein introduced will be by no means displeasing to them;

Then to the others, especially to those who neither know nor practice the proper beat for the aforementioned modern music and its notes of lesser value and also the steady broadened way of bowing the violin which we Germans have (but who may wish nonetheless to perform something of this), this is my friendly request: that before they undertake to employ one or the other of these pieces in public they not be ashamed to seek instruction in advance from those familiar with this manner and spare themselves no pains in private practice lest perchance on the contrary there accrue to them and to the author himself, through no fault of his, instead of the expected thanks, an unexpected ridicule.

Further, inasmuch as in the concerto "May God Rise Up," etc., I have been guided in some few details by Signor Claudio Monteverdi's madrigal "Armato il cor," etc., and also by one of his chaconnes with two tenor voices, I leave the question of how far I have gone in this to those familiar with the aforementioned compositions. But let no one on this account suspect my remaining work unduly, for I am not accustomed to dress my works in borrowed plumage.

Finally, I make this further offer: that, if God continue to prolong my life, I shall, with His help, publish without delay still others of my admittedly unworthy *opera,* and, first among these, works of such a sort that even those who neither are nor intend becoming musicians *ex professo* may use them, it is hoped, and with the better effect.

Vale.

Translated by Oliver Strunk and William Strunk, Jr.

Samuel Scheidt

To Duke August of Brunswick (1642)

Halle, June 19, 1642

Most Serene Highness, Most Esteemed Prince and Lord:

From my youth until my present age I have composed many motets, concertos for singing, and all sorts of pieces to be played on instruments alone, such as canzonas, pavans, galliards, courantes, and similar things, as well as tablatures for the organ.

Now, however, I have taken it upon myself to compose some spiritual songs for five voices in the manner of a madrigal, a particularly beautiful kind of style, so that when there are five singers present and an organ or instrument of that nature is lacking, these can be sung without instruments. And when an organ and instrumentalists are at hand, if it is so desired, they can play along very appropriately and conveniently. Another beautiful sort of style is to play a symphony on the instruments, as a sort of prelude, just before the concerto, motet, or spiritual madrigal. Thus I have composed a considerable number of symphonies in various styles in all the customary keys and clefs, ten in each key, so that when a song is performed very frequently, it will cause no regret.

Since I do not desire to have these symphonies appear in print, whereby they would become common, I have made bold to dedicate them, together with some spiritual madrigals, to Your Lordship for your court chapel, and I entertain the most humble hope that Your Serene Highness will accept and receive my poor work and effort with goodwill, and that you will judge it according to my most humble intention rather than for the work itself, and that henceforth you will remain my most gracious Prince and Lord. And should these new spiritual madrigals meet with your approval and acceptance, in future I shall send more of the same to your Kapellmeister, for I am laboring at them daily, and so, if it please God to grant me life, I hope to assemble over a hundred of them very shortly, even before next winter.

I pray Almighty God to grant Your Serene Highness an auspicious reign and all general welfare; commending myself and mine to your kind favor, with utmost devotion,

Your Serene Highness's most humble and obedient servant,
Samuel Scheidt
Kapellmeister

Translator anon.

To Heinrich Baryphonus (1651)

Halle, January 26, 1651

I am astonished at the foolish music written in these times. It is false and wrong and no longer does anyone pay attention to what our beloved old masters wrote about composition. It certainly must be a remarkably elevated art when a pile of consonances are thrown together any which way.

I remain faithful to the pure old composition and pure rules. I have often walked out of the church since I could no longer listen to that mountain yodelling. I hope this worthless modern coinage will fall into disuse and that new coins will be forged according to the fine old stamp and standard.

Translator anon.

Georg Philipp Telemann

From the *Autobiography* (1740)

I was born in Magdeburg on March 14, 1681, and baptized three days later in the Evangelical Lutheran Church. My father, Henricus, was the preacher there at the Church of the Holy Spirit and died on the 17th of January, 1685, having barely reached the age of thirty-nine, while I had not yet reached the age of four. My mother, Maria, was likewise the child of a pastor, Johann Haltmeyer of Altendorf, and passed away in 1710.

In the first years of school I learned the usual things, namely reading, writing, the catechism, and some Latin; but ultimately I took up the violin, flute, and zither, with which I entertained my neighbors, without being aware of the existence of printed music. The Gymnasium in the old part of the city, which I entered at the age of ten, provided me with a high level of instruction, first by the cantor, Herr Benedikt Christiani, then in the uppermost class of Rector Herr Anton Werner Cuno, and finally also in the class of Herr N. Müller, Rector of the Cathedral, who implanted in me my initial love for German poetic art. All of the teachers were satisfied with my diligence, or rather with my ability to grasp things quickly, and certified that I had established a firm foundation in Latin and particularly in Greek. But alas, one forgets everything without practice.

In music I had grasped so much within a few weeks that the cantor permitted me to conduct the singing lessons in his place, although the boys entrusted to my care were far taller than I. At such times he would compose; but as soon as he turned his back

I examined his scores and always found something there to delight me. But why this was so remained obscure to me. In short, this prompted me to gather together all sorts of music, which I wrote out in score and read diligently, whereby I became ever more enlightened. Finally, I began to compose myself (which I note with honor), but still privately.

In the meantime I had learned how to play my clumsy compositions into the hands of the cantor and prefect by use of an assumed name, whereupon I heard the works and likewise the new composer praised in the highest terms, both in the church and on the street. This emboldened me so much that, at about the age of twelve, I set to music a Hamburg opera libretto I had noticed, *Sigismundus,* which was also performed splendidly enough on an established stage. I myself rather defiantly sang the role of the hero in this production. I would have to be out of my mind to want to see this music now. . . .

But oh! What a storm I brought down upon myself with this opera. The enemies of music came in hordes to my mother and explained to her: I would become a charlatan, a tightrope-walker, minstrel, rodent-trainer, etc. if music were not taken away from me. No sooner said than done! My music, instruments, and with them half my life were taken from me. However, to remove me even further from these things it was decided that I be sent to school in Zellerfeld, in the Harz region: perhaps because my music tyrants believed that the witches tolerated no music beyond the Blocksberg. . . .

I finally had enough of my years as a choirboy and longed to attend an institution of higher learning, to which end I selected Leipzig. I traveled to my hometown to get the necessary things in order. An examination given at that time resulted in the verdict that I was to study law and totally renounce music. The former was my intention in any case; and I accommodated myself to the latter without any opposition, with the firm intention of studying to become a privy councillor. Leaving behind all of my musical belongings, I went to Leipzig in 1701. While enroute in Halle, I almost succumbed again to musical poison through my acquaintance with Herr Georg Friedrich Händel, already an eminent figure at that time. But I held firm and went on my way again, following my previous intentions.

I soon began my studies and attended lectures on law, rhetoric, and philosophy given by three professors and doctors. Then my roommate came upon my trunk and found the Sixth Psalm I had composed, which had found its way, I don't know how, into my linens. I informed him of my intention, and he approved, but he requested the Psalm from me in order to have it performed at the Thomaskirche the following Sunday. The then mayor and privy councillor Herr D. Romanus took a liking to the music and persuaded me to compose a piece every two weeks for the same church, for which I was provided with a considerable sum of money, without the hope that this would be of further advantage to me. However, his advice was also to the effect that I should not put down my other studies.

Now I thought of my mother again, whose commands I honored, for I had received a money draft from her. I sent it back again, reported on my circumstances at the time, and asked for a change of will on her part with regard to my musical activity. Her blessing of my new work followed: and now half of me was once again a musician.

Shortly thereafter I began to direct operas, of which I composed a total of twenty or so, and likewise the librettos for many of these. I also worked on operas while in Sorau and Frankfurt. For the court at Weissenfels I wrote about four operas and ultimately established the Collegium Musicum in Leipzig, which still exists. . . .

On July 10, 1721, I was chosen to become director of the musical chorus and cantor of the Johanneum in Hamburg upon the demise of Herr Joachim Gerstenbüttel. On Michaelmas I was solemnly installed in that capacity following an address entitled *De musica in ecclesia* and earlier invitational programs.

Approximately one year later, the operas, at the time in a state of decline, were put into a better and more splendid condition with the aid of several ministers and aristocratic persons. I was commissioned with the supervision of the music in addition to the composition of new theater pieces for an annual income of 300 Reichsthaler. . . .

Translated by Michael Gilbert

Sonnet on the Deceased Herr Kapellmeister Bach (1751)

Let Frenchmen and Italians have their ardent way,
Bestowing fame on virtuosos and their skill:
On German soil, they're likewise able to hold sway
And drink of our applause and our acclaim their fill.

O Bach, whose face has blanched! Your manly organ play,
Prompting the great one's favor-word, echoing still.
How joy and envy were awakened by the way
In which your sound was rendered captive by your quill!

Sleep, then. Oblivion cannot ever touch your name:
Your discipline's disciples, and who later came,
Forge for your head the crown your living fame has won.
Also your children's hands add to your coronation.
But as for special reasons for our admiration,
Berlin has shown them us in one most worthy son!

Translated by Felix Pollak

Georg Friedrich Händel

To Johann Mattheson (1719)

London, February 24, 1719

Monsieur,

The letter that I have just received from you dated the 21st of this month obliges me with all haste to satisfy you more precisely than I had done in my previous letters on the two points in question. I must therefore declare that, in the matter of solmization and the Greek modes, my opinion conforms in general to what you have so ably deduced and proved in your book. The question, in my opinion, comes to this: whether one should prefer a method at the same time simple and of the most perfect kind to another which is fraught with great difficulties, apt not only to give pupils a distaste for music but also to make them waste much precious time, which could be better employed in acquiring a profound knowledge of this art and in improving their natural gifts? I do not mean to argue that solmization is of no practical use whatever, but as one can acquire the same knowledge in far less time by the method in use at present with such success, I see no point in not adopting the way which leads with greater ease and in less time to the proposed goal. Touching the Greek modes, I find, Monsieur, that you have said all that there is to be said on that score. Knowledge of them is no doubt necessary for those who wish to study and execute ancient music composed according to these modes; but as we have been liberated from the narrow limits of ancient music, I cannot see of what use the Greek modes can be to modern music. Such,

Monsieur, are my views; you will oblige me by informing me if they agree with what you wish from me.

As regards the second point, you can yourself judge that it demands more leisure than I can dispose of among the many pressing affairs that I have on hand. As soon as I am a little freer, I shall pass in review the main periods of my professional life, so that you may be assured of the particular esteem and consideration in which I have the honor to remain,
Monsieur,

> Your most humble and
> > obedient servant,
> > > G. F. Händel

Translated by Alexis Vlastro

To King George I of England (1720)

To the King's Most Excellent Majesty

Sir,

The protection which Your Majesty has been graciously pleased to allow both to the art of music in general, and to one of the lowest, though not the least dutiful of Your Majesty's servants, has emboldened me to present to Your Majesty, with all due humility and respect, this my first essay to that design. I have been still the more encouraged to this, by the particular approbation Your Majesty has been pleased to give to the music of this drama: which, may I be permitted to say, I value not so much as it is the judgement of a great Monarch, as of One of a most refined taste in the art: my endeavors to improve which, is the only merit that can be pretended by me, except that of being with the utmost humility,

> Sir,
> Your Majesty's most devoted, most
> obedient, and most faithful subject
> and servant,
> > George Frideric Handel

Written in English

To Charles Jennens, Jr. (1741)

Dublin, December 29, 1741

Sir,

It was with the great pleasure I saw the continuation of your kindness by the lines you was pleased to send me, in order to be prefixed to your oratorio *Messiah,* which I set to music before I left England. I am emboldened, Sir, by the generous concern you please to take in relation to my affairs, to give you an account to the success I have met here. The nobility did me the honor to make amongst themselves a subscription for 6 nights, which did fill a room of 600 persons. So that I need not sell one single ticket at the door. And without vanity the performance was received with a general approbation.

Signora Avolio, which I brought with me from London pleases extraordinary. I have formed another tenor voice which gives great satisfaction, the basses and countertenors are very good, and the rest of the chorus singers (by my direction) do exceeding well, as for the instruments they are really excellent. Mr. Dubourgh being at the head of them, and the music sounds delightfully in this charming room, which puts me in such spirits (and my health being so good) that I exert myself on my organ with more than usual success. I opened with the *Allegro, Penseroso, & Moderato,* and I assure you that the words of the Moderato are vastly admired. The audience being composed (besides the flower of ladies of distinction and other people of the greatest quality) of so many bishops, deans, heads of the college, and the most eminent people in the law as the chancellor, auditor general, etc. all which are very much taken with the poetry. So that I am desired to perform it again the next time.

I cannot sufficiently express the kind treatment I receive here, but the politeness of this generous nation cannot be unknown to you, so I let you judge of the satisfaction I enjoy, passing my time with honor, profit and pleasure.

They propose already to have some more performances when the 6 nights of the subscription are over, and My Lord Duke the Lord Lieutenant (who is always present with all his family on those nights) will easily obtain a longer permission for me by His Majesty, so that I shall be obliged to make my stay here longer than I thought. One request I must make to you, which is that you would insinuate my most devoted respects to My Lord and My Lady Shaftesbury. You know how much their kind protection is precious to me. Sir Windham Knatchbull will find here my respectful compliments. You will increase my obligations if by occasion you will present my humble service to some other patrons and friends of mine. I expect with impatience the favor of your news, concerning your health and welfare, of which I take a real share.

As for the news of your operas, I need not trouble you for all this town is full of their ill success, by a number of letters from your quarters to the people of quality here, and I can't help saying but that it furnishes great diversion and laughter. The first opera I heard myself before I left London, and it made me merry all along my journey, and of the second opera called *Penelope*, a certain noble man writes very jocosely, *il faut que je dise avec Harlequin, nôtre Penelôpe n'est qu'une Sallôpe*. But I think I have trespassed too much on your patience, I beg you to be persuaded of the sincere veneration and esteem with which I have the honneur to be, Sir,

Your most obliged and most humble servant
George Frideric Handel

Written in English

To Georg Philipp Telemann (1754)

London, September 20, 1754

Monsieur,

It is some time since I had a provision of exotic plants prepared to send to you, when Captain Jean Carsten (whom I had spoken to so that you should get them) told me that you had died. You cannot doubt that this report afflicted me extremely. You judge then of the joy with which I have learned that you find yourself in perfect health. The same Captain Jean Carsten who has just arrived here on his return from your region, sends me this good news through a friend, and also that you have consigned to him a list of exotic plants to procure for you. I have embraced this occasion with great pleasure, and I have made an effort to find these plants, and you will have almost all of them. As Captain Carsten need not leave here until the coming month of December, he has had the kindness to offer to send them to you by the first ship leaving here, and you will find on the note herewith both the name of the captain and of the ship. I hope that this little present which I have dared to offer you will be agreeable to you; I beg you to be kind enough to give me news of your health, which I hope is very perfect, and I also wish you every kind of prosperity, who am with inviolable esteem,

Monsieur,

Your very humble and very obedient Servant

G. F. Händel

Translated by Maurice J. E. Brown

Johann Sebastian Bach

Dedication of the Brandenburg Concertos (1721)

To His Royal Highness My Lord Christian Louis Elector
of Brandenburg &c.&c.&c.

Your Royal Highness,
   As I had a couple of years ago the pleasure of appearing before
Your Royal Highness, by virtue of Your Highness' commands, and
as I noticed then that Your Highness took some pleasure in the
small talents which heaven has given me for music, and as in taking leave of Your Royal Highness, Your Highness deigned to honor
me with the command to send Your Highness some pieces of my
composition: I have then in accordance with Your Highness' most
gracious orders taken the liberty of rendering my most humble duty
to Your Royal Highness with the present concertos, which I have
adapted to several instruments; begging Your Highness most humbly not to judge their imperfection with the rigor of the fine and
delicate taste which the whole world knows Your Highness has
for musical pieces; but rather to infer from them in benign consideration the profound respect and the most humble obedience which
I try to show Your Highness therewith. For the rest, Sire, I beg
Your Royal Highness very humbly to have the goodness to continue Your Highness' gracious favor toward me, and to be assured
that nothing is so close to my heart as the wish that I may be em-

ployed on occasions more worthy of Your Royal Highness and of Your Highness' service—I, who without an equal in zeal am,

Sire, Your Royal Highness' most humble and obedient servant

Jean Sebastien Bach

Coethen, March 24, 1721

Translator anon.

Contract with the Thomasschule (1723)

Whereas the Honorable and Most Wise Council of this Town of Leipzig have engaged me as Cantor of the Thomasschule and have desired an undertaking from me in respect to the following points, to wit:

(1) That I shall set the boys a shining example of an honest, retiring manner of life, serve the School industriously, and instruct the boys conscientiously;

(2) Bring the music in both the principal churches of this town into good estate, to the best of my ability;

(3) Show to the Honorable and Most Wise Council all proper respect and obedience, and protect and further everywhere as best I may its honor and reputation; likewise if a gentleman of the Council desires the boys for a musical occasion unhesitatingly provide him with the same, but otherwise never permit them to go out of town to funerals or weddings without the previous knowledge and consent of the Mayor and Honorable Directors of the School currently in office;

(4) Give due obedience to the Honorable Inspectors and Directors of the School in each and every instruction which the same shall issue in the name of the Honorable and Most Wise Council;

(5) Not take any boys into the School who have not already laid a foundation in music, or are not at least suited to being instructed therein, nor do the same without the previous knowledge and consent of the Honorable Inspectors and Directors;

(6) So that the churches may not have to be put to unnecessary expense, faithfully instruct the boys not only in vocal but also in instrumental music;

(7) In order to preserve the good order in the churches, so arrange the music that it shall not last too long, and shall be of such a nature as not to make an operatic impression, but rather inspire the listeners to devotion;

(8) Provide the New Church with good scholars;

(9) Treat the boys in a friendly manner and with caution, but, in case they do not wish to obey, chastise them with moderation or report them to the proper place;

(10) Faithfully attend to the instruction in the School and whatever else it befits me to do;

(11) And if I cannot undertake this myself, arrange that it be done by some other capable person without expense to the Honorable and Most Wise Council or to the School;

(12) Not go out of town without the permission of the Honorable Mayor currently in office;

(13) Always so far as possible walk with the boys at funerals, as is customary;

(14) And shall not accept or wish to accept any office in the University without the consent of the Honorable and Learned Council;

Now therefore I do hereby undertake and bind myself faithfully to observe all of the said requirements, and on pain of losing my post not to act contrary to them, in witness whereof I have set my hand and seal to this agreement.

Johann Sebastian Bach

Leipzig, May 5, 1723

Translator anon.

To Georg Erdmann (1730)

Most Honored Sir,

Your Honor will have the goodness to excuse an old and faithful servant for taking the liberty of disturbing you with the present letter. It must be nearly four years since Your Honor favored me with a kind answer to the letter I sent you; I remember that at that time you graciously asked me to give you some news of what had happened to me, and I humbly take this opportunity of providing you with the same. You know the course of my life from my youth up until the change in my fortunes that took me to Cöthen as Kapellmeister. There I had a gracious Prince, who both loved and knew music, and in his service I intended to spend the rest of my life. It must happen, however, that the said *Serenissimus* should marry a Princess of Berenburg, and that then the impression should arise that the musical interests of the said Prince had become somewhat lukewarm, especially as the new Princess seemed to be unmusical; and it pleased God that I should be called hither to be *Director Musices* and Cantor at the Thomasschule. Though at first, indeed, it did not seem at all proper to me to change my position of Kapellmeister for that of Cantor. Wherefore, then, I postponed my decision for a quarter of a year; but this post was described to me in such favorable terms that finally (particularly since my sons seemed inclined toward [university] studies) I cast my lot, in the name of the Lord, and made the journey to Leipzig, took my examination, and then made the change of position. Here, by God's will, I am still in service. But since (1) I find that the post is by no means so lucrative as it had been described to me; (2) I have failed to obtain many of the fees pertaining to the office; (3) the place is very expensive; (4) the authorities are odd and little interested in music, so that I must live amid almost continual vexation, envy, and persecution; accordingly I shall be forced, with God's help, to seek my fortune elsewhere. Should Your Honor know or find a suitable post in your city for an old and faithful servant, I beg you most humbly to put in a most gracious word of recommendation for me—I shall not fail to do my best to give satisfaction and justify your most gracious intercession on my behalf. My present post amounts to about 700 thaler, and when there are rather more funerals than usual, the fees rise in proportion; but when a healthy wind blows, they fall accordingly, as for example last year, when I lost fees that would ordinarily come in from funerals to an amount of more than 100 thaler. In Thuringia I could get along better on 400 thaler than here with twice that many, because of the excessively high cost of living.

Now I must add a little about my domestic situation. I am married for the second time, my late wife having died in Cöthen. From the first marriage I have three sons and one daughter living, whom

Your Honor will graciously remember having seen in Weimar. From the second marriage I have one son and two daughters living. My eldest son is a *Studiosus Juris,* and of the other two, one is in the *prima* class [the last class of school] and the other in the *secunda,* and the eldest daughter is also still unmarried. The children of my second marriage are still small, the eldest, a boy, being six years old. But they are all born musicians, and I can assure you that I can already form an ensemble both *vocaliter* and *instrumentaliter* within my family, particularly since my present wife sings a good, clear soprano, and my eldest daughter, too, joins in not badly. I shall almost transgress the bounds of courtesy if I burden Your Honor any further, and I therefore hasten to close, remaining with most devoted respect my whole life long

Your Honor's most obedient and devoted servant,

Joh. Sebast. Bach

Leipzig, October 28, 1730

Translator anon.

Dedication of *A Musical Offering* (1747)

To King Friedrich II of Prussia

Most Gracious King!

In deepest humility I dedicate herewith to Your Majesty a musical offering, the noblest part of which derives from Your Majesty's Own August Hand. With awesome pleasure I still remember the very special Royal Grace when, some time ago, during my visit in Potsdam, Your Majesty's Self deigned to play to me a theme for a fugue upon the clavier, and at the same time charged me most graciously to carry it out in Your Majesty's Most August Presence. To obey Your Majesty's command was my most humble duty. I noticed very soon, however, that, for lack of necessary preparation, the execution of the task did not fare as well as such an excellent theme demanded. I resolved therefore and promptly pledged myself to work out this right Royal theme more fully and then make it known to the world. This resolve has now been carried out as well as possible, and it has none other than this irreproachable intent, to glorify, if only in a small point, the fame of a Monarch whose greatness and power, as in all the sciences of war and peace, so especially in music, everyone must admire and revere. I make bold to add this most humble request: may Your Majesty deign to dignify the present modest labor with a gracious acceptance, and continue to grant Your Majesty's Most August Royal Grace to

Your Majesty's most humble and obedient servant,

The Author

Leipzig, July 7, 1747

Translator anon.

Johann Joachim Quantz

How a Performer and a Piece of Music Ought to Be Judged (1752)

1. There is perhaps no art so subject to every man's judgment as music. It would seem as though there were nothing easier than to judge it. Not only every musician, but also everyone who gives himself out as a musical amateur, wishes likewise to be regarded as a judge of what he hears.

2. We are not always satisfied that each performer whom we hear should be at pains to offer what lies within his powers; we often expect to hear more than we ourselves have ever been used to hearing. If, in a company, not all sing or play with equal perfection, we often attribute all the excellence to one performer, considering the others as of no account, without reflecting that one may have his merits in this style, another in that, one, for example, in Adagio, another in Allegro. We fail to consider that the attraction of music consists, not in equality or similarity, but in variety. If it were possible for all musicians to sing or play with the same ability and in the same taste, as a result of this lack of an agreeable variety the greater part of our enjoyment in music would be lost.

3. We are seldom guided by our own impression, which would after all be the surest guide, but we are at once anxious to hear which one is the ablest of those who are singing or playing, just as though we could at one time oversee and estimate the skill of several persons, like things that only show their worth and merit on the scales. And now we listen only to him who is in this fash-

ion pronounced the ablest. A piece which he performs carelessly enough, often intentionally, and which is into the bargain a very poor one, is puffed up as a marvel; to another, for all the great industry with which he is at pains to perform some choice piece, we grant barely a few moments' attention.

4. We seldom allow a performer time enough to show his strength or weakness. We also fail to consider that a performer is not always in a position to offer what he understands; that often the slightest accident may easily cause him to lose all his self-possession; and that, as a result of this, we ought in fairness to hear him more than once before venturing to pass judgment on him. Some performers are forward and have perhaps a few pieces in which they can show everything that they can do and, so to speak, unburden themselves of their whole art at one time, so that we hear them once and for all. Others who are not thus forward and whose art cannot, as in the former case, be confined to a few pieces have not the same advantage. For most listeners are only too inclined to be hasty in their judgments and allow themselves to be altogether too much prepossessed by what they hear at first. Had they the patience and the opportunity to hear each performer several times, no great insight would be required as a rule; they would need only to be guided by their own feelings, without prejudice, and to see which performer gave them the most pleasure in the long run.

5. As regards composition, we are no better off. We are unwilling to be regarded as ignorant; at the same time we feel, no doubt, that we may not always be competent to make a proper decision. Hence we are usually inclined to begin by asking who the composer is, in order to be guided by this in our judgment. Should the piece prove to be by someone to whom we have conceded our approval in advance, it is at once unhesitatingly pronounced beautiful. Should the contrary apply, or have we perhaps some objection to the author's person, the whole piece passes for worthless. Anyone who wishes to convince himself of this in a positive way need only publish two pieces of equal excellence under different names, one of which is in favor, the other out of favor. The ignorance of many judges will surely soon betray itself.

6. More modest listeners, who do not credit themselves with sufficient insight to judge a thing, often have recourse to a musi-

cian, whose word they accept as irrefutable truth. Assuredly, by listening to many good performances and to the judgment which experienced, instructed, and honest musicians pass on them, we can attain a certain degree of knowledge, especially when we ask also about the reasons why a piece is good or bad. This, then, ought to be one of the most reliable means of avoiding error. But are all those who make music their business at the same time musical experts or musical scholars? Have not ever so many of these learned their art as a mere trade? It can then easily happen that we address our questions to the wrong person and that the musician, quite as much as the amateur, is swayed in his decision by ignorance, envy, prejudice, or flattery. Like wildfire, such a verdict spreads abroad at once and so takes in the uninformed who rely on a supposed oracle of this kind that in the end there arises from it a prejudice which is not easily again removed. What is more, it is not even possible for every musician to be a competent judge of all that can occur in music. Singing requires its special insight. The variety of the instruments is so great that the powers and the lifetime of a single person would be insufficient for attaining insight into all their properties. Before placing his trust in the judgment of a musician, the musical amateur must therefore accurately determine whether his musician is really in a position to judge correctly. With one who has thoroughly mastered his art, we are on safer ground than with one who has only followed his good instincts; the latter, however, is also not to be entirely rejected. And because it is not easy for anyone to be so free from the passions that his judgments do not sometimes even run counter to his knowledge, the musical amateur must also in this respect accept the judgment of a musician with caution. There are some whom almost nothing pleases but what they have written themselves. Alas, then, for all music that has not the honor to thank their celebrated pens for its existence! Whenever, to avoid scandal, they find themselves obliged to praise a thing, do they not do so in a way which, after all, betrays that praise is difficult for them? Others, just the other way, praise everything indiscriminately, to fall out with nobody and to make themselves agreeable to everyone. Many a rising young musician regards nothing as beautiful but what has flowed from his master's inventive genius. Many a composer seeks his reputation in unrelieved remote modulations, obscure melodies, and other things of this sort. With him, everything has to be extraordinary and un-usual. No doubt he has won applause by his real merits and also surreptitiously gained a following by other means. Does anyone expect him and those who blindly honor him to pronounce a thing beautiful which does not agree with this way of thinking? The older generation complains of the melodic extravagances of the younger; the younger generation makes fun of the dry style of the older. Nevertheless, we occasionally find musicians who grasp a thing impartially according to its real worth, who praise what ought to be praised, and who reject what ought to be rejected. Such musical scholars are the safest to trust. Yet the upright and able musician must be very much on his guard lest his passions lead him to com-mit some injustice and especially lest professional jealousy deceive him, for his judgment, to be sure, while it can be the most correct, can also, because of the reputation he enjoys, be the most danger-ous.

7. Now since music is the sort of art which must be judged, not according to our own fancy, but, like the other fine arts, according to good taste, acquired through certain rules and refined by much experience and exercise; since anyone who wishes to judge an-other ought to understand at least as much as the other, if not more; since these qualities are seldom met with in those who occupy themselves with the judging of music; since, on the contrary, the greater part of these are governed by ignorance, prejudice, and passions which hinder correct judgment; many a one would do much better if he would keep his judgment to himself and listen with greater attention, if, without judging, he can still take plea-sure in music. When he listens more to judge the performer need-lessly than to enjoy the music, he arbitrarily deprives himself of the greater part of the pleasure he would otherwise take in it. And when, even before the musician has finished his piece, our critic is already occupied in imposing his mistaken opinions on his neigh-bors, he makes the musician lose not only his self-possession, but also his power to finish with a stout heart and to demonstrate his ability as he might otherwise have done. For who can remain in-sensible and self-possessed when, here and there among his lis-teners, he sees expressions of disapproval? The hasty judge, more-over, is in constant danger of betraying his ignorance to others who are not of his opinion and perhaps understand more than he does;

he can expect, therefore, no advantage from his judgment. From this, we may conclude how really difficult it is to take upon ourselves the office of a music critic and to discharge it honorably.

8. In judging music, besides obeying the usual dictates of reason and fairness, we should always pay particular attention to three points, namely, to the piece itself, to the performer, and to the listener. A fine composition may be mutilated by a bad performance; a poor composition, on the other hand, deprives the performer of his advantage; we must first determine, therefore, whether it is the performer or the composition that is responsible for the good or bad effect. With regard to the listener, as with regard to the performer, much depends on the various constitutions of the temperament. Some prefer the magnificent and lively style, some the mournful and profound, some the cheerful and delicate; each is governed by his inclinations. Some have considerable knowledge, which others lack. We are not always carried away immediately the first time we hear this piece or that. It often happens that a piece pleases us today which tomorrow, if we chance to be in a different mood, we can scarcely sit through; on the other hand, a piece may displease us today in which tomorrow we discover beauties. A piece may be well written and well played; even so it fails to please everyone. A poor piece badly played may displease many; at the same time it finds a few admirers. The place in which a piece of music is performed can put many obstacles in the way of our judging it correctly. We hear, for example, one and the same piece, today from near by, tomorrow from far off. In each case we notice a difference. We may hear a piece intended for a vast place and a large orchestra in its proper setting. It will please us immensely. But if, at some other time, we hear the same piece in a room, performed perhaps by other persons, with a few instruments accompanying, it will have lost half its beauty. A piece that has well-nigh enchanted us in the chamber may be barely recognizable when we hear it in the theater. If, on the one hand, we were to ornament a slow movement, written in the French taste, with many arbitrary embellishments as though it were an Italian Adagio, or if, on the other hand, we were to perform an Italian Adagio in a good, dry, straightforward style with pretty, pleasing trills in the French taste; the former would become wholly unrecognizable—the latter would sound very plain and thin; as a re-

sult, neither one would please either the Frenchman or the Italian. Each piece, then, must be played in the style that belongs to it; unless this is done, there can be no judgment. Supposing, further, that each piece were played, according to the taste proper to it, in these two ways, no Italian could judge the French and no Frenchman the Italian, for both are prepossessed by prejudices in favor of their country and their national music.

9. After this, everyone will grant me, I believe, that the correct and impartial judgment of a piece of music requires, not merely a little insight, but perhaps the highest degree of musical skill; that far more is involved than merely being able to sing or play a little ourselves; and that, as a result of this, if we would judge, we must apply ourselves assiduously to the attainment of that knowledge which reason, good taste, and art have placed within our reach. And further, I hope that no one will wish to dispute my contention that not every one of those who commonly set themselves up as judges of music is equipped with this knowledge and that, for this reason, there must arise a great detriment to music, musicians, and musical amateurs, who are kept thereby in a constant state of uncertainty.

10. I shall attempt to indicate, by means of certain characteristic signs, the chief qualities of the complete performer and of the well-written piece of music, in order that musicians, and musical amateurs as well, may have at least some guidance in forming their judgments and in determining to which performer or to which piece of music they may properly give their approval. Let everyone who seeks to judge try always to do so without prejudice, without passion, with fairness. Let him proceed cautiously and not hurry himself unduly. Let him regard the thing itself and not allow himself to be blinded by secondary considerations which have nothing to do with it; for example, whether the performer or composer is of this or that nationality, whether or not he has traveled abroad, whether he claims to be a pupil of a famous master, whether he is in the service of a great lord, or of a little one, or of no one at all, whether he has a musical character or no character, whether he is friend or foe, young or old, and so forth. In general, we shall not easily be unfair if, instead of saying of a performer or a piece of music, "It is worthless," we say only, "It does not please me." The latter everyone has the right to say, for no one is obliged to be

pleased with anything. The former, however, we ought in fairness to leave solely to the real musical experts, who are in any case duty bound to indicate the reasons for their verdict.

Translated by Oliver Strunk

Johann Adolf Hasse

To the Abbé Giovanni Maria Ortes (1769)

Vienna, September 30, 1769

I have made the acquaintance here of a certain Herr Mozart, Kapellmeister to the Archbishop of Salzburg, a clever man, charming and cultivated, who, I believe, knows his business in music as well as other matters. He has a daughter and a son. The former plays the harpsichord proficiently, and the latter, who cannot be more than twelve or thirteen years old, already holds forth as a composer and teacher of music.

I have seen the compositions he is supposed to have written. They are not at all bad, and I should not have recognized in them a twelve-year-old author. I dare not question his having written them, for after giving me proof of various styles on the harpsichord, he showed me some things which were incredible for his age and admirable even for a grown man.

Since his father wishes to take him to Italy to make him known and wrote me requesting some letters of recommendation, I am taking the liberty of sending you one. I am depending on your kindness. The sole purpose of this letter is to have him meet you and to have him obtain some useful advice which may prove necessary in that country. But if you could also introduce him to some lady of your acquaintance, that would be more than I had hoped for. The father says he will leave Salzburg on October 24 and should arrive by the end of the month.

This Herr Mozart is an extremely courteous and gracious man, and his children are very well bred. The boy, moreover, is handsome, lively, charming, and has excellent manners. I am certain that if he continues to progress as he grows older, he will be a prodigy—provided the father does not push him too much and spoil him with undue and exaggerated praise, which is the one thing I dread.

What a long letter! Accept my greetings and forgive me for having written at such length. Believe me, with the most faithful and lifelong devotion, my very dear Monsieur Abbé. The ladies send their respects.

Your most humble and obliged servant and friend,
J. A. Hasse

Translator anon.

Carl Philipp Emanuel Bach

Autobiography (1773)

I, Carl Philipp Emanuel Bach, was born in March 1714 in Weimar. My late father was Johann Sebastian, Kapellmeister at a few courts and finally music director in Leipzig. My mother was Maria Barbara Bach, the youngest daughter of Johann Michael Bach, an accomplished composer. After finishing my schooling at the Leipzig Thomasschule, I studied law both in Leipzig and later in Frankfurt an der Oder. At the latter place I both directed a musical academy and composed and directed all public musical performances on ceremonial occasions. In composition and in playing the clavier, I never had any teacher other than my father. When I completed my academic studies in 1738 and went to Berlin, I received a very favorable opportunity to escort a young nobleman on his travels abroad. The journey I was planning was cancelled when I was unexpectedly and graciously summoned to Ruppin by the then Crown Prince (now King) of Prussia. Certain circumstances, however, led to my not formally entering the Prussian service until 1740, when His Majesty's reign began, and I alone was favored to accompany on the harpsichord the first flute solo His Majesty played as King in Charlottenburg Palace. From this time on, up to November of 1767, I was constantly in Prussian service, although I had several opportunities to take highly remunerated positions elsewhere. His Majesty was gracious enough to bring these calls to naught by a substantial raise in my salary. In 1767, I was offered the position of music director in Hamburg previously occupied by the late Herr Kapellmeister Telemann! After most obediently presenting my wishes to His Majesty on repeated occasions, I was discharged by the King, and the King's sister, Princess Amalia, Highness of Prussia, graciously appointed me Her Highness' Kapellmeister upon my departure. Since arriving here I have continued to receive very favorable offers at other places, but I have always declined them. My Prussian service never left me enough time for travel to foreign countries. I have therefore always remained in Germany and have undertaken some journeys only within this, my fatherland. This lack of foreign travel would have been a greater professional setback if I had not had the especially good fortune, from my youth on, to hear the finest music of all kinds close at hand and to make the acquaintance of numerous masters of the first rank, some of whom have become close friends. I already enjoyed this advantage during my youth in Leipzig, for a master in music could scarcely travel through this city without meeting my father and playing for him. My father's particular greatness in composition, on the organ, and in playing the clavier was far too well-known for a musician of any standing to pass up the opportunity to get better acquainted with this great man if at all possible. I need not say much about all the music that could be heard then, particularly in Berlin and Dresden; who does not know that period, during which a new era began, so to speak, both for music in general and especially for its most accurate and fine performance, leading the art to such heights that I fear it has already declined somewhat. Along with many discerning men, I believe that this is largely attributable to the comic opera, now so popular. Without citing men who could perhaps be faulted for having composed very little or nothing at all within the genre, I will mention the greatest living master of opera buffa, Signor Galuppi, who totally agreed with me while visiting at my house in Berlin, and on this occasion mentioned several very ludicrous incidents he had actually experienced in some Italian churches. In short, I had to be and was quite content with hearing, apart from the great masters of our fatherland, outstanding music of all sorts sent to us in Germany from foreign regions; and I do not believe that any sort of music remains that I have not heard played by some of the greatest masters.

It would not be difficult for me to fill a considerable space merely with the names of the composers, male and female singers, and instrumentalists of all sorts I have come to know, were I to go into detail and exert my memory. This much I know for certain: among them were geniuses whose like and greatness have not been equalled since. Despite all this, I will not deny that it would have been very agreeable and also advantageous for me to have the opportunity to visit foreign lands.

In the year 1744, I was married in Berlin to Miss Johanna Maria Dannemann, the youngest daughter of a wine dealer who lived there at the time. Two sons and one daughter of this marriage are living. My elder son practices law here as a licentiate, my daughter still lives at home with me, and my younger son is now in Saxony studying his chief metier, painting, at the art academies in Leipzig and Dresden. With my knowledge and consent, the following works of mine have appeared in print:

(1) In the year 1731, a minuet with crossed hands set for keyboard. A natural and, at the time, very popular legerdemain. I myself engraved this minuet in copper.

(2) In 1742, six harpsichord sonatas, engraved and published by Schmidt in Nürnberg.

(3) In 1744, six harpsichord sonatas, published by Haffner in Nürnberg.

(4) In 1745, a harpsichord concerto in D major with accompaniment, with Schmidt's press in Nürnberg.

(5) In 1751, with the same publisher, two trios, of which the first is set in C minor for two violins and bass (with annotations) and the second is set in B-flat major for flute, violin, and bass.

(6) In 1752, with the same publisher, a harpsichord concerto in B-flat major with accompaniment.

(7) In 1753, *Essay on the True Art of Playing Keyboard Instruments* with examples and six sonatas in 16 copper plates, part one, published by the author.

(8) Between 1755 and 1765, Haffner in Nürnberg published ten clavier sonatas by me in his collections, namely in F major, D minor, E major, B-flat major, B minor, C major, B-flat major, A major, A minor, and E major.

(9) In 1757 and 1758, two of my clavier sonatas were published in the Breitkopf *Raccolta,* namely in D major and D minor, together with a few individual clavier pieces and a fugue.

(10) In 1758, a two-part clavier fugue by me set in D minor was published in Marpurg's *Fugue Collection.*

(11) In 1759, Winter in Berlin printed my melodies to Gellert's *Sacred Songs.*

(12) In 1758, my twelve small and short two- and three-voice pieces were issued in octavo format by Winter.

(13) In 1759, part one of my reprise sonatas appeared with Winter.

(14) In 1759, Schmidt in Nürnberg engraved in copper a sinfonia by me with two violins, viola, and bass set in E minor.

(15) In 1760, Winter printed a harpsichord concerto by me set in E major.

(16) In 1761, Winter likewise printed the continuation of my clavier sonatas.

(17) In 1761, I published part two of my *Essay,* which treats the art of accompaniment and free fantasy.

(18) In 1761, Wever in Berlin published a collection of my odes. Apropos of odes, I must mention that similar works of mine were already to be found in the collections of odes published by Gräfe, Krause, Lange, and Breitkopf.

(19) In 1761, Winter printed the second continuation of my clavier sonatas.

(20) In 1764, the same publisher released my first sonatina, set in C major, for harpsichord and several instruments.

(21) In the same year and with the same publisher, the supplement to Gellert's odes appeared.

(22) In 1765, Winter printed the second and third sonatinas set in D minor and E-flat major.

(23) In 1765, my six easy clavier sonatas were released by Breitkopf.

(24) In 1765, Birnstiel printed part one of my father's four-voice chorales, which I collected.

(25) In 1765, the first collection of clavier pieces of various sorts was released by Winter.

(26) In 1765, the first collection of my twelve short and easy clavier pieces for beginners likewise appeared with Winter.

(27) In 1766, my *Phillis and Tirsis,* a cantata, appeared with the same publisher. Further:

(28) A vocal ode by Gleim, *The Innkeeper and the Guests,* appeared with Winter in the same year.

(29) In1768, Winter printed the second collection of my twelve short and easy clavier pieces.

(30) In 1770, my sonatas for ladies were issued in engravings by Hummel in Amsterdam.

(31) In 1771, the *Musical Miscellany,* which I had edited and which contained many of my pieces, appeared here with Bock.

Since I am listing all of my works in print, I must take this opportunity to mention that there is a canonic invention by me in the third volume of Marpurg's *Contributions;* in Marpurg's *Treatise on the Fugue,* there are likewise various examples of my fugues and canons, especially those located at the end of part two, which treat and occasioned the supplement to part one. Many additional works by me appeared in Marpurg's *Critical Letters,* in the *Musical Miscellany* and *Musical Varia,* in Marpurg's *Practical Lessons on Playing the Clavier,* in Wever's *Musical Pieces,* in Birnstiel's *Idle Hours* and *Short Clavier Pieces,* in Spener's *Clavier Pieces,* in the *Conversations,* and in *Münter's Collection of Sacred Songs.* The second essay in hexameters is also by me.

(32) In 1770, Schönemann engraved in copper twelve small two- and three-voice pieces by me in octavo format.

(33) In 1772, I published six easy clavier concertos with accompaniment.

(34) In 1773, I set six four-part sinfonias upon request.

I have composed a considerable number of vocal pieces for the church and various ceremonial occasions, but none of them has been printed. Altogether, my compositions consist of approximately a few dozen sinfonias; 30 trios for the clavier and other instruments; eighteen solos for instruments other than the clavier; twelve sonatinas for one clavier with accompaniment; 49 concertos for the clavier and other instruments (the latter part of which I have also set for the clavier); among the keyboard concertos, one is for two harpsichords; 170 solos for clavier, most of which are sonatas but some of which consist of small collections of character pieces and other small works as well as settings of concertos, sinfonias, and fugues.

Because I was obliged to compose most of my works for certain persons and for the public, I have always been more restricted than in the few pieces composed only for myself. Occasionally I have even had to fulfill ridiculous specifications; yet for all that, it may be that such unpleasant circumstances have challenged my genius to certain inventions I might not otherwise have happened upon.

Since I have never loved excessive uniformity in composition and taste, have heard so much good work of such varied sorts, and have always been of the opinion that one should accept the good wherever it may be, even if to be found in only small measure in a piece; all this, along with my God-given natural talent, presumably accounts for the diversity of my compositions, which has often been noted. At this juncture I must observe that the worthy critics, if they write without passion (as happens all too seldom), very often treat the compositions they are reviewing too uncharitably, because they are unacquainted with the circumstances, the specifications, and the occasions for the pieces. How seldom indeed one encounters feeling, knowledge, honesty, and courage in proper measure in a critic—four attributes that every critic simply must have in adequate measure. It is therefore quite sad for the realm of music that criticism, which might otherwise be very useful, is often the occupation of minds that are not gifted with all these attributes.

Among all my works, especially for clavier, there are only a few trios, solos, and concertos that I have composed with total freedom and for my own use.

Especially in the last few years, I have been turning my attention to playing the clavier, and composing for it, as lyrically as possible, despite the impossibility of sustaining notes. This matter is not at all easy if one does not want to leave the ear empty or spoil the noble simplicity of song by too much noise.

It seems to me that music must first and foremost stir the heart, and a clavier player can never achieve this by mere pounding, drumming, and arpeggiating—at least not for me.

Translated by James Steakley

Christoph Willibald Gluck

Dedication of *Alceste* (1767)

To Grand Duke Leopold of Toscana

Royal Highness!

When I began to write the music for *Alceste*, I resolved to free it of all the abuses which have crept in either through ill-advised vanity on the part of singers or through excessive complaisance on the part of composers, with the result that for some time Italian opera has been disfigured, and the most splendid and beautiful of all stage performances has been made the most ridiculous and wearisome. I sought to restrict the music to its true purpose, serving to give expression to the poetry and to strengthen the dramatic situations without interrupting the action or hampering it with unnecessary and superfluous ornamentations. I believed that it should achieve the same effect as lively colors and a well-balanced contrast of light and shade on a very correct and well-disposed painting, so animating the figures without altering their contours. So I have tried to avoid interrupting an actor in the warmth of dialog with a boring intermezzo or stopping him in the midst of his discourse, merely so that the flexibility of his voice might show to advantage in a long passage, or that the orchestra might give him time to collect his breath for a cadenza. I did not think I should hurry quickly through the second part of an air, which is perhaps the most passionate and important, in order to have room to repeat the words of the first part regularly four times or to end the aria quite regardless of its meaning, in order to give the singer an opportunity of showing how he can render a passage with so-and-so many variations at will; in short, I have sought to eliminate all these abuses, against which sound common sense and reason have so long protested in vain.

I imagined that the overture should prepare the spectators for the action to be presented and give an indication of its subject; that the instrumental music should vary according to the interest and passion aroused, and that between the aria and the recitative there should not be too great a disparity, lest the flow of the period be spoiled and rendered meaningless, the movement interrupted inopportunely, or the warmth of the action dissipated. I believed further that I should devote my greatest effort to seeking to achieve a noble simplicity; and I have avoided parading difficulties at the expense of clarity. I have not placed any value on novelty, if it did not emerge naturally from the situation and the expression; and there is no rule I would not have felt dutybound to break in order to achieve the desired effect.

These are my principles. Happily all my intentions fitted admirably with the libretto, in which the famous author, having devised a new plan for the lyrical drama, has replaced florid descriptions, superfluous comparisons, sententious and frigid moralization with the language of the heart, with strong passion, interesting situations, and an ever-varied spectacle. My maxims have been vindicated by success, and the universal approval expressed in such an Enlightened city [Vienna] has convinced me that simplicity, truth, and lack of affectation are the sole principles of beauty in all artistic creations. Nonetheless, in spite of repeated demands by the most respectable persons that I should decide to publish this opera of mine in print, I have realized how much danger lies in fighting against such widespread and deep-rooted prejudices, and I have found it necessary to avail myself in advance of the powerful protection of Your Royal Highness by imploring the favor of prefixing my opera with His August Name, which so justly carries with it the approval of all Enlightened Europe. The great protector of the fine arts, who rules over a nation famed for having freed them from universal oppression and for having set in each of them the finest examples, in a city that has always been the first to break the yoke of vulgar prejudice and pave the way to perfection, can alone undertake the reform of this noble spectacle, in which all the fine arts play such a large part. When this has been accomplished, I shall have the glory of having moved the first stone, and this public testimony of Your Highness's protection, for which I have the honor to declare myself with the most humble respect

Your Royal Highness's
Most humble, most devoted,
most dutiful servant
Christoph Gluck

Translated by Stewart Thomson

To the *Mercure de France* (1773)

February 1773

Monsieur

I would lay myself open to just reproach, and I would reproach myself most severely, if, after having read the letter written from here to one of the directors of the Royal Academy of Music, which you published in the *Mercure* of October last and the subject of which is the opera *Iphigénie*—if, I say, after having expressed to the author of this letter my appreciation of the praises he was pleased to heap upon me, I did not hasten to point out that his friendship and too strong a prejudice in my favor have undoubtedly carried him away, and that I am very far from flattering myself that I deserve the praise he accords me. I would reproach myself even more if I consented to accept the credit for having invented the new form of Italian opera, the success of which has fully justified the experiment; it is to M. de Calzabigi that the chief merit belongs; and if my music has met with some approbation, I feel bound to admit that it is to him I am indebted for this, since it is he who made it possible for me to develop the resources of my art. This author, full of genius and talent, has in his poems *Orphée, Alceste,* and *Paris* pursued a course which is virtually unknown to the Italians. These works are full of happy situations, of those elements of terror and pathos which give a composer the opportunity to express great passion and to create forceful and moving music.

Whatever talent the composer may have, he will never create more than mediocre music if the poet does not arouse in him that enthusiasm without which all artistic productions are weak and spiritless; to imitate nature is the acknowledged aim which they must all set themselves. This is the aim which I seek to attain: always as simple and natural as possible, my music merely strives to achieve the fullest expression and to reinforce the poetic declamation. That is the reason why I do not employ the trills, passages, or cadenzas in which the Italians revel. Their language, which lends itself to these so easily, therefore has no advantage for me in this respect, though it has doubtless many others; but, born in Germany, any study I may have made of the Italian language, as also of the French language, is not, I believe, sufficient to enable me to appreciate the delicate nuances which may render one preferable to the other, and I think that all foreigners should abstain from judging their respective merits; but what I think is permissible for me to say is that the language which will always appeal to me most is that in which the poet provides me with the most varied opportunities to express the emotions; this is the advantage I believe I have found in the text of the opera *Iphigénie,* in which the poetry seemed to me to have all the vigor required to inspire good music. Although I have never been in the position of offering my works to any theater, I cannot hold it against the writer of the letter to one of the directors that he proposed my *Iphigénie* to your Academy of Music. I confess that I would have been pleased to produce it in Paris, because, by its effect and with the help of the famous M. Rousseau of Geneva whom I intended to consult, we might together, in seeking a noble, moving, and natural melody with a declamation in keeping with the prosody of each language and the character of each people, have succeeded in finding the medium I have in mind for producing a type of music suited to all nations and in eliminating the absurd distinctions between national forms of music. The study I have made of this great man's works on music, amongst others the letter in which he analyzes the monolog of Lully's *Armide,* prove the depth of his knowledge and his sureness of taste and have filled me with admiration. I was left with the profound conviction that if he had chosen to devote himself to the application of this art, he would have been able to achieve the prodigious effects that the ancients attributed to music. I am delighted to have this opportunity of paying him publicly this tribute, which I believe he deserves.

I beg you, Monsieur, to have the goodness to publish this letter in your next *Mercure*.

I have the honor to be, etc.

Chevalier Gluck

Translated by Stewart Thomson

To Friedrich Gottlieb Klopstock (1773)

Vienna, August 14, 1773

Nobly Born,

Most Highly Honored Councillor,

Father Denis has informed me that you desire to receive the verses which I composed on your *Battle of Arminius*. I would long since have done you this service if I had not been geometrically assured that many would not find them to their taste, because they must be sung with a certain decorum which is not as yet very much in fashion; for, although you have excellent musical artists, music which calls for enthusiasm seems to me to be still quite unknown in your parts, as I could clearly perceive from the criticism which was directed at my *Alceste* in Berlin. I am so great an admirer of your person that I promise you: (If you do not propose to come to Vienna) I will make a journey to Hamburg next year, in order to make your acquaintance, and I give my assurance that I will sing to you not only much from *The Battle of Arminius* but also some of your sublime odes, to make clear to you in how far I have measured up to your greatness or in how far I have obscured it with my music.

Meanwhile I am sending you a few songs, which are quite simple in style and easy to execute. Three of them are German in character and three with a more foreign flavor, and of the latter I have added two melodies in the old bardic style by way of experiment which can, however, always be thrown away. It will be necessary to choose a good pianoforte player for these, in order that they may appear to you less intolerable. I have the honor to continue to call myself with great respect,

Your Nobly Born's most obedient servant

Chevalier Gluck

Translated by Stewart Thomson

To the Baroness Anna von Fries (1777)

Madame,

I have been so plagued over music and I am so disgusted with it, that at present I would not write a single note for a louis. So you can imagine the extent of my devotion to you, Madame, since I could resolve to arrange for the harp the two songs which I have the honor to send you. Never was a more terrible and more hotly disputed battle fought than that over my opera *Armide*. The cabals against *Iphigénie, Orphée,* and *Alceste* were by comparison mere petty encounters with minor forces. The ambassador of Naples, in order to ensure that Piccinni's opera should be a great success, has been intriguing indefatigably against me both at court and amongst the nobility. He has won over Marmontel, La Harpe, and several academicians to write against my musical system and my way of composing. M. l'Abbé Arnaud, M. Suard, and a few others have rallied to my defence, and the quarrel became so heated that insults would have led to deeds if mutual friends had not restored order amongst them. The *Journal de Paris,* which is sold daily, is full of it. This dispute is making the editor a fortune, for he already has more than 2,500 subscribers in Paris. There, then, you have the revolution in French music carried out with the most blatant pomp. The enthusiasts tell me: Monsieur, you are fortunate to enjoy the honors of persecution; all great geniuses have experienced this. I would gladly send them to the devil with their fine speeches. The fact is that the opera which was said to have failed produced in seven performances 37,200 livres without reckoning the boxes rented for the year and the subscribers. Yesterday the eighth performance brought in 5,767 livres. Never has such a terrible crush nor such a sustained silence been known before. The pit was so crowded that one man, who had his hat on and was told by the attendant to remove it, replied: 'Come and remove it yourself, for I cannot use my arms.' That raised a laugh. I saw people coming out with their hair dishevelled and their clothes wringing wet, as if they had fallen into a river. Only a Frenchman would pay such a price for his pleasure. There are six points in the opera at which the public are forced to lose countenance and are carried away. Come, Madame, and see this tumult; it will amuse you as much as the opera itself. I am in despair that I cannot leave yet on account of the bad road: my wife is too frightened. I beg you to pay my compliments to the Baron and to Monsieur Gontard. I remain with the most perfect esteem,

Madame,
Your very humble and very obedient servant
Le Chevalier Gluck

P.S. My wife sends you a thousand tender regards.
Paris, November 16, 1777

Translated by Stewart Thomson

To Valentin (1782)

Vienna, April 17, 1782

Monsieur,

Your obliging letter gave me great pleasure and I must thank you for it.

It is very flattering to me and I see in it the imprint of an ardent genius, eager to learn, as well as the essential qualities of a good heart and an excellent character, which do you much honor.

If the state of my health permitted it and if I could still undertake something relating to dramatic art, I could think of nothing more pressing than to accept the offer you have just made me, and I am convinced that we would be both well pleased.

I have been ill for several months following an apoplectic stroke, which came upon me last year. My head is weakened and my right arm is paralyzed. I am incapable of doing the least work which is continuous; I am not allowed, and still less am I able, to apply myself in any way. So you see, Monsieur, that I cannot lend myself to your request, which does you so much credit and me so much honor. It is against my wishes but it is impossible to do otherwise.

You are young, Monsieur, and you are full of good will; work, and I have no doubt you will make progress, gain advancement, and achieve success.

Determination and courage in your studies, reflection and a sense of unity in a work as a whole, and above all the seeking of truth in expression: all these, allied to the rules of art, will take you far. The simplicity of nature and the force of emotion must be your guides more than all else. He who departs from them invariably slips into absurd incongruities, which condemn him to mediocrity.

These are my masters; they must be yours. In this school and with the natural and acquired qualities that are necessary, one finds the right road.

Several stray from it by failing to observe these rules of conduct while following an everyday routine.

Sound them, these masters, consult them, question them. They are gentle with those who seek them. They listen to you; they will reply; they will lead you.

Adieu, Monsieur.

Pray accept these few pieces of advice given to you by an invalid, who is no longer good for anything else, and rest assured of the feeling of esteem which you deserve, which you have inspired in me, and with which I have the honor, Monsieur, to be

Your very humble and very obedient servant
Le Chevalier Gluck

Translated by Stewart Thomson

Franz Joseph Haydn

To Leonore Lechner (1776)

Estoras, July 6, 1776

Mademoiselle!

You will not take it amiss if I hand you a hodgepodge of all sorts of things as an answer to your request: to describe such things properly takes time, and that I don't have; for this reason, I do not dare write to Monsieur Zoller personally, and therefore ask forgiveness.

I send you only a rough draft, for neither pride, nor fame, but solely the great kindness and marked satisfaction that so learned a national institution has shown towards my previous compositions, have induced me to comply with their demand.

I was born on the last day of March 1733, in the market town of Rohrau, Lower Austria, near Bruck on the Leitha. My late father was a wheelwright by profession, and served Count Harrach, a great lover of music by nature. He played the harp without knowing a note of music, and as a boy of 5, I correctly sang all his simple little pieces: this induced my father to entrust me to the care of my relative, the schoolmaster in Haimburg, in order that I might learn the rudiments of music and the other juvenile acquirements. Almighty God (to Whom alone I owe the most profound gratitude) endowed me, especially in music, with such proficiency that even in my 6th year I was able to sing some masses in the choir loft, and to play a little on the harpsichord and violin.

When I was 7, the late Kapellmeister von Reutter passed through Haimburg and quite accidentally heard my weak but pleasant voice.

He forthwith took me to the choir house [of St. Stephen's Cathedral in Vienna] where, apart fom my studies, I learned the art of singing, the harpsichord, and the violin, from very good masters. Until my 18th year I sang soprano with great success, not only at St. Stephen's but also at the court. Finally I lost my voice, and then had to eke out a wretched existence for eight whole years, by teaching young pupils (many geniuses are ruined by their having to earn their daily bread, because they have no time to study): I experienced this, too, and would have never learned what little I did, had I not, in my zeal for composition, composed well into the night; I wrote diligently, but not quite correctly, until at last I had the good fortune to learn the true fundamentals of composition from the celebrated Herr Porpora (who was at that time in Vienna): finally, by the recommendation of the late Herr von Fürnberg (from whom I received many marks of favor), I was engaged as *Directeur* at Herr Count von Morzin's, and from there as Kapellmeister of His Highness the Prince [Esterházy], in whose service I wish to live and die.

Inter alia the following compositions of mine have received the most approbation:

The operas
- *Le pescatrici*
- *L'incontro improvviso*
- *L'Infedeltà delusa,* performed in the presence of Her Imperial and Royal Majesty.

The oratorio   *Il ritorno di Tobia,* performed in Vienna.

The *Stabat mater,* about which I received (through a good friend) a testimonial of our great composer Hasse, containing quite undeserved eulogiums. I shall treasure this testimonial all my life, as if it were gold; not for its contents, but for the sake of so admirable a man.

In the chamber-musical style I have been fortunate enough to please almost all nations except the Berliners; this is shown by the public newspapers and letters addressed to me. I only wonder that the Berlin gentlemen, who are otherwise so reasonable, maintain no moderation in their criticism of my music, for in one weekly paper they praise me to the skies, while in another they dash me sixty fathoms deep into the earth, and this without explaining why; I know very well why: because they are incapable of performing some of my works, and are too conceited to take the trouble to understand them properly, and for other reasons which, with God's help, I will answer in good time. Herr Kapellmeister von Dittersdorf, in Silesia, wrote to me recently and asked me to defend myself against their hard words, but I answered that to do so would be premature; and that perhaps one of these days some unprejudiced person would stop their tongues, as happened to them once before when they accused me of monotony. Despite this, they try very hard to get all my works, as Herr Baron van Swieten, the Imperial and Royal Ambassador at Berlin, told me only last winter, when he was in Vienna: but enough of this.

Dear Mademoiselle Leonore: You will be good enough to give this present letter, and my compliments, to Monsieur Zoller for his consideration: my highest ambition is only that all the world regard me as the honest man I am.

I offer all my praises to Almighty God, for I owe them to Him alone: my sole wish is to offend neither my neighbor, nor my gracious Prince, nor above all our merciful God.

Meanwhile I remain, Mademoiselle, with high esteem,

Your most sincere friend and servant
Josephus Haydn

Translated by H. C. Robbins Landon

To Herr Rott (1787)

December 1787

. . . You ask me for an opera buffa. Most willingly, if you want to have one of my vocal compositions for yourself alone. But if you intend to produce it on the stage at Prague, in that case I cannot comply with your wish, because all my operas are far too closely connected with our personal circle (Esterház, in Hungary), and moreover they would not produce the proper effect, which I calculated in accordance with the locality. It would be quite another matter if I were to have the great good fortune to compose a brand new libretto for your theater. But even then I should be risking a good deal, for scarcely any man can brook comparison with the great Mozart.

If I could only impress on the soul of every friend of music, and on high personages in particular, how inimitable are Mozart's works, how profound, how musically intelligent, how extraordinarily sensitive! (for this is how I understand them, how I feel them)—why then the nations would vie with each other to possess such a jewel within their frontiers. Prague should hold him fast—but should reward him, too; for without this, the history of great geniuses is sad indeed, and gives but little encouragement to posterity to further exertions; and unfortunately this is why so many promising intellects fall by the wayside. It enrages me to think that this incomparable Mozart is not yet engaged by some imperial or royal court! Forgive me if I lose my head: but I love the man so dearly. I am, &c.

Joseph Hayden

P.S. My respectful compliments to the Prague Orchestra and all the virtuosi there.

Translated by H. C. Robbins Landon

To Maria Anna von Genzinger (1790)

Nobly born,
Most highly respected, and kindest Frau von Genzinger,
    Well, here I sit in my wilderness—forsaken—like a poor waif—almost without any human society—melancholy—full of the memories of past glorious days—yes! past alas!—and who knows when these days shall return again? Those wonderful parties? Where the whole circle is one heart, one soul—all these beautiful musical evenings—which can only be remembered, and not described—where are all these enthusiastic moments?—all gone—and gone for a long time. Your Grace mustn't be surprised that I haven't written up to now to thank you. I found everything at home in confusion, and for 3 days I didn't know if I was Kapell-master or Kapell-servant. Nothing could console me, my whole house was in confusion, my

pianoforte which I usually love so much was perverse and disobedient, it irritated rather than calmed me, I could only sleep very little, even my dreams persecuted me; and then, just when I was happily dreaming that I was listening to the opera, *Le nozze di Figaro*, that horrible north wind woke me and almost blew my nightcap off my head; I lost 20 lbs. in weight in 3 days, for the good Viennese food I had in me disapperared on the journey; alas! alas! I thought to myself as I was eating in the mess here, instead of that delicious slice of beef, a chunk of a cow 50 years old; instead of a ragout with little dumplings, an old sheep with carrots; instead of a Bohemian pheasant, a leathery joint; instead of those fine and delicate oranges, cole slaw or so-called big salad; instead of pastry, dry apple-fritters and hazelnuts—and that's what I have to eat. Alas! alas! I thought to myself, if I could only have a little bit of what I couldn't eat up in Vienna.—Here in Estoras no one asks me: Would you like some chocolate, with milk or without? Will you take some coffee, black, or with cream? What may I offer you, my dear Haydn? Would you like a vanilla or a pineapple ice? If I only had a good piece of Parmesan cheese, especially in Lent, so that I could more easily swallow those black dumplings and noodles; just today I told our porter here to send me a couple of pounds.

Forgive me, kindest and most gracious lady, for filling the very first letter with such stupid nonsense, and for killing time with such a wretched scrawl, but you must forgive a man whom the Viennese terribly spoiled. I am gradually getting used to country life, however, and yesterday I studied for the first time, and quite Haydnish, too. Your Grace will certainly have been more industrious than I. The pleasing Adagio from the Quartet has, I hope, by now received its true expression from your fair fingers. My good friend Fräulein Peperl will (I hope) be reminded of her teacher by singing the Cantata frequently; she should remember to have a distinct articulation and a correct vocal production, for it would be a crime if so beautiful a voice were to remain hidden in her breast; so therefore I ask her to smile frequently, lest I be disappointed in her. Likewise I advise Monsieur Francois to cultivate his musical talents; even when he sings in his dressing-gown, he does very nicely. I shall often send him some new things to encourage him. Meanwhile I again kiss your hands for all your kind favors, and am, as always, most respectfully,

Your Grace's
most sincere and wholly
obedient servant,
Josephus Haydn

Estoras, February 9, 1790

Translated by H. C. Robbins Landon

To the Administrator of the Esterházy Estate (1796 or 1797)

Nobly born,
Highly respected Administrator!
  From the letter addressed to me and the enclosure of the worthy Privy Economic Administration of His Serene Highness Prince Esterházy, I saw that I am more or less *condemned* to pay the debt of Luegmayer, who because of *insolvency* is not able to do so. Why? Because I am thought to possess the necessary *means:* I wish to God it were so! But I *swear* by the Kyrie eleison which I am at this moment supposed to compose for my *fourth* Prince, that since the death of my *second* Prince—God rest his soul!—I have fallen into the *same state of insolvency* as that of Luegmayer, but with the difference that he has fallen from his horse to the back of an ass, whilst I have managed to remain on the horse, but without saddle or harness.
  I therefore beg the worthy Privy Economic Administration of His Highness to wait at *least* till I have finished the Dona nobis pacem, and until the Prince's house-master Luegmayer shall begin to receive the salary rightly due to him from his most gracious Prince, instead of drawing it, as he has hitherto done, from the *small* salary of Kapellmeister Haydn (who has been 36 years in the Princely service). For nothing is sadder or more dissonant than when one *servant* pays another *servant,* in this case the Kapellmeister having to pay the house-master. If I should, perhaps today or tomorrow, be placed in a *better* position, either as a result of my own merits or by the voluntary impulse of my most gracious Prince *(for flatter*

and beg I will not), of course I shall not fail to comply with the above demand.

I am, Sir, with every respect,

Your most obliging servant,
Fran[z] J. Haydn
Doctor of Oxford and Princely Esterházy
Kapellmeister

Translated by H. C. Robbins Landon

To Christoph Gottlob Breitkopf (1799)

Vienna, June 12, 1799

Dearest Friend!

I am really very much ashamed to have to offend a man who has written so often and honored me with so many marks of esteem (which I do not deserve), by answering him at this late date; it is not negligence on my part but the vast amount of *business* which is responsible, and the older I get, the more business I have to transact daily. I only regret that on account of my growing age and (unfortunately) the decrease of my mental powers, I am able to dispatch but the smallest part of it. Every day the world pays me compliments on the fire of my recent works, but no one will believe the strain and effort it costs me to produce them: there are some days in which my enfeebled memory and the unstrung state of my nerves crush me to the earth to such an extent that I fall prey to the worst sort of depression, and thus am quite incapable of finding even a single idea for many days thereafter; until at last Providence revives me, and I can again sit down at the pianoforte and begin to scratch away again. Enough of this!

Yesterday Herr Griesinger brought me the 2nd, 3rd and 4th volumes of our immortal Mozart, together with the musical periodical. Please let me know how much I owe you for them, and to whom I should give the money here in Vienna.

The publication of both these things does you great credit. I *would only wish, and hope, that the critics do not deal too severely with my* Creation: *they might perhaps object a little to the musical orthography of certain passages, and possibly some other minor points elsewhere; but the true connoisseur will see the reasons for them as readily as I do, and will push aside this stumbling-block.* Nulla regola s[enza] e[ccezione]. *N.B.: As for the tattered section in the Duet of the* Creation, *you will find it entirely different in the edition from that which Herr Traeg had the twopenny Kramer prepare for him: but all this underlined* inter nos.

Apart from all this, I shall be very happy to serve you in any possible way. Meanwhile, my dear friend, I remain, with every esteem,

Your obliging and obedient servant,
Joseph Haydn

Translated by H. C. Robbins Landon

To the Members of the Bergen Musical Association on Rügen (1802)

Gentlemen,

It was indeed a most pleasant surprise to receive such a flattering letter from a part of the world where I could never have imagined that the products of my poor talents were known. But when I see that not only is my name familiar to you, but my compositions are performed by you with approval and satisfaction, the warmest wishes of my heart are fulfilled: to be considered a not wholly unworthy priest of this sacred art by every nation where my works are known. You reassure me on this point as regards your fatherland, but even more, you happily persuade me—and this cannot fail to be a real source of consolation to me in my declining years—that I am often the enviable means by which you, and so many other families sensible of heartfelt emotion, derive, in their homely circle, their pleasure—their enjoyment. How reassuring this thought is to me!—Often, when struggling against the obstacles of every sort which oppose my labors; often, when the powers of mind and body weakened, and it was difficult for me to continue in the course I had entered on;—a secret voice whispered to me: "There are so few happy and contented peoples here below; grief and sorrow are always their lot; perhaps your labors will once be a source from which the care-worn, or the man burdened with affairs, can derive a few moments' rest and refreshment." This was indeed a powerful motive to press onwards, and this is why I now look back with cheerful satisfaction on the labors expended on this art, to which I have devoted so many long years of uninterrupted effort and exertion. And now I thank you in the fullness of my heart for your kindly thoughts of me, and beg you to forgive me for delaying my answer so long: enfeebled health, the inseparable companion of the grey-haired septuagenarian, and pressing business deprived me till now of this pleasure. Perhaps nature may yet grant me the joy of composing a little memorial for you, from which you may gather the feelings of a gradually dying veteran, who would fain even after his death survive in the charming circle of which you draw so wonderful a picture. I have the honor to be, with profound respect,

Your wholly obedient servant,
Joseph Haydn

Vienna, September 22, 1802

Translated by H. C. Robbins Landon

Karl Ditters von Dittersdorf

From the *Autobiography* (1799)

The eventful day was ushered in gloriously by the most perfect weather, and the noble guests with their suites, consisting of minions of high degree, reached Schlosshof at one o'clock. The Emperor, the Empress, the Archduke Joseph, the Archduke Karl, the Archduchesses Marianne and Christine were all there; Prince Salm, the Mistress of the Robes, and six other gentlemen and ladies were of the suite; they did not bring many servants.

The grandees made no formal entry; there were no triumphal arches, no volleys of mortars and cannon, no blaring trumpets nor shouting. The Prince had forbidden all parade in order to enhance the surprise of the other fine sights. He received the visitors at the principal gate, attended only by Hofkavalier Beust.

After luncheon, the guests drove to Niederwenden, and when the Prince had shown them all over it, he set them down at an open-air theater, with a noble view of the blue mountains of Pressburg in the background. Then, when the overture to the play began, a crowd of peasants pressed forward; some of them kept at a distance, others clambered up the trees, to the great amusement of the Emperor. How surprised and delighted he was when all the peasants—men, women, youths, and maidens, either standing in a circle or perched on the boughs of the trees—broke out into a chorus of over two hundred voices and repeated the last strophe of the drama, whenever it occurred, with such correctness and purity of intonation, that they might have been taken for professional singers. This was so extraordinarily effective that everyone was struck, and the Emperor grew quite emotional.

The Emperor was naturally simple and unconventional, full of delicacy and kindness. Seeing the Prince about to withdraw, to change his dress, he good-naturedly interposed:

"Pray stay as you are, Prince—and I shall be obliged if you will let me be as I am, for if not, I shall be the only person unadorned in the company, and everyone will think me eccentric."

The Empress added, with all her husband's kindliness:

"Do keep on your pilgrim's coat, if you want to be thought my particular friend!"

It would weary my readers were I to make a long yarn about all the many *fêtes*, fireworks, bacchanal scenes, and hunting parties which were the order of the day; but I cannot help a word or two before leaving the subject for good, because, in the sad circumstances of my present condition, it cheers me up to let my fancy dwell on these scenes of my merry youth, and I think I can promise myself that it will please my readers too. What is every biography but the tale of a journey in a foreign land? Now and then it is pleasant to get rid of the guide, and to talk about other things for a change.

So I mean to tell all about a water-*fête*, given on an artificial lake at Kroissenbrunn, which had been planned by Prince Eugen, and walled round with large blocks of freestone, by his orders. It was eighty feet broad and a hundred long. From bank to bank, in the center of the lake, two galleries were thrown across; on each of these were seated a number of trumpeters and drummers, with other players on wind instruments; they were heard playing alternate strains.

In the lake itself, at a little distance from the shore, there stood, at regular intervals on each side, eight pedestals, painted so as to look like stone, and adorned with bronzed grotesques. On the first two pedestals, two live bears stood opposite each other, dressed as clowns; on the second two, two wild-boars, dressed as columbines; on the third, two big goats, dressed as harlequins; and on the fourth were two huge bulldogs.

You may fancy the noise made by growling bears, grunting pigs, bleating goats, howling dogs, and the music going on at the same time! All the masqueraders stood in the attitudes that best became their parts.

The picturesque hills, on both sides of the lake, were thronged with some thousands of spectators. Opposite the fishing-cottage stood a gallery, resting on pillars, with railings through which you could look. It was a wooden construction, but Quaglio, the famous stage architect, properly called *il Bibiena redivivo* ('the great architect, Cavaliere Bibiena, restored to life'), had so disguised it with a coat of paint that anyone looking at it from a distance would have taken it for stonework.

After allowing his guests an interval in which to enjoy the scene, the Prince waved his handkerchief as a signal, and the show began.

Two gondolas emerged at either end of the gallery, and made towards the cottage; each was manned by four gondoliers dressed in Venetian fashion. One of them sat on the beak of the vessel, with a bundle of spears, lances, and similar weapons laid crosswise before him; two others rowed, and the steerer, turning the gondola wherever he chose, sat behind them. These two gondolas advanced, circling in different ways round the pedestals; they were afterwards joined by two others, then by two more, and then the last two. The eight went through their maneuvers with such accuracy, that no ballet-master, marshalling his *danseuses,* could have improved upon them. When they had gone their rounds, they were ranged face to face, and a tournament began, in which each water-knight, seated on the beak, broke from four to five lances; then they went once more round the pedestals on which the comic actors stood. At one and the same moment, each knight, armed with a staff, struck at one of the grotesque masks, a spring gave way under the blow, and a trap door fell. Numbers of white ducks and geese, and one swan as well, were concealed in each of the hollow pedestals, and you may fancy the alacrity with which these winged creatures took to their native element, though a marionette rode upon each of them. These marionettes were various figures, proportioned to the size of the birds which they bestrode—clowns, harlequins, Anselmos, dottores, Leanders, Pasquins, Scaramouches, and other carnival mummers.

A fray ensued, and the knights seized their clubs and threatened one another. The gondolas darted about in studied disorder. When one collided with another, the knights dipped their clubs, which were hand-syringes, into the lake, and squirted their enemies. Whenever they neared a pedestal, the creature on it got the whole benefit of a shower bath, and the animals loudly resented the rudeness of the whole proceeding. The effect on the audience may be imagined, for orders had been given to the musicians on either bank to blow in any key they chose. Directly after the skirmish had begun, one trumpeter blew a shrill blast in D, while another, with the aid of a crook, did the same in C, and another in E *la fa*. Some of the drummers had tuned up, others had tuned down; oboists, clarinettists, bassoon players, followed suit. What an infernal discord it was! The beasts growled, the ducks and geese quacked and spluttered, coming into collision with the moving gondolas every moment, and the three thousand spectators roared with laughter. Show me the hypochondriac who could remain unmoved by such a spectacle!

When the scene had lasted long enough, the gondolas withdrew, and to the astonishment of all the spectators, the gallery was metamorphosed into a willow grove. Laughter died away on their lips. Even the chorus of animals and birds, who now beheld their tormentors vanishing in the distance, went out in a diminuendo in spite of the efforts of the Elector of Mannheim's orchestra (which was then very famous for this sort of thing). Everyone was on the *qui vive,* and staring at the magic grove, in eager expectation of the wonders about to be revealed there.

From the center of the grove there slowly rose a pretty little garden, which looked like a floating island; it went on moving, as though of itself, for about a quarter of an hour, towards the fishing house. It was fenced all round with palisades, painted white and green, half the height of a man. The garden was planted with regular borders of box, within which flourished all sorts of most lovely flowers that happened to be in bloom just then. Between the borders were vases, painted white and green, containing twelve pomegranate and orange trees, laden with ripe fruit. In the middle of the garden was a round basin, filled with shoals of little fish. A small dolphin, too, was seen disporting himself, and throwing up a jet of water. That was not all. At the end of the garden was Parnassus, with the winged Pegasus. At the blow of his hoof, two streams bubbled out to the right and left of the rocks, and fell into the basin by means of a little canal.

Baron Beust, dressed as a gardener, and Mademoiselle Heinisch, as a gardener's wife, stood at the entrance. The lady wore a white and green satin dress, covered with real flowers. The gardener had a gilded rake, and the lady a gilded watering can.

Two fishermen and fisherwomen, dressed in white and sky-blue satin, stood near the basin. I represented one, the second was my younger brother, and Mademoiselle Heinisch the younger and my sister took the women's parts. Each of us had a small draw-net, with a handle of black fretted wood, the nets being composed of thin silver lace.

When the garden had reached them, the royal guests were invited by the gardener to enter and pick the flowers. They gathered several nosegays, and the Archdukes and Archduchesses, to whom we had handed the nets, drew fish out of the basin, and threw them into the lake. At last they sat down on the benches provided for them along the palisade. The gardener and his wife retreated to Parnassus, where there were plenty of ices, which they handed round in the most dainty glasses.

I shall never forget the scene—the mild summer evening, the grateful coolness after the glaring heat of the day, the soothing music of the wind instruments, the happy faces all around, and the graciousness and kindness displayed by the good Prince to everyone, the humblest guest included.

I still have before my eyes the exquisite performance of *La danza,* the slight comic opera, arranged by Metastasio from his play *Il ballo cinese,* and set to music by Gluck. Quaglio's decorations were quite in the Chinese taste, and transparent. Workers in lacquer, carpenters, and gilders had lavished all their resources upon them, but their chief brilliancy depended on prismatic poles of glass, which had been polished by Bohemian craftsmen and were carefully fitted into one another in empty places, previously soaked in colored oils. They were very effective, even in sunshine and the broad light of day, but no pen can describe the surpassing and astounding brilliancy of these prisms when lit up by innumerable lamps. The reader must imagine the reflected brilliancy of the azure-coloured meadows of lacquer, the glitter of the gilded foliage, and, lastly, the rainbow-like colors repeated by hundreds of prisms, and flashing like diamonds of the finest clarity. The most vivid fancy will fall short of the real magic. And then, Gluck's divine music! It was not only the delicious playfulness of the sparkling symphony, accompanied now and again by little bells, triangles, small hand drums, etc., sometimes singly, sometimes all together, which, at the very outset, and before the rising of the curtain, transported the audience: the music was from first to last an enchantment.

When the piece was over, the Emperor and the Prince left their seats, and asked that the curtain might be raised again, which was done. The monarch, opera glass in hand, stepped on to the stage, and Quaglio explained to him every detail. He asked for a fragment of one of the prisms; a hatful was brought to him, and he carried off three or four pieces. Then he entreated the Prince to be allowed to summon a draftsman from Vienna, to make a drawing of the scenery. Quaglio, however, undertook the business, and finished his sketch on the following evening. The Emperor rewarded him with a handsome gold watch and chain.

In the following winter, the Emperor ordered a performance of the play in the Hoftheater near the Burg (the present National Theater), and the *mise-en-scène* caused a great sensation in Vienna. I have often seen the play there, but in all honesty I must own that the staging was very inferior to that at Schlosshof, though the coloring was the same, after the same design, and they used the very same prisms. I cannot account for the fact. Besides this, the actors, except as singers (they had the great Gabrieli and others of equal merit among them), were not to be compared with ours—they had not been trained by Tesi.

The six days of feasting and revelry were over; the guests returned to Vienna, highly delighted with their entertainment. The Emperor ordered the Paymaster General in Vienna to grant the officers of the little brigade a month's salary on their return, and a similar gratuity was given to the lower officers and enlisted men. The Empress presented Tesi with two bracelets, valued at two thousand gulden, containing portraits of the Emperor and herself, set in brilliants. Baron Beust received from Prince Salm a gold snuffbox with a lid of brilliants. Mesdemoiselles Heinisch and Starzer were given magnificent dresses; Gluck and Bonno had a gold snuffbox apiece, containing a hundred ducats. Twelve hundred ducats were distributed among the servants and huntsmen.

To prevent any complaint as to favoritism, the Prince ordered the Treasurer to pay according to the rate of wages. He was just going, when the Prince called after him: "Karl, poor fellow! will get too little, with his two hundred gulden; you had better reward him as if he earned four hundred."

When the people moved off, it was discovered that four horses, decked in the Imperial harness, had been left, tied by their tails to the manger, and it was briefly believed that the grooms had forgotten their charge in a drunken fit; but on closer examination, a paper was found attached to each horse's cloth, on which the Emperor himself had written:

"*Ces quatre chevaux, mon cher Prince, sont de ce moment à votre disposition.—François Premier.*"

The Prince had the horses led out, and when the cloths were taken off, everyone praised their beauty and their splendid appointments. The present was worthy of an Emperor of the Romans and of a Prince of Saxony-Hildburghausen.

We resumed our ordinary life after a lapse of three months, with this difference, that the Prince received many more visits from the neighborhood and from Vienna. On such occasions there were frequent repetitions of the new operas, both at Niederwenden and in the theater.

Translated by A. D. Coleridge

Karl Stamitz

To King Friedrich Wilhelm II of Prussia (1791)

Greiz en Vogtland, April 12, 1791

Sire!

In accordance with Your Majesty's commands, I have the honor to present four selected compositions. A *Symphonie à double orchestres,* the first I ever composed in my life.

Next is a *Symphonie figurée en quatre parties;* the idea for this comes from Versailles in 1772. That year the summer was not at all agreeable, but toward the beginning of October the weather was lovely and every morning the Queen used to go walking in the country. For this I imitated a pastoral. Toward evening a storm springs up, and the night is very dark. But the next day brings fine weather again and the King continues the hunt he ordered the day before.

The third piece is an *Echo à deux orchestres,* for which the second orchestra is closed up in another room.

The fourth, an *Ouverture d'un bal masqué,* I composed at The Hague for Their Most Serene Highnesses the Prince and Princess of Orange. It was performed in the presence of the Grand Duke of Russia. They deigned to express their pleasure, especially the Prince, who graciously considered this piece his favorite.

Since the Ambassador of Turkey is now in Berlin and Your Majesty will certainly desire to honor him with several different kinds of entertainment, and the Turks are fond of this very noisy music, I thought it well to send you these pieces. I would have offered Your Majesty the last three pieces a long time ago, but they were in no state for me to have ventured to present them until now.

Sire, I most humbly request that when these pieces are performed, the orchestra be arranged in the manner I have indicated so as to create the proper effect and meet with your entire satisfaction. I shall attain the height of happiness should these compositions receive the approval of Your Majesty, who is so great a critic and connoisseur. I have the honor of commending myself to your august protection and am, with the deepest respect, Sire,

Your Majesty's most humble and obedient servant,
Charles Stamitz

Translator anon.

Christian Gottlob Neefe

From the *Autobiography* (1789)

Result of an Observation of Myself

My body is small and of Aesopian build and inordinately spare. My temperament is choleric-melancholic. It has also something of the phlegmatic and sanguinic. I have a vivid imagination, quick sensibility, weak memory; stronger is my power of judgment and a feeling for all that is morally and physically good and beautiful. But this feeling is not always equally warm. I cherish the religion of the heart, love all human beings, hate evil-mindedness, willingly indulge errors of reasoning, and gladly excuse weaknesses of the heart. I am ready to help, have compassion with the unfortunate, am coldhearted against the poor who are so because of idleness.

I honor the fair sex. My heart is very much inclined toward friendship; yet I no longer establish friendships so easily, because betrayals by so-called friends have made me suspicious and reserved. Toward proven friends, however, I am faithful, outgoing, openhearted, and communicative. Candid I am with everyone.

I am no friend of ceremony, of etiquette, or of empty compliments. I often become peculiar for that reason, and perhaps even offensive. Flatterers and telltales I detest.

I love my family and insist on strict discipline and order in my household. I love order in general and demand it of all those with whom I have any connection.

In my married life I am abstinent. I do not like to let marital and social relationships intrude into my more general duties.

I like to be usefully busy, am never really idle: but mechanical work goes against my grain. Without being in the mood, I don't compose. And the works which I had at times to get ready when I was not in the mood are the ones I no longer care to acknowledge as mine.

I have a bent for solitude and life in the country. I am sad and gay; but the former more than the latter. These two passions, sadness and gayness, alternate sometimes very quickly with me, as with all hypochondriacs. In a hypochondriacal mood, I easily see things in a false light. Also at such times, a tendency toward exaggerated thriftiness comes over me; I normally do not value money very much. The weather has a particularly strong influence upon my body and humor, sometimes I am a spirited companion, sometimes also a very tedious one. Occasionally, I am gruff and bitter in my expressions.

Rank and title are meaningless to me if they do not contribute something to solid effectiveness. Yet I always love honor, and it is the driving force of many of my actions. I am not at all indifferent about reasonable acclaim. However, sometimes I am too proud, sometimes too humble. At times too forward, at times too timid. Often I deem myself capable of carrying out the most difficult tasks, and soon thereafter I believe I cannot make a minuet, or write a letter to a shoemaker.

To every outside merit I gladly give its due, may it equal my own or surpass it, even if I encounter it among my enemies.

Lofty sentiments, generous deeds, displays of filial and parental love and of rectitude rewarded have my special approval.

One-sided taste I can as little abide as compendious erudition. I like to be independent, without wanting to disregard all circumstances. I am sensitive, hot-tempered, easily offended by mockeries, by attacks against my honor and my heart, by interference with my office, and by neglected professional duties; but am also easy to mollify and reconcile again. Except I don't like to take the first step toward a reconciliation if I have been offended, but will, if I was the offender. Vindictive I am not, and I never let private insults affect the whole which totally or partly depends upon my activity. I hate cliquishness. Confidence to one who has once deliberately betrayed me, I regain with difficulty.

Matters the truth of which I am convinced, or believe to be convinced, I will argue with warmth, even with heat. My memory is not too short for benefits received. I return them willingly, according to my ability, if I find occasion for it.

I like to drink wine, sometimes more than I, for my health, should; I must beware of that beverage, however, when I have business or work before me. I can otherwise restrict my needs according to my circumstances. I don't let myself be tyrannized by fashion.

I love the great ones of this earth, if they're good people, I cherish their laws, if they promote the best for civic society. Yet I never force myself upon them. Evil rulers I hate like bandits.

I strive for the expansion of my knowledge and the improvement of my heart, even though I have also therein not infrequently to fight against weaknesses, negligences, passions, and circumstances.

Translated by Felix Pollak

Wolfgang Amadeus Mozart

To Archbishop Hieronymus von Colloredo (1777)

Salzburg, August 1, 1777

Your Most Royal Grace, Most Venerable Prince
of the Holy Roman Empire, Most Gracious Sovereign,
and Lord Master!

I will not importune Your Most Royal Grace with a lengthy description of our unhappy circumstances, which my father, on his honor and conscience, made known in all truthfulness in his most humble petition handed to you on March 14, 1777. Since, however, upon this most humble petition the hoped for graciously favorable decision was not forthcoming, my father would have beseeched you most graciously to permit us a journey of several months in order to help us recuperate somewhat, if Your Lordship had not graciously commanded the musicians to be ready for the visit of His Majesty the Emperor with one or the other piece. Thereupon my father again humbly requested your permission for leave of absence, which, however, Your Most Royal Grace denied while most graciously suggesting that possibly I—only half in your employ in any case—should travel alone. Our situation is urgent, and my father has therefore decided to let me go alone. But even here Your Most Royal Grace etc. has been pleased to raise certain objections. Most Gracious Sovereign and Lord Master! Our parents strive to put their children in a position to earn their own bread; and this they owe to themselves as well as to the state. The greater the talents the children have received from God, the more they are obliged to utilize them to improve their own and their parents' circumstances, and to provide for their own advancement and future. The investment of talent the Gospel indeed prescribes for us. I am dutybound before God and my conscience to show gratitude with all my might to my father—who untiringly applies all his hours to my education—by easing his burden and providing for myself and later on also for my sister. For I would deplore it if my sister, after having spent so many hours at the harpsichord, were unable to make good use of it.

May Your Most Royal Grace etc. therefore graciously permit me most humbly to request my discharge from your services, since I am compelled to take advantage of the coming autumn month so as not to be exposed to the inclement weather of the ensuing cold months. Your Most Royal Grace will not be displeased by my most humble request, seeing that three years ago, when I asked for permission to travel to Vienna, Your Royal Highness decided against me and most graciously declared that I had nothing to hope for here and would do better to seek my fortune elsewhere. I thank Your Most Royal Grace in deepest humility for all the high benefits received and, in the fervent hope of being able to serve Your Most Royal Grace in my adult years with a modicum of success and commending myself to your continuing highest favor and grace, am

> Your Most Royal Grace's,
> Most Gracious Sovereign's,
> and Lord Master's
> Most humble and obedient servant,
> Wolfgang Amadé Mozart

Translation by Emily Anderson
adapted by Felix Pollak and James Steakley

To Maria Anna Thekla Mozart (1777)

Mannheim, December 3, 1777
Ma très chère Cousine!

Before I write to you, I must go to the john. Well, that's over. Ah! At last I feel relieved, a weight is off my heart; and now I can gobble again. Oh, oh, when you've emptied yourself, life is far more worth living. Your letter of November 25 would have left me in good spirits if you hadn't written that you had had pains in your head, throat, and arms; but as you say that now, at the moment, for the present, for the nonce, at this instant you feel no more pains, I have received your letter of November 26 gladly. Yes, yes, my dearest Miss Cousin, thus has it been since the days of old, one has the purse, the other the gold; and what do you hold it with? with your ⟨drawing⟩, don't you? Ta-ra-ra-boom, copper-smith, hold on tight, ⟨drawing⟩ pinch me not, ass my kiss, copper-smith. Yes, and true it is that whosoever believes it sees the pearly gates, and whosoever does not will go to heaven, but straight, and not the way I'm scribbling. You see now that I can write just as I please, both fair and untidy, both straight and crooked. The other day I was in a bad mood, and I wrote a fair, straight, and serious hand; today I am in good spirits, and I am writing an untidy, crooked, and jolly one. So all depends now on what you prefer. You must make the choice (I have nothing in between to offer you): fair or untidy, straight or crooked, serious or jolly, and the three first or the three last. I expect to hear your decision in your next letter. My mind is made up; when it's necessary, I go somewhere; but it all depends on circumstances. If I have diarrhea, I run: and if I can't hold it any longer, I shit in my pants. God preserve thee, foot, because my calf is lying on the window sill. I am much obliged to you, my dear Miss Cousin, for the compliments from your Miss Freysinger, which your dear Miss Juliana has been so kind as to send me. You say: "I could tell you a great deal more, but too much is more than enough." In *one* letter it is too much, I admit, but little by little one can write a great deal. You see what I mean? As for the sonata, patience is indicated a little longer. If it had been for my dear little cousin, it would have been finished long ago. Who knows whether Mademoiselle Freysinger hasn't forgotten all about it? All the same I'll get it done as soon as possible, write a letter to accompany it, and beg my dear cousin to deliver them safely. Apropos, since leaving Augsburg I haven't taken off my pants, except at night before going to bed. What will you think when you hear that I am still in Mannheim, in the thick of it? The reason is that I haven't gone somewhere else, anywhere! But now I think Mannheim will soon be gone. Yet Augsburg, through you, can continue to write to me and address letters to Mannheim until further notice. My uncle, my aunt, and my cousin send their greetings to my mama and me. They were very worried about us and thought that we must be ill, as they had received no letter from us for so long. But at last to their delight they received the day before yesterday our letter of November 26, and today, December 3, they were pleased to answer me. So I'll keep my promise to you. Well, are you glad to hear this? Be sure you don't forget to compose Munich according to sonata, for what one has kept, one must promise, one must always be a word of one's man. But seriously now.

I have to tell you something quickly. I didn't eat at home today, but at a certain Monsieur Wendling's. Now you must know that he always eats at one-thirty, that he is also married and has a daughter who, however, is always sickly. His wife will be singing in the coming opera and he will be playing the flute. Now, imagine, when it was half past one we all sat down and ate, except for the daughter who stayed in bed.

Please give a whole shitload of regards from both of us to all our good friends. Our regards to your parents are on page three, line twelve. Well, now I have no more news except that an old cow has shat a new cowpie. And herewith adieu, Anna Maria Locksmith, née Keymaker. Take good care of yourself and keep loving me. Your letter don't withhold, 'cause I'm feeling mighty cold; keep your word or I'll drop a turd. Adieu, mon Dieu, I kiss you a thousand times and send you my dirty rhymes!

Mannheim	Ma très chère cousine,
Without slime,	Were you never in Berlin?
The 3rd of December	Your cousin of virtues rare
Be sure to remember,	In weather foul or fair,
1777 in deep nocturnity,	W. A. Mozart,
From now on to all eternity.	Who shits without a fart.
Amen.	

Translation by Emily Anderson
adapted by Felix Pollak and James Steakley

To Leopold Mozart (1781)

Vienne, ce 9 de Juin, 1781

Mon très cher Père!

Well, Count Arco has made a nice mess of things! So that is the way to persuade people and to win them over! To refuse petitions out of innate stupidity, not to say a word to your master for lack of courage and love of toadyism, to keep a fellow hanging for four weeks, and finally, when he is forced to present the petition in person, instead of *at least* granting him admittance, to throw him out of the room and give him a kick in the butt—that is the Count, who, according to your last letter, has my interest so much at heart—and that is the court where I ought to go on serving—the place where anyone who wants to make a written application, instead of having its delivery facilitated, is treated in this fashion! The scene took place in the antechamber. So the only thing to do was to break away and run—for, although Arco had already done so, I did not wish to show disrespect to the Prince's apartments. I have written three memoranda, which I have handed in five times; and they have always been thrown back at me. I have carefully kept them, and anyone who wishes to read them may do so and convince himself that they do not contain the slightest personal insinuation. When at last I was handed back my memorandum in the evening by Herr von Kleinmayr (for that is his job here), I was beside myself with rage, as the Archbishop's departure was set for the following day. I could not let him leave that way and, when I heard from Arco (or so at least he told me) that the Prince knew nothing about it, I realized how angry he would be with me for staying on so long and then appearing at the very last moment with a petition of this kind. I therefore wrote another memorandum, in which I explained to the Archbishop that it was now four weeks since I had drawn up a petition, but, finding myself for some unknown reason forever put off, I was now compelled to present it to him in person, though at the very last moment. This memorandum procured me my dismissal from his service in the best way in the world. For who knows whether the whole thing was not done by order of the Archbishop in the first place? If Herr von Kleinmayr still wishes to maintain the character of an honest man, he can testify, as can also the Archbishop's servants, that his command was carried out. So now I need not send in any petition, for the affair is at an end. I don't want to write anything more on the subject, and if the Archbishop were to offer me a salary of 1200 florins, I would not accept it after such treatment. How easy it would have been to persuade me to stay on! But with civility, not with insolence and rudeness. I sent a message to Count Arco saying *that I had nothing more to say to him.* Because he so barked at me the first time and treated me as if I were a scoundrel, which he had no right to do. And—by God! as I have already told you, I wouldn't have gone to him the last time if in his message he hadn't added that he'd received a letter from you. Well, that finishes it. What business is it of his if I wish to get my discharge? And if he were really so well disposed towards me, he ought to have reasoned quietly with me—or have let things take their own course, instead of throwing such words as "knave" and "varlet" around and booting a fellow out of the room with a kick in the ass; but I am forgetting that this may have been done by order of our worthy Prince Archbishop.

I shall reply very briefly to your letter, for I am so sick of the whole affair that I never want to hear anything more about it. Given the original *cause* of my leaving (which you know well), no father would dream of being angry with his son; on the contrary, he would be angry if his son *had not left.* Still less ought you to have been angry, *since you knew that even without any particular cause I definitely wanted to leave.* Really, you can't be serious; and I must assume that you are acting this way because of your position at court. But I beg you, most beloved father, not to fawn too much; for the Archbishop cannot do you any harm. Let him try! I almost wish he would; for that would truly be a misdeed which would ruin him completely in the eyes of the Emperor, who, as it is, not only dislikes him, but actually hates him. If after such treatment you were to come to Vienna and tell the story to the Emperor, you would in any event receive from him the salary you are drawing at present, for in such cases the Emperor behaves most admirably. Your comparing me with Madame Lange absolutely amazed me and distressed me all day. That girl lived on her parents as long as she could earn nothing for herself. But as soon as the time came when she could show them her gratitude (remember that her father died before she had earned anything in Vienna), she deserted her poor mother, attached herself to an actor, and married him—and her mother never got a *thing* from her. Good God! *He* knows that my sole aim is to help you and to help us all. Must I repeat it a hundred times that I can be of more use to you here than in Salzburg? I implore you, dearest, most beloved father, spare me such letters in the future. I implore you to do so, for they only irritate my mind and disturb my heart and spirit; and I, having to compose all the time, need a serene mind and a calm disposition. The Emperor is not here, nor is Count Rosenberg. The latter has commissioned Schröder (the eminent actor) to look around for a good libretto and to give it to me to compose.

Herr von Zetti had to leave unexpectedly by command and set off so very early that I can neither send the portrait, nor the ribbons for my sister, nor *the other thing you know of* until a week from tomorrow by the mail coach.

Now farewell, dearest, most beloved father! I kiss your hands a thousand times and embrace my dear sister with all my heart and am ever your most obedient son,

Wolfgang Amadé Mozart

Translation by Emily Anderson
adapted by Felix Pollak and James Steakley

To Leopold Mozart (1781)

Vienne, ce 15 de Dec^{bre}, 1781

Mon très cher Père!

I have this moment received your letter of the 12th. Herr von Daubrawaick will bring you this letter, the watch, the Munich opera, the six engraved sonatas, the sonata for two claviers, and the cadenzas. As for the Princess of Württemberg and myself, it's all over. The Emperor has spoiled everything, because for him there's no one but Salieri. The Archduke Maximilian recommended *me* to her, and she replied that had it been up to her, she would never have engaged anyone else, but that on account of her singing the Emperor had suggested Salieri. She added that she was extremely sorry. What you tell me about the House of Württemberg and yourself may possibly prove useful to me.

Dearest father! You demand an explanation of the words in the closing sentence of my last letter! Oh, how gladly would I have opened my heart to you long ago, but I was deterred by the reproaches you might have made to me for *thinking of such a thing at the wrong time*—although there can never be a wrong time for thinking. Meanwhile, my aim here is to secure a small but *steady* income, which, together with what chance may provide, will enable me to live here comfortably—and then—to marry! You are shocked at the idea? But I beg you, dearest, most beloved father, listen to me. I was compelled to disclose my intentions to you. Now you must also allow me to disclose my reasons, and very weighty reasons they are, too. Nature speaks as loud to me as to anyone else, maybe even louder than to many a big strapping lout of a fellow. I simply cannot live as most young men do these days. In the first place, I have too much religion; in the second place, I have too great a love of my neighbor and too honest intentions to lead on an innocent girl; and, in the third place, I have too much horror and disgust, too much dread and fear of disease, and too much concern for my health to mess around with whores. So I can swear that I've never done anything like that with a woman. Besides, if such a thing had occurred, I wouldn't have concealed it from you; for, after all, to slip is natural enough in a man, and to slip *once* would be mere weakness—although indeed I wouldn't dare promise that if I had slipped once, I would stop there. However, I stake my life on the truth of what I have told you. I am well aware that this reason (powerful as it is) is not weighty enough. But owing to my disposition, which is more inclined to a peaceful and domestic existence than to revelry, I who from my youth on have never been accustomed to bother about my things, such as laundry, clothes, and so on, cannot think of anything more necessary for me than a wife. I assure you that I often spend money unnecessarily, simply because I don't pay attention to things. I am absolutely convinced that I'd manage better with a wife (on my present income) than I do now. And how many useless expenses would be avoided! True, other expenses would have to be met, but—one knows what they are and can be prepared for them—in a word, I would lead a well-ordered existence. A bachelor, in my opinion, is only half alive. That's the way I see things, I can't help it. I've thought the matter over and reflected sufficiently, and this is the way my mind works.

But who is the object of my love? Again, I beg you not to be shocked. Surely not one of the Webers? Yes, one of the Webers—but not Josefa, nor Sophie, but Constanze, the middle one. In no other family have I ever come across such differences in character. The eldest is a lazy, coarse, deceitful person, and sly as a fox. The Lange woman is a false, evil-minded person and a coquette. The youngest—is still too young to be anything in particular—she is just a good but frivolous creature! May God protect her from seduction! But the middle one, my good, dear Constanze, is the martyr of the family and, probably for that very reason, is the kindest, the cleverest, and, in short, the best of them all. She takes care of the whole household and yet in their opinion can't do anything right. Oh, my most beloved father, I could fill whole sheets with descriptions of all the scenes that I have witnessed in that house. If you really want me to tell you about them, I'll do so in my next letter. But before I put an end to my chatter, I must acquaint you better with the character of my dear Constanze. She is not ugly, but at the same time far from beautiful. Her whole beauty lies in two little black eyes and a pleasing figure. She has no wit, but she has enough common sense to enable her to fulfill her duties as a wife and mother. It is a downright lie that she is inclined to be extravagant. On the contrary, she is accustomed to being poorly dressed, for the little that her mother has been able to do for her children, she has done for the two others, but never for Constanze. True, she would like to be neatly and cleanly dressed, but not fancily, and most things that a woman needs she is able to make for herself; and she does her own hair every day. Understands housekeeping, has the best heart in the world. I love her and she loves me with all her heart. Tell me whether I could wish myself a better wife?

One more thing I must tell you, which is that when I resigned, our love had not yet begun, but was created by her tender care and attentions when I was living in their house.

Thus, I wish for nothing more than a small regular income (for which, thank God, I have good hopes), and then I shall never cease entreating you to allow me to save this poor girl—and to make myself and her—and, if I may say so, all of us very happy. For aren't you happy too when I am? And half of my regular income, dearest father, you are to enjoy. I have opened my heart to you and explained my words. Now it's my turn to beg you to explain your words in your last letter. Surely you wouldn't believe that I could be aware of *a proposal that was made to you* at that time and *to which you didn't respond.* I don't understand a word of that—I know of no such proposal. Now, please take pity on your son! I kiss your hands a thousand times and am ever

Your most obedient son,
W. A. Mozart

*Translation by Emily Anderson
adapted by Felix Pollak and James Steakley*

To Constanze Weber (1782)

Vienna, April 29, 1782

Dearest, most beloved Friend!

Surely you will still allow me to address you by this name? Surely you do not hate me so much that I may be your friend no longer, and you—no longer mine? And even if you will not be my friend any longer, yet you cannot forbid me to wish you the best, my friend, as I've grown accustomed to doing. Consider carefully what you said to me today. In spite of all my pleas, you turned me down three times and told me to my face that you don't want to have anything more to do with me. Since I am not as indifferent as you about losing an object of affection, I am not so hot-tempered, so rash, and so unreasonable as to accept the rejection. I love you too much to make such a move. I therefore beg you again to reconsider and to think carefully about the reason for this upset, which was that I became distraught that you were so flagrantly thoughtless as to tell your sister—and, be it noted, in my presence—that you had let a *chapeau* measure the calves of your legs. Any woman who values her reputation could never do such a thing. It is quite a good maxim to do as one's company does. At the same time there are many other factors to be considered—as, for example, whether only close friends and acquaintances are present—whether I am a child or already a *marriageable* girl—and particularly, whether I am already engaged—but, above all, whether only people of my own station or people of a lower order are present. If it be true that the Baroness herself allowed it to be done to her, the case is still quite different, for she is already past her prime and can no longer be attractive—and besides, she is enamored of you-know-what. I hope, dearest friend, that even if you do not wish to become my wife, you will never lead a life like hers. If you couldn't possibly resist the urge to carry on (although carrying on is not always seemly for a man, let alone for a woman), then why in the name of heaven didn't you take the measuring tape and measure you own calves (as *all women of honor* have done on such occasions in my presence) instead of allowing a *chapeau* to do so? I— I personally would never have done such a thing to you *in the presence of others.* I myself would have handed you the tape. Still less, then, should a stranger be allowed to do so—a man whom I know nothing about. But that's all past now; and a little admission of your rash conduct on that occasion would have remedied it all; and, if you don't take it amiss, dearest friend, still would. From that you can see how much I love you. *I do not fly off the handle as you do.* I think, I reflect, and I feel. *If you feel—if you have feelings,* then I know for sure that I will be able to say today: Constanze is the virtuous, respectable, reasonable, and faithful beloved of her honest and devoted

Mozart

Translation by Emily Anderson
adapted by Felix Pollak and James Steakley

Ludwig van Beethoven

To Franz Wegeler (1801)

Vienna, November 16, 1801

My dear, kind Wegeler!

. . . Now my life is a little more agreeable again, because I spend more time with others. You would hardly believe how dreary, how sad my life has been in the last two years: my bad hearing haunted me everywhere like a ghost, I fled from men, had to appear a misanthropist, though I am far from being one. This change has been brought about by a charming, fascinating girl, who loves me and whom I love. At last, after two years, there have been some moments of complete bliss, and this is the first time I have ever felt that marriage could make one happy. Unfortunately she is not of my social standing and, besides, I could not marry at present, I must still struggle valiantly. If it were not for my hearing, I would have travelled half-way round the world by now, and this I must do. For me there is no greater pleasure than to pursue and display my art.

Do not think I should be happier with you: what, indeed, should make me happier? Even your care for me would hurt me, I should always be conscious of the compassion on your faces and feel only more unhappy. What did those fine native surroundings of mine bestow on me? Nothing but the hope of a better state: and this would have been fulfilled now—were it not for this affliction. Oh, if I were free from this, I should embrace the world! My youth—yes, I feel it, is only beginning now. Have I not always been a sickly person? My physical strength has been increasing more than ever for some time, and so are my mental powers. Every day I draw nearer to the goal which I can sense, but not describe. Only in this can your Beethoven live. Do not mention rest! I know of no other kind than sleep and it pains me enough to be obliged to give up more of my time to it than before. Grant me only partial release from my affliction, and I shall come to you as an accomplished, mature man to renew our old feelings of friendship. You shall see me as joyful as it is possible to be here on earth, not unhappy— no, I could not bear that. I shall seize Fate by the throat, it shall never wholly subdue me. Oh, it is good to live one's life a thousand times! As for a quiet life, no, I feel I am no longer made for it. . . .

Bthvn

Translated by Michael Hamburger

The Heiligenstadt Testament (1802)

For my brothers Karl and (Johann) Beethoven.

O, you men who believe or declare that I am malevolent, stubborn, or misanthropic, how greatly you wrong me! You do not know the secret cause behind the appearance. From childhood onwards my heart and my mind have tended towards a gentle benevolence. I have always been disposed even to accomplish great deeds. Yet only consider that for six years I have been suffering an incurable afflication, aggravated by imprudent physicians. Year after year deceived by the hope of an improvement, finally forced to contemplate the prospect of a lasting illness, whose cure may take years or may even be impossible, born with a fiery, impulsive temperament, sensible, even, to the distractions of social life, I was yet compelled early in my life to isolate myself, to spend my life in solitude. Even if at times I wished to overcome all this, oh, how harshly I was driven back by the doubly grievous experience of my bad hearing, and yet I could not prevail upon myself to say to men: speak louder, shout, for I am deaf. Oh, how could I possibly admit to being defective in the very sense which should have been more highly developed in me than in other men, a sense which once

I possessed in its most perfect form, a form as perfect as few in my profession, surely, know or have known in the past. Oh, I cannot do it. Therefore you must forgive me if you should see me draw back when I would gladly mingle with you. My affliction is all the more painful to me because it leads to such misinterpretations of my conduct. Recreation in human society, refined conversation, mutual effusions of thought are denied to me. Almost quite alone, I may commit myself to social life only as far as the most urgent needs demand. I must live like an exile. When I do venture near some social gathering, I am seized with a burning terror, the fear that I may be placed in the dangerous position of having to reveal my condition. So, too, it has been with me during the past half-year, which I spent in the country. When my reasonable physician ordered me to spare my hearing as much as possible, he almost accorded with my natural disposition, although sometimes, overpowered by the urge to seek society, I disobeyed his orders. But what a humiliation when someone standing next to me heard a flute in the distance and I heard nothing, or when someone heard the shepherd sing and, again, I heard nothing. Such occurrences brought me to the verge of despair. I might easily have put an end to my life. Only one thing, art, held me back. Oh, it seemed impossible to me to leave this world before I had produced all that I felt capable of producing, and so I prolonged this wretched existence—truly wretched, because I am cursed with a body so irritable that a somewhat sudden change can plunge me from the best into the worst of states. Patience—so I am told, it is patience that I must now choose to be my guide: I have patience enough. My determination to hold out until it pleases the inexorable Fates to cut the thread shall be a lasting one, I sincerely hope. Perhaps there will be an improvement, perhaps not: I am prepared. Already in my 28th year I have been compelled to become a philosopher; this is no easy matter, more difficult for an artist than for anyone else. Divine One, Thou canst see into my inmost thoughts, Thou knowest them; Thou knowest that love of my fellow men and the desire to do good are harbored there. O, men, when one day you read these words, reflect that you did me wrong; and let the unhappy man take comfort in his meeting with one of his kind; one who, despite all his natural disabilities yet did everything in his power to be admitted into the ranks of worthy artists and men. You, my brothers Karl and Johann: as soon as I am dead, if Professor Schmidt is still alive, ask him in my name to describe my illness, and add this document to his account, so that, as far as possible, the world may be reconciled with me after my death. At the same time I declare you both to be the heirs to my small fortune (if one can call it such). Divide it fairly, bear with and help each other. The evil you have done me, as you know yourselves, has long been forgiven you. To you, brother Karl, I give special thanks for the devotion shown to me in these recent times. It is my wish that you may lead lives better and more free from cares than my own. Recommend virtue to your children: for virtue alone, not money, can grant us happiness; I speak from experience. It was virtue that raised me up even in my misery; it is owing to virtue, and to my art, that I did not end my life by suicide. Farewell and love each other! I give thanks to all my friends, but especially to Prince Lichnowsky and to Professor Schmidt. I desire that the instruments given to me by Prince Lichnowsky be preserved by one of you; yet let no quarrel arise among you on this account. However, as soon as they can be of more use to you in this way, by all means sell them. How glad I am at the thought that even in the grave I may render you some service!

Now it is done. It is with joy that I hasten to meet my death. Should death come before I have had time to develop all my artistic faculties, then, in spite of my cruel fate, it will come too soon and I would wish that its coming might be delayed. Yet even then I shall be content: does not death liberate me from a state of endless suffering? Come whenever it pleases thee to come: bravely I shall come out to meet thee. Farewell and do not quite forget me when I am dead. I have deserved this of you, for often in my lifetime I thought of you, wondering how I could make you happy; be so!

Heiligenstadt, October 6, 1802

Ludwig van Beethoven

Heiligenstadt, October 10

So I must bid you farewell—though sadly. Yes, the cherished hope—which I brought with me when I came here, of being healed at least to a certain degree, must now abandon me entirely. As the leaves of autumn fall and are withered, so, too—my hope has dried up. Almost as I was when I came here, I leave again—even the courage—which often inspired me on lovely summer days—is vanished. O Providence—let a single day of untroubled joy be granted to me! For so long already the resonance of true joy has been unknown to me. O when—O when, Divine one—may I feel it once more in the temple of nature and of mankind? Never?—no—that would be too hard!

Translated by Michael Hamburger

To His "Immortal Beloved" (1812)

On the morning of July 6

My angel, my all, my very self! Only a few words today, and those in pencil (with yours). Not until tomorrow will the matter of my lodgings be finally settled: what a shameful waste of time are all such things! Why this deep sorrow, where necessity speaks? Can our love subsist otherwise than by sacrifices, by our not desiring everything? Can you do anything to alter the fact that you are not wholly mine, that I am not wholly yours? Oh, God! gaze at the beauties of nature and reconcile yourself to that which must be! Love demands everything and quite rightly so; that is how I feel towards you and you towards me. Only you so readily forget that I must live for me and for you. If we were wholly united you would feel the pain of it as little as I do.

My journey was terrible: I did not arrive here until four o'clock yesterday morning. As there was a shortage of horses, the mail coach chose a different route, but what terrible roads! At the stage before the last I was warned not to travel at night, told to fear a certain forest, but this only made me eager, and I was in the wrong. The coach was bound to break down on this dreadful road, a bottomless, sheer mud-track! Without four such excellent postillions as I had with me, I should still be lying somewhere on the way. Esterhazy suffered the same fate on the other, usual route with his eight horses, while I had only four. Nevertheless, I got a certain amount of enjoyment even from this, as I do whenever some great difficulty or danger has been overcome.

But to plunge from external to internal matters: we shall probably be meeting soon. But today I cannot tell you of the observations I have made during the past days with regard to my life. If our hearts were always close together I should scarcely have occasion to make any such observations. My heart is full of many things to say to you. Oh, there are moments when I feel that words are nothing at all. Take courage! remain my true, my only treasure, as I remain yours! The gods must send us the rest, whatever has been ordained for us and must be.

Your faithful Ludwig

Monday night, July 6

You are suffering, you, my dearest creature. (At this very moment I learn that letters must be posted very early in the morning, on Mondays, Thursdays, the only days on which the mail-coach goes from here to K.) You are suffering. Oh, wherever I am, you are with me; I speak to you and to myself. Make it possible that I may live with you! and what a life we shall live!!!! thus!!!! without you—pursued by the kindness of persons here and there, a kindness which I wish to deserve as little as I deserve it. The humility of men towards men, it hurts me. And when I contemplate myself in connection with the universe, what I am and what is he whom they call the greatest! And yet it is herein that the divinity of men resides. I weep when I reflect that you will probably receive no news of me before Saturday. Much as you love me, I love you still more. But never hide your thoughts from me!

Good night! As I am here for the baths, I must go to bed. Oh, God, so near and so far! Is it not truly a heavenly edifice, our love? but as firm, too, as the firmament of heaven.

Good morning! July 7

Though I am still in bed, my thoughts surge towards you, my immortal beloved, now joyfully, then again sorrowfully, waiting to know whether fate will hear us. I must live with you entirely, or not at all. Yes, indeed, I am resolved to stray in distant places until that moment when I can throw myself into your arms and say that I am really at home with you, when I can send my soul, wrapped in your presence, into the realm of the spirits. Yes, unfortunately there is no other way. You will not give in, for you know my fidelity to you. Never shall another be able to possess my heart, never—never! Oh, God, why is one forced to part from her whom one loves so well! And yet my life in Vienna, as it is at present, is a wretched affair. Your love makes me both the happiest and unhappiest of men. At my age I need a certain regularity, a certain balance in my life: can these be reconciled with our relationship? My angel, at this moment I learn that the mail-coach leaves every day and so I must end, to make sure that you will receive this letter at once. Be calm! Only by calmly contemplating our existence shall we be able to achieve our purpose of living together. Be calm! Love me! Today, yesterday, what a tearful desire to be with you, you, you! My life, my all! Farewell! Oh, never cease to love me, never misjudge the most faithful heart of your beloved.

Eternally yours, eternally mine, eternally ours!

L.

Translated by Michael Hamburger

To Johann Wolfgang von Goethe (1823)

Vienna, February 8, 1823

Your Excellency,

Still, as in my boyhood years, absorbed in your immortal, never aging works and, as ever, remembering the hours once spent in your company, I have now occasion to recall myself to your memory. I hope, Your Excellency, that you have received my dedication of "Calm Sea" and "Happy Voyage," set to music by me. Both, because of the contrast between them, seemed to me very suitable for a musical setting which might express this very contrast. How very pleased I should be to hear whether I have fittingly combined my harmony with yours! Instruction, too, which, so to speak, would be regarded as the truth, would be most welcome to me; for I love the truth more than anything, and never shall it be said of me: *veritas odium parit.* A number of your poems, unique as ever, should soon be appearing, set to music by me, among them "Rastlose Liebe." How highly I should value a general remark upon the composing or setting to music of your poems! Now a request to your Excellency. I have written a grand Mass, which, however, I do not wish to publish as yet, but which is intended only for the most prominent courts. The cost amounts only to 50 ducats. For this purpose I have applied to the Grand-Ducal Weimar Embassy, which accepted my petition to His Highness the Grand Duke and promised to convey it to him. The Mass could also be performed in the manner of an oratorio and who knows that nowadays the charitable societies may not require such works! My request consists in this, that Your Excellency draw the attention of His Highness the Grand Duke to this petition, so that His Highness may subscribe for the work. The Grand-Ducal Weimar Embassy also disclosed to me that it would be very advantageous if the Grand Duke were previously disposed in its favor. I have written so much, but earned—almost nothing. Now, however, I am no longer alone; already for six years I have been a father to the son of my late brother, a promising youth in his sixteenth year, wholly devoted to the humanities and already quite at home in the rich mines of Hellenism. However, in these parts such an education costs a great deal and with boys who are studying one must think not only of the present, but of the future, and much as in the past all my thoughts were directed above, I am now compelled to lower my gaze. My subsistence is without substance. My ailing condition in recent years did not permit me to go on tour in the interest of my art, nor, indeed, to take up anything that might be of profit to me. Should my health be entirely restored to me, perhaps I may yet look forward to better things. You must not think, however, Your Excellency, that I have now dedicated "Calm Sea" and "Happy Voyage" to you on account of the service which I am asking of you. I did so already in May 1822, and there was no question of circulating the Mass in this manner until some weeks ago. The reverence, love, and esteem which, ever since my boyhood, I have felt for our unique, immortal Goethe have never changed. Such things cannot easily be expressed in words, especially not by a bungler of my sort who has never endeavored to master anything but music. Yet a strange feeling always compels me to say so much to you, for I live in your writings. I know that you will not fail to do this one service to an artist who feels only too strongly how far mere money-making is from true art, when necessity constrains him to seek such aid, for others, as well as himself. The virtuous course is always clear to us, and so I know, your Excellency, that you will not refuse my request. A few words from you to me would en-velop me in bliss. As ever Your Excellency's

Sincerely, boundlessly devoted

Beethoven

Translated by Michael Hamburger

Ernst Theodor Amadeus Hoffmann

Beethoven's Instrumental Music (1813)

When we speak of music as an independent art, should we not always restrict our meaning to instrumental music, which, scorning every aid, every admixture of another art (the art of poetry), gives pure expression to music's specific nature, recognizable in this form alone? It is the most Romantic of all the arts—one might almost say the only genuinely Romantic one—for its sole subject is the infinite. The lyre of Orpheus opened the portals of Orcus—music discloses to man an unknown realm, a world that has nothing in common with the external sensual world that surrounds him, a world in which he leaves behind him all definite feelings to surrender himself to an inexpressible longing.

Have you even so much as suspected this specific nature, you miserable composers of instrumental music, you who have laboriously strained yourselves to represent definite emotions, even definite events? How can it ever have occurred to you to treat after the fashion of the plastic arts the art diametrically opposed to plastic? Your sunrises, your tempests, your *Batailles des trois Empereurs,* and the rest, these, after all, were surely quite laughable aberrations, and they have been punished as they well deserved by being wholly forgotten.

In song, where poetry, by means of words, suggests definite emotions, the magic power of music acts as does the wondrous elixir of the wise, a few drops of which make any drink more palatable and more lordly. Every passion—love, hatred, anger, despair, and so forth, just as the opera gives them to us—is clothed by music and the purple luster of Romanticism, and even what we have undergone in life guides us out of life into the realm of the infinite.

As strong as this is music's magic, and, growing stronger and stronger, it had to break each chain that bound it to another art.

That gifted composers have raised instrumental music to its present high estate is due, we may be sure, less to the more readily handled means of expression (the greater perfection of the instruments, the greater virtuosity of the players) than to the more profound, more intimate recognition of music's specific nature.

Mozart and Haydn, the creators of our present instrumental music, were the first to show us the art in its full glory; the man who then looked on it with all his love and penetrated its innermost being is—Beethoven! The instrumental compositions of these three masters breathe a similar Romantic spirit—this is due to their similar intimate understanding of the specific nature of the art; in the character of their compositions there is nonetheless a marked difference.

In Haydn's writing there prevails the expression of a serene and childlike personality. His symphonies lead us into vast green woodlands, into a merry, gaily colored throng of happy mortals. Youths and maidens float past in a circling dance; laughing children, peering out from behind the trees, from behind the rose bushes, pelt one another playfully with flowers. A life of love, of bliss like that before the Fall, of eternal youth; no sorrow, no suffering, only a sweet melancholy yearning for the beloved object that floats along, far away, in the glow of the sunset and comes no nearer and does not disappear—nor does night fall while it is there, for it is itself the sunset in which hill and valley are aglow.

Mozart leads us into the heart of the spirit realm. Fear takes us in its grasp, but without torturing us, so that it is more an intimation of the infinite. Love and melancholy call to us with lovely spirit voices; night comes on with a bright purple luster, and with inexpressible longing we follow those figures which, waving us familiarly into their train, soar through the clouds in eternal dances of the spheres.

Thus Beethoven's instrumental music opens up to us also the realm of the monstrous and the immeasurable. Burning flashes of light shoot through the deep night of this realm, and we become aware of giant shadows that surge back and forth, driving us into narrower and narrower confines until they destroy *us*—but not the pain of that endless longing in which each joy that has climbed aloft in jubilant song sinks back and is swallowed up, and it is only in this pain, which consumes love, hope, and happiness but does not destroy them, which seeks to burst our breasts with a many-voiced consonance of all the passions, that we live on, enchanted beholders of the supernatural!

Romantic taste is rare, Romantic talent still rarer, and this is doubtless why there are so few to strike that lyre whose sound discloses the wondrous realm of the Romantic.

Haydn grasps in a Romantic way what is human in human life; he is more commensurable, more comprehensible for the majority.

Mozart calls rather for the superhuman, the wondrous element that abides in inner being.

Beethoven's music sets in motion the lever of fear, of awe, of horror, of suffering, and wakens just that infinite longing which is the essence of Romanticism. He is accordingly a completely Romantic composer, and is not this perhaps the reason why he has less success with vocal music, which excludes the character of indefinite longing, merely representing emotions defined by words as emotions experienced in the realm of the infinite?

The musical rabble is oppressed by Beethoven's powerful genius; it seeks in vain to oppose it. But knowing critics, looking about them with a superior air, assure us that we may take their word for it as men of great intellect and deep insight that, while the excellent Beethoven can scarcely be denied a very fertile and lively imagination, he does not know how to bridle it! Thus, they say, he no longer bothers at all to select or to shape his ideas, but, following the so-called daemonic method, he dashes everything off exactly as his ardently active imagination dictates it to him. Yet how does the matter stand if it is *your* feeble observation alone that the deep inner continuity of Beethoven's every composition eludes? If it is *your* fault alone that you do not understand the master's language as the initiated understand it, that the portals of the innermost sanctuary remain closed to you? The truth is that, as regards self-possession, Beethoven stands quite on a par with Haydn and Mozart and that, separating his ego from the inner realm of harmony, he rules over it as an absolute monarch. In Shakespeare, our knights of the aesthetic measuring-rod have often bewailed the utter lack of inner unity and inner continuity, although for those who look more deeply there springs forth, issuing from a single bud, a beautiful tree, with leaves, flowers, and fruit; thus, with Beethoven, it is only after a searching investigation of his instrumental music that the high self-possession inseparable from true genius and nourished by the study of the art stands revealed.

Can there be any work of Beethoven's that confirms all this to a higher degree than his indescribably profound, magnificent Symphony in C Minor? How this wonderful composition, in a climax that climbs on and on, leads the listener imperiously forward into the spirit world of the infinite! . . . No doubt the whole rushes like an ingenious rhapsody past many a man, but the soul of each thoughtful listener is assuredly stirred, deeply and intimately, by a feeling that is none other than that unutterable portentous longing, and until the final chord—indeed, even in the moments that follow it—he will be powerless to step out of that wondrous spirit realm where grief and joy embrace him in the form of sound. The internal structure of the movements, their execution, their instrumentation, the way in which they follow one another—everything contributes to a single end; above all, it is the intimate interrelationship among the themes that engenders that unity which alone has the power to hold the listener firmly in a single mood. This relationship is sometimes clear to the listener when he overhears it in the connecting of two movements or discovers it in the fundamental bass they have in common; a deeper relationship which does not reveal itself in this way speaks at other times only from mind to mind, and it is precisely this relationship that prevails between sections of the two Allegros and the Minuet and which imperiously proclaims the self-possession of the master's genius.

How deeply thy magnificent compositions for the piano have impressed themselves upon my soul, thou sublime master; how shallow and insignificant now all seems to me that is not thine, or by the gifted Mozart or that mighty genius, Sebastian Bach! With what joy I received thy seventieth work, the two glorious trios, for I knew full well that after a little practice I should soon hear them in truly splendid style. And in truth, this evening things went so well with me that even now, like a man who wanders in the mazes of a fantastic park, woven about with all manner of exotic trees and plants and marvelous flowers, and who is drawn further and further in, I am powerless to find my way out of the marvelous turns and windings of thy trios. The lovely siren voices of these movements of thine, resplendent in their many-hued variety, lure me on and on. The gifted lady who indeed honored me, Kapell-meister Kreisler, by playing today the first trio in such splendid style, the gifted lady before whose piano I still sit and write, has made me realize quite clearly that only what the mind produces calls for respect and that all else is out of place.

Translated by Oliver Strunk

Louis Spohr

From the *Autobiography* (ca. 1850)

After my return from Gotha, my first work was the composition of *Faust*. Before my journey there, I had had another subject in view, which Theodor Körner was to have worked out for me as an opera. I had made the young poet's acquaintance soon after my first arrival in Vienna; he was then already as much admired for his amiable manners as for the success of his theatrical pieces. I met him at almost every party where I played, and as Körner was very fond of music we soon took to each other. When it was decided that I should remain in Vienna, I asked Körner to write an opera for me and proposed as the subject the legend of Rübezahl. Körner, who had been present at both performances of *The Last Judgment* and had a good opinion of my talent for composition, acquiesced without hesitation and went to work with zest upon the materials proposed. But suddenly it was reported that Körner was about to join the Lützow Fusiliers and to fight for the freedom of Germany. I hastened to him and endeavored like many other of my friends to dissuade him from that intention, but without success. We soon saw him depart. It became known afterwards that it was not just his enthusiasm for the Liberation of Germany but an unfortunate and unrequited love for the beautiful actress Adamberger that drove him from Vienna, and to an early death.

I thus saw my hope of an opera libretto from the pen of the youthful and gifted poet destroyed, and was now obliged to look elsewhere for another. It was therefore quite opportune that Herr Bernhard had offered me his version of *Faust* for composition, and we were soon agreed upon the terms. Some alterations that I wished to have made were completed by the author during my journey to Gotha, so that I could begin on it immediately after my return. From the list of my compositions, I find that I wrote the opera in less than four months, from the end of May to the middle of September. I still remember with what enthusiasm and perseverance I worked on it. As soon as I had completed some of the parts I hastened with them to Meyerbeer, who then resided in Vienna, and begged him to play them to me from the score, a thing in which he greatly excelled. I then undertook the vocal parts and executed them in their different characters and voices with great enthusiasm. When my voice was not sufficiently flexible for the purpose, I helped myself by whistling, in which I was well practiced. Meyerbeer took great interest in this work, which appears to have kept its ground up to the present time, as he again put *Faust* on the stage during his direction of the Opera at Berlin and had it studied with the greatest care.

Pixis the Younger also, who then resided with his parents in Vienna, as well as Hummel and Seyfried, showed a great predeliction for this opera, so that I offered it for presentation at the Theater an der Wien with the fairest hopes of a brilliant success. Count Palffy, with whom I was then still on good terms, accepted it immediately and promised to distribute the characters as soon as possible and to bring it out. While engaged on the work, it is true, I had the personnel of my theater in mind; and I wrote the Faust for Forti, the Mephistopheles for Weinmüller, Hugo for Wild, Franz for Gottdank, Cunigunda for Madame Campi, and Rosa for Mademoiselle Teiner; but nevertheless (apart from the circumstance that I did not yet at that time understand how to keep myself within the bounds of the natural compass of the voice) all manner of things had escaped my pen that did not suit the aforementioned singers, as, for instance, the long ornamental passages in the air of Hugo, for Wild, who at that time had but a limited power of execution. This at a time later period was urged by the Count, when I had a disagreement with him, as an excuse for withdrawing his consent, and actually the opera was never produced while I was in Vienna. Some years afterwards, it was brought out with great success, and in more recent times was staged again with increased approbation. I had always felt an interest in my compositions only so long as I was engaged on them and, so to speak, full of them, so I bore with great equanimity the banishing of my score to the shelves of the library of the theater, and immediately set to work on new subjects. Even the pianoforte arrangement of the opera that Pixis had taken great pleasure in preparing, I did not publish until many years later at Peter's in Leipzig.

Translator anon.

Carl Maria von Weber

On the Opera *Undine* by E. T. A. Hoffmann (1817)

A fair judgment of a work of art that unfolds in time requires that quiet and unprejudiced mood which, receptive to every kind of impression, should remain aloof from any definite aim or predisposition of feeling, except for a certain opening of the soul toward the subject matter in question. Only in this way is the artist in a position to gain ascendancy over the soul and the power to draw it, through his emotions and characters, into the world he has created and in which he, a mighty ruler over strong passions, allows us to feel, with and through him, pain and pleasure as well as love, joy, terror, and hope. Quickly and clearly it will then be shown whether he has succeeded in creating a grand work that profoundly and permanently affects us or whether, his artistry resulting from strokes of undisciplined genius, he has made us admire certain individual traits at the expense of the total effect.

In opera, this kind of effect is harder to avoid, and hence more common, than in any other art form. By opera I naturally mean that type of musical drama which is dear to the Germans: a fully rounded and self-contained work of art in which all the ingredients furnished by the contributing arts disappear in the process of fusion and, in thus perishing, help to form an entirely new universe. . . .

The nature and essence of opera, consisting, as it does, of wholes within a whole, causes this enormous difficulty, which only the masters have managed to overcome. Each musical number, on account of the structure that is peculiar to it, appears to be a self-contained, organic unit. Yet as part of a larger unit it is supposed to vanish as we contemplate the latter. Nevertheless, the operatic ensemble, revealing several external aspects at one and the same time, can and should be a Janus head to be taken in at one single glance.

This is the innermost secret of music, which can be felt but cannot be explicitly stated: the undulation and the contrasting natures of wrath and love, of blissful pain, in which salamander and sylph embrace and merge, are here united. In other words: what love is to man, music is to man as well as to the arts; for it is love itself, the purest, most ethereal language of the passions, containing their innumerable and constantly changing colors, yet expressing only one truth that is immediately understood by a thousand people endowed with the most widely divergent feelings.

Translated by Ulrich Weisstein

Autobiography (1818)

I was born on December 18, 1786, at Eutin in Holstein, and was given the most thorough education, with special preference shown to the fine arts, since my father was himself an excellent violinist. My family's withdrawn manner of life, the regular society of cultivated adults, and the scrupulous care with which I was kept from the rough company of my contemporaries early taught me to live predominantly in the world of my own imagination and to seek in it my interests and my happiness. My time was chiefly devoted to painting and music. I was successful in several branches of the former—painting in oils, miniatures, and pastel and having some skill in engraving. But imperceptibly my interest in painting dwindled and was finally ousted by music almost before I was aware of it. It was a fancy of my father's to change his place of residence with some frequency; and the constant change of teachers that this necessitated was a drawback, though one that was later more than made up for by the stimulus it gave to my individual powers and the need to draw on my own mental resources and industry. I owe my firm grounding and my achieving a powerful, well-articulated, and well-characterized piano style and the equal training of both hands, to the excellent Heuschkel in Hildburghausen (1796–97), a strict and assiduous teacher. As soon as my father saw the gradual budding of my talent, he made every sacrifice to further its development. He took me to Michael Haydn in Salzburg; but Haydn was a serious man too far removed from my childish condition for me to learn much from him, and that little involved a considerable effort. It was at Salzburg, in 1798, that my father encouraged me by having my first works published—six fughettas, which were kindly reviewed in the musical press. At the end of 1798, I went to Munich, where I studied singing with Valesi and composition with the present court organist, Kalcher. It is to Kalcher's clear, well-ordered, and scrupulous teaching that I am indebted for my mastery and ease in the handling of academic forms, more particularly four-part *a cappella* writing. Such things must become second nature to any composer who wishes to express himself and his ideas clearly, just as prosody and meter must become second nature to a poet. I finished my studies with an industry that never flagged.

A preference for the dramatic began to become unmistakable in my musical individuality, and under the eyes of my master I wrote an opera entitled *The Power of Love and of Wine,* a grand Mass, several pianoforte sonatas, variations, string trios, songs, etc., all of which were later destroyed in a fire. The lively ambition of youth, always anxious to adopt anything that is new and attracts attention, prompted the idea of stealing Sennefelder's thunder. He had just invented the process of lithography, and I believed that in fact I had made the same discovery and had even devised a better method than his. My desire to exploit this on a large scale took us to Freiberg, where all the materials needed were most easily to be had. The scale of the enterprise and the purely mechanical, soul-destroying work involved soon caused me to abandon the scheme, and I returned with redoubled enthusiasm to composition. I set Ritter von Steinberg's *The Forest Maiden,* and the opera was performed in November 1800. It was later given further afield than I could have wished (fourteen performances in Vienna, translated into Czech for Prague and successful in St. Petersburg), since it is a very immature work with no more than occasional glimpses of inventiveness. In fact, Act 2 was written in ten days—one of the many regrettable consequences of the effect on a young mind of those impressive stories told of the great masters, whose example always stimulates imitation. In just the same way, an article that I read in the *Musikzeitung* spurred me on to write in an entirely new way and to revive the use of old, forgotten instruments, etc. Family business having taken me to Salzburg, I there put my new plans into action and wrote the opera *Peter Schmoll and His Neighbors*. That was in 1801. The novelties in this score delighted my old master Michael Haydn, who wrote an unusually laudatory notice of the work, which is printed in Gerber's *Composer's Lexicon*. This opera was given in Augsburg, but naturally had no great success. I later rewrote the overture, which I published with Gombart. In 1802, my father and I made a musical tour to Leipzig, Hamburg, and Holstein, during which I made a collection of theoretical works which I studied with great diligence. Unfortunately a doctor of medicine overthrew all my fine theories by a volley of questions— why this? why that? and so forth—overwhelming me with doubts; and it was only gradually that I found my feet again and was able to compose in my own way, according to a system which is well founded in both nature and philosophy. My aim was to penetrate to the heart of all that the old masters had recommended and established, and to construct a complete system on those principles. I was overcome by a longing for the musical life of Vienna, and for the first time made my appearance there. It was in the company of leading Viennese musicians, including the unforgettable "Papa" Haydn, that I met the Abbé Vogler, who showed that willingness to help all serious efforts which is characteristic of all really great men, opening the treasure-house of his knowledge for my benefit with the most selfless generosity.

Only myself and a few others had the opportunity of observing at close quarters the profundity of that great soul, that inexhaustible store of learning and ardent recognition of all that is good— coupled with great shrewdness in assessing it—and he inspired an undying reverence in us. As for the dross and the eccentricities that upbringing, social position, enmities, and misunderstandings had mingled with this precious metal, surrounding it and apparently adulterating its quality—these we came to accept as wholly minor details, easy to overlook or even to find natural.

If only I could succeed in drawing a clear portrait of this rare psychological phenomenon in the arts, something worthy of the man himself and a lesson to students of music! On Vogler's advice, but not without some considerable sacrifice on my part, I wrote no major works for the next two years, but devoted almost all my time to a thorough study of different works by the great masters. Under his guidance I analyzed their structure, the development of their ideas, and the means employed in each case; and I then attempted to match these and to form a clear conception of them in my own mind and in isolated studies. Nothing of mine was published during this period, except a few sets of variations and the vocal score of Vogler's opera *Samori*.

With my appointment as director of music at Breslau, new possibilities of gaining orchestral experience came my way. In Breslau I built up a new orchestra and chorus, revised my earlier works, and composed the opera *Rübezahl,* for which Professor Rhode wrote the greater part of the libretto. My official duties left me little time for composition; but I did have time to digest the many different ideas and artistic principles that I had, as it were, swallowed perhaps too hastily, and so gradually to develop my own musical individuality.

In 1806, the art-loving Prince Eugen of Württemberg invited me to his court at Karlsruhe in Silesia, and there I composed two symphonies, several concertos, and pieces for wind band. Neither the charming little theater at Karlsruhe nor the fine orchestra survived the war. I embarked on a musical tour at a time when circumstances could hardly have been more unfavorable. For a time I abandoned practical music-making and found a home with Duke Ludwig of Württemberg at Stuttgart. Stimulated by the encouragement of the excellent Danzi, I wrote my opera *Silvana,* on Hiemer's new version of my earlier *The Forest Maiden; The First Tone;* overtures; rewrote some earlier choral pieces; and also composed some pianoforte pieces. This lasted until 1810, when I returned to practical music-making and embarked on another tour. At this point I think I may reckon to have reached artistic maturity; and all that has followed, and what is still to come, may be regarded as the rounding-off of sharp corners and the gradual clarification and increased understanding of basic principles no longer subject to change.

I travelled all over Germany; and the warmth with which my efforts were received, whether as performer or composer, and the seriousness that marked even violent differences of opinion or hostile attacks stimulated me to exert all my powers and all the idealism of an unshakable determination—the faculties that alone consecrate a man to the true priesthood of art. My operas were given in Frankfurt, Munich, Berlin, etc., and my concerts attracted the public. I met the Abbé Vogler once again, a short time before his death, and saw how he devoted himself to two brilliant pupils, Meyerbeer and Gänsbacher. More mature now and better able to discriminate, I could still join these two young men and profit from Vogler's deep experience. It was then that I wrote the opera *Abu Hassan* (Darmstadt, 1810). I only saw Vogler once more, in Vienna, and found him full of enthusiasm for my work. Peace to his ashes!

From 1813 to 1816 I directed the Opera in Prague, after completely reorganizing it. I lived now entirely for music, in the conviction that my true vocation lay in cultivating and furthering the cause of that art. My object in Prague once attained, and having achieved all that was feasible in the restricting circumstances of a privately run institution, I resigned my position there, knowing that all my successor needed was to be a scrupulous guardian.

Once again I sallied out into the world, content to wait for it to be made clear to me where my sphere of influence was to be. I received various flattering offers; but it was only the challenge of initiating a German Opera in Dresden that finally captured my imagination. And so I gave myself with enthusiasm and industry to my new task; and if I am one day to have an inscription on my tombstone, it could well run thus—"Here lies a man who was always honest and selfless in his dealings with his fellow men and with the art he loved."

Translated by Martin Cooper

Essay on Johann Sebastian Bach (1821)

Bach (Johann Sebastian), born Eisenach, March 21, 1685. From time to time Providence sends into the world heroes who seize in a mighty grasp the artistic tradition that has passed comfortably from master to pupil, from one generation to the next; purify and transform it; and thus shape something novel. This new art continues for many years to serve as a model, without losing its taste of novelty or its ability to shock contemporaries by its sheer power, while the heroic originator becomes the bright focal point of his age and its taste. It is generally forgotten in such cases, though quite unjustly, that these great men were at the same time also children of the age in which they lived, and that their great achievements argue the previous existence of much that was excellent.

Sebastian Bach was one of these heroic figures. He originated so much that was new and, in its way, perfect that the history of music before his day has come to seem a kind of Dark Age, and his contemporary Händel is oddly enough regarded as belonging to a different era. Sebastian Bach's individuality was, even in its austerity, in fact Romantic, truly German to its very roots, in opposition perhaps to Händel's greatness, which was rather in the antique mold. Bach's style is grandiose, sublime, and rich. He achieved his effects by the most unexpected progressions in his part-writing, thereby producing long successions of unusual rhythms in the most ingenious contrapuntal combinations. The work of this sublime artist in fact resembles a Gothic cathedral dedicated to the arts, whereas all his predecessors were lesser men who lost themselves in the arid ingenuities that were the fashion, seeking the inner life of art in mere form and therefore finding nothing. It should not of course be forgotten in this connection that in those days music was primarily written for, and commissioned by, the church. The organist was the directing spirit, and the world of sound that is locked up in the organ for the creative artist to release was a plentiful source of the material that a composer today must look for in the rich field of the orchestra.

Sebastian Bach worked hard to achieve that complete mastery of the organ which determined the whole character of his art. This has as its most characteristic and distinguishing feature a grandeur closely associated with the fact that the organ is essentially an instrument that achieves expressiveness by effects of mass. The greatness of Bach's music in the harmonic field comes directly from his intellectual adroitness in combining the most contradictory melodic lines into a single whole.

The freedom of his part-writing combined with its strict logic naturally compelled him to discover means of making his music performable. Pianists are therefore indebted to him for a method of fingering first communicated to the world by his son Carl Philipp Emanuel Bach in his *Essay on the True Art of Playing Keyboard Instruments.* The particular feature of this method is the use of the thumb, never properly used before by keyboard players, who for the most part made use of their four fingers. Bach was also the inventor of the so-called "viola pomposa," since cellists of the day could not manage the figured basses in his works. This instrument was in fact an enlarged viola, with five strings and a range of a fifth (up to E) above the range of the cello. This made the performance of wide-spaced figures more practicable.

Sebastian Bach founded what is commonly called a "school." It is hard to imagine Mozart's supreme achievements without the stages represented by Bach and Händel. The art of performing his works effectively is in fact dead, because the pleasure that they offer does not lie on the surface, and because the richness of the harmonic structure does not allow the melodic line the absolute predominance demanded by our pampered taste.

Sebastian Bach was the son of Johann Ambrosius Bach, court and town musician at Eisenach. Orphaned before he was ten, he was given his first lessons by his elder brother, Johann Christoph, who was organist at Ohrdruf; and his apprenticeship was not, apparently, without its excitements, as he was obliged to study the better works of Froberger, Kerll, Pachelbel, and so on, in secret on moonlight nights. His first appointment was to a post as a treble in the choir of the Michaelisschule in Lüneburg, and from there his passion for self-improvement took him on several occasions to Hamburg, to hear the famous organist Reincken. In 1703, he was appointed court musician at Weimar and the next year he became organist at Arnstadt. From this time onwards his development was swift and sustained. In 1707, he became organist at Mühlhausen, and in the following year he returned to Weimar as court organist, and later (1714) Konzertmeister. Shortly after this he was appointed Kapellmeister by the Prince of Anhalt-Cöthen, but in 1723 he moved to Leipzig as director of music and cantor at the Thomasschule. He died in Leipzig on July 28, 1750, of a stroke. In 1736, the Duke of Weissenfels had bestowed the title of Kapellmeister on him and the King of Poland the title of Royal Polish and Electoral Saxon Court Composer.

He had eleven sons and nine daughters, all gifted and four of them outstandingly so. Wilhelm Friedemann, sometimes called "the Halle Bach," was born at Weimar in 1710 and died at Berlin in 1784—a solid organist, mathematician, and writer of fugues. Carl Philipp Emanuel was born at Weimar in 1714 and is commonly referred to as "the Berlin Bach." He had leanings towards the *galant* or rococo style and was popular with the public. His greatest service to music was his publication of the book describing the perfecting of the art of keyboard playing as discovered by his father. He died at Hamburg in 1788. Johann Christoph Friedrich, "the Bückeburg Bach," was born at Weimar in 1732 and died at Bückeburg in 1795—the nearest in taste to his brother Emanuel. Johann Christian, called "the English Bach" or "the Milanese Bach," was born at Leipzig in 1735 and died in 1782 in London, where he had been Kapellmeister to the Queen. He was of all the brothers the most devoted in his music to the so-called *galant* style, and for this reason he was the most popular in his lifetime and is the most completely forgotten now. The musical endowments of the Bach family are in fact of an almost incredible wealth.

Translated by Martin Cooper

Carl Czerny

From *Reminiscences from My Life* (1842)

I was about ten years old when I was taken to see Beethoven by Krumpholz. How joyfully and fearfully did I look forward to the day on which I was to see the great master! Today, that moment is still vividly present in my memory. On a winter's day, my father, Krumpholz, and I made our way from the Leopoldstadt, where we were still living, into the city proper, to the so-called Tiefer Graben—a street—and climbed way up to the sixth or seventh floor, where a rather unkempt-looking servant announced our arrival to Beethoven and then let us in. It was a very disorderly looking room; papers and articles of clothing strewn about all over the place; some trunks, bare walls, hardly a chair, with the exception of the wobbly one at the Walter pianoforte, at that time the best. And in this room was a gathering of six to eight persons, among them both of the Wranitzky brothers, Süssmeyer, Schuppanzigh, and one of Beethoven's brothers.

Beethoven himself was wearing a jacket of fuzzy, dark-grey material and matching trousers, so that he immediately reminded me of the illustration of Robinson Crusoe in the Campe edition, which I happened to be reading at the time. His pitch-black hair cut à la Titus bristled shaggily about his head. His beard, which hadn't been shaved for a few days, further darkened the lower part of his already brown face. With the visual acuity common to children I noticed right away that he had cotton in both ears, which seemed to have been dipped into a yellowish liquid. At the time, however, he didn't show the slightest evidence of being hard of hearing. I was immediately asked to play something, and since I was too shy to begin with one of his compositions, I played Mozart's great C Major Concerto, which begins with a series of chords. Beethoven soon became attentive, came closer to my chair, and played the orchestral theme with his left hand during those passages in which I had only the accompaniment to play. His hands were densely covered with hair and his fingers very broad, particularly at the tips. The satisfaction he expressed gave me courage enough to then play his *Pathétique* Sonata, which had just appeared, and, finally, the "Adelaide," which my father sang with his quite fine tenor voice. When I had finished, Beethoven turned to my father and said: "The boy has talent, I want to teach him myself and I'll take him on as my pupil. Send him to me a few times a week. Above all, however, get him a copy of Emanuel Bach's book *On the True Art of Playing Keyboard Instruments,* which he must bring with him next time." All those present congratulated my father on this favorable verdict. Krumpholz was especially delighted, and my father hurried off immediately to locate a copy of Bach's book.

During my first lessons with him, Beethoven worked with me exclusively on the scales, in all keys. He also showed me the only proper positioning of the hands and fingers, and in particular the use of the thumb (still unknown to most players at that time)— rules whose usefulness I would only learn to appreciate fully at a much later time. He then went through with me the exercise pieces in Bach's method book and, in particular, called my attention to the use of legato, which he himself mastered in an incomparable way, and something which all other pianists at that time considered impossible to achieve, since the choppy, abruptly detached style of playing of Mozart's era was still in fashion. Beethoven also told me years later that he had heard Mozart play on several occasions and that Mozart had become accustomed to this style of playing on the more commonly used harpsichord—a style which was not at all suited to the pianoforte, still in its infancy in Mozart's time. I also made the acquaintance of several people over the years who had taken lessons from Mozart and found confirmation of Beethoven's observations in their manner of playing. . . .

In 1804 I was presented by Krumpholz to Prince Lichnowsky, the friend and most ardent supporter of Beethoven. Both the prince as well as his brother, Count Moritz, had earlier been students of Mozart and later of Beethoven, and were just as much connoisseurs of art as they were likeable, humane men. It was Prince Lichnowsky who had brought the young Beethoven to Vienna, who had arranged for him to study with Haydn, Salieri, and Albrechtsberger, and treated him like a friend and brother and persuaded all of the high nobility to support him. I possessed such a thorough musical memory that I knew how to play everything Beethoven—to say nothing of other composers—had written for the fortepiano completely by heart—a natural gift which I still had at that time. The Prince became so favorably inclined toward me upon his first listening that I had to spend a few hours with him almost every morning and play from memory anything he wanted to hear. Every month he gave me a present, which was welcome assistance to my good but poor parents. On one of these mornings, Beethoven, who had not seen me for two years and was angry at my father for discontinuing my lessons, also came to Prince Lichnowsky and appeared to be quite satisfied with my progress. "I told you right away," he said, "that the boy has talent. But," he added with a smile, "his father wasn't strict enough with him." "Oh, Herr van Beethoven," my father replied good-humoredly, "he is after all our only child." Beethoven was also satisfied with my sight-reading when he gave me the manuscript of the C Major Sonata, op. 53.

From this time on Beethoven remained well-disposed toward me and treated me in a friendly manner up until his last days. I had to take care of all the corrections for his newly appearing works, and when the opera *Leonore* was performed in 1805, he had me arrange it for the pianoforte. I am indebted to his guidance in this task for my arranging skills, which became so useful to me later on.

Translated by Michael Gilbert

Franz Schubert

To Franz von Schober and Others (1818)

September 8, 1818

Dear Schober,	Dear Senn,
Dear Spaun,	Dear Streinsberg,
Dear Mayrhofer,	Dear Wayss,

Dear Weidlich,

How infinitely happy your letters, separately and together, make me is beyond telling. I was attending a cattle auction when they brought me in your fat packet. I opened it and, catching sight of Schober's name, gave vent to a loud cry of joy. With childish pleasure and laughing to myself all the time, I read it through in a room nearby. It was as though my dearest friends were really within arm's reach again! But now I must answer you all in the proper order.

Dear Schobert,

I see that this alteration in your name holds good. Well, dear Schobert, your letter was from beginning to end very precious and delightful, and especially the last sheet. Yes, indeed, the last sheet sent me into the Seventh Heaven of joy. You are a splendid fellow (in Swedish of course), and, believe me, my friend, you will not fail, for your understanding of art is the finest and sincerest imaginable. That you should look upon this change as a small one pleases me very much: for a long time now you have had one foot in our particular inferno.—The fact that the management of the opera house in Vienna is so stupid and produces the finest operas but none of mine, makes me pretty furious. Here in Zelez I have to be everything at once. Composer, editor, audience, and goodness knows what besides. There is not a soul here with a genuine interest in music except, perhaps, now and then, the Countess (if I am not mistaken). So I am all alone with my beloved, and must hide her in my room, in my pianoforte, and in my own heart. Although this is often very depressing, yet on the other hand it inspires me towards greater things. Do not be afraid that I shall stay away any longer than I absolutely must. Several new songs—and I hope very successful ones—have come into being during this time. That the bird of Greece should be fluttering his wings in Upper Austria does not surprise me at all, since it is his own country and he is on a holiday. I wish I were with him. I should certainly know how to make good use of my time. But that you—by nature a sensible fellow—should imagine my brother to be wandering about there alone, with neither guide nor companion, does surprise me very much. First, since an artist likes best of all to be left to himself; second, since there are too many lovely districts in Upper Austria for him not to be able to discover the most beautiful; third, since he has an agreeable acquaintance in Herr Forstmeyer in Linz. He must know quite certainly, therefore, what he is about.

If you could manage a greeting to Max, when his melancholia is better, I should be infinitely glad. And since you will shortly be seeing your mother and sister, please give them my kindest regards. It is quite possible that this letter will not reach you in Vienna in time, for I only received yours at the beginning of September, just when you were due to leave. I will then have it sent on to you. I am very glad, among other things, that Milder is, for you, irreplaceable. I feel the same about her too. She sings best and trills worst of all.

Now a description for you all:

Our castle is by no means one of the largest, but it is very attractively built. It is surrounded by a lovely garden. I live in the estate agent's house. It is fairly quiet except for some forty geese, which at times set up such a cackling that one cannot hear oneself speak. All the people about me are thoroughly kindhearted. It is rare for a nobleman's household to run as smoothly as this one. The agent, a Slav from Slavonia and a good fellow, very much fancies his former musical talents. He can blow on the lute two German dances in a masterly fashion. His son, a student of philosophy, has just arrived on his holidays, and I hope I shall get on very well with him. His wife is just like any other woman who wants to be taken for a lady. The steward is perfectly suited to his job: a man of extraordinary perspicacity in whatever concerns his own purse and pocket. The doctor, twenty-four years old, and a really able man, is as full of ailments as an old lady. A great deal of it put on. The surgeon, whom I like best of all, a venerable old man of seventy-five, always happy and serene. God grant to all such a fortunate old age! The magistrate a very unaffected and pleasant man. A cheerful old bachelor, companion to the Count, and a good musician, often comes to see me. The chef, the lady's maid, the chambermaid, the lodgekeeper, etc., and two coachmen are all good folk. The chef, rather a loose fellow; the lady's maid, thirty years old; the chambermaid very pretty, and often in my company; the children's nurse a nice old body; the lodgekeeper my rival. The two grooms are better suited to the stables than to human society. The Count is rather a rough sort of man, the Countess proud, but a more sensitive nature, the little Countesses good children. So far I have been spared any invitation to the dining room. I can think of nothing more to tell you now. I need hardly say to all of you that know me that with my naturally frank disposition I get along very well with all these people.

Dear Spaun, I am heartily glad that you are able at last to build palaces for little clerks of the Court Chancery to run about in. You probably mean by this a choral quartet. Remember me to Herr Gahy.

Dear Mayerhofer, you cannot be longing for November much more than I am. Stop being so seedy, or at least give up taking medicine, and the other will follow of itself.

For Hans Senn to read too if he pleases: as above.

Maybe friend Streinsberg is already dead: and that is why he cannot write. Let friend Weidlich tack his name on to his own coattails.

Good old Waiss remembers me with gratitude. He is an excellent man.

And now, dear friends, good-bye. Write to me very soon. My

best and favorite form of entertainment is to read your letters through a dozen times.

Greetings to my dear parents, and tell them how much I long for a letter from them. With enduring love,

Your faithful friend,
Franz Schubert

Translated by Venetia Savile

"My Dream," an Allegorical Story (1822)

July 3, 1822

I was one of many brothers and sisters. We had a good father and mother. I felt a deep love for them all.—One day my father took us to a feast. My brothers became very merry there. But I was sad. My father then came up to me and bade me taste the delicious foods. But I could not, and at that my father in his anger banished me from his sight. I turned on my heel, and with a heart filled with infinite love for those who scorned it, I wandered off into a far country. For years I was torn between the greatest love and the greatest sorrow. Then came news of my mother's death. I hastened back to see her, and my father, softened by grief, did not hinder my return. I saw her lying dead. Tears poured from my eyes. I saw her lying there, looking just as she used to, one with the dear past in which, according to her wishes, we ought still to live and move and have our being.

Mourning, we followed her to the grave, and the coffin slowly sank.—From this time onwards I stayed at home again. Then one day my father took me once more into his pleasure-garden. He asked me if it pleased me. But the garden was hateful to me, and I did not dare to reply. Then he asked me a second time, and more impatiently, if I liked the garden.—Trembling I told him no. At that my father struck me and I fled. For the second time I turned away, and my heart filled with infinite love to those who scorned it, I wandered once more into distant lands. Through long, long years I sang my songs. But when I wished to sing of love it turned to sorrow, and when I wanted to sing of sorrow it was transformed for me into love.

So was I divided between love and sorrow.

And once a pious maiden who had just died appeared to me. And a circle formed about her tomb in which many youths and old men wandered as though in perpetual bliss. They spoke softly so as not to wake the maiden.

Heavenly thoughts like bright sparks seemed to flicker unceasingly out of the virgin's tomb, and to fall in a soft-sounding shower on to the young men. I longed to walk there too. But only by a miracle, so people said, could one enter the circle. I went forward, however, slowly and devoutly, with my eyes lowered towards the gravestone, and before I knew it I was in the circle, from which the loveliest melody sounded. And I felt, pressed as it were into a moment's space, the whole measure of eternal bliss. My father I saw too, loving and reconciled. He folded me in his arms and wept. And I still more.

Franz Schubert

Translated by Venetia Savile

To Franz von Schober (1824)

September 21, 1824

Dear Schober,

I hear that you are not happy? That you have to get over a bad attack of despair? So Swind wrote to me. Although I am exceedingly grieved to hear this, I am not at all surprised, this being the fate of most intelligent people in this miserable world. And, after all, of what use is happiness when the only incitement left to us is misfortune? If only we were together, you, Swind, Kuppel, and I, each stroke of ill-luck would be easy enough to bear, but instead we are all separated, each one in a different corner, and in that lies my real unhappiness. I want to cry out with Goethe: "Who'll bring back just an hour of that delightful time!" That time when in our intimate circle each showed the other, with motherly diffidence, the children of his art, and waited, not without apprehension, for the verdict that love and truth would pronounce upon them: that time when each inspired the other with a common striving towards the ideal that animated one and all. Now I am sitting here alone in farthest Hungary, whither I let myself be enticed, alas, for a second time, without a single person near me to whom I can really talk. Since you went away I have written scarcely any songs, but have tried my hand at some instrumental music. Heaven knows what will happen to my opera! Although I have been in good health for the past five months, my spirits suffer from your and Kuppel's absence, and I have very wretched days sometimes. In one of these fits of depression, when the sterility and insignificance that characterize the life of today was painfully brought home to me, there came into my head the following lines which I am only showing you because I know that you treat even my weaknesses with love and indulgence.

Lament over the Nation

Youth of our time! Your former power has fled.
The strength of countless nations ebbs away.
None rises up to point a better way.
Valor is lost and inspiration dead.

My days are spent in sorrow's leaden ban,
Sterile and poor, a victim of this age,
Which shrouds in dust our golden heritage,
And brings no greatness unto any man.

The folk, grown old and feeble, wander by,
Their youthful prowess but a vanished dream,
And even poesy no more esteem,
Its golden glories turn to mockery.

O power of Art! The sacred task is thine!
Hold up thy mirror to the nobler past!
Thy strength alone can sorrow's strength outlast,
And mock its triumph over our decline.

Up to the time of writing things are going very badly with Leidesdorf. He cannot pay, and no one buys either my things or anybody else's, but only wretched "popular" productions.

I have now informed you pretty exactly how matters stand with me, and I am anxiously awaiting the earliest possible news of your own affairs. The best of all for me would be if you were to come back to Vienna again. I feel confident that you are in good health.

And now good-bye, and write to me as soon as you can.

Your
Schubert
Adieu!!!

Translated by Venetia Savile

From His Lost Diary (1824)

Sorrow sharpens the understanding and strengthens the character, whereas happiness seldom troubles about the former, and only makes for weakness or frivolity in the latter.

With all my heart I hate that narrow-mindedness which makes so many wretched people believe that what they think and do is best, and that everything else is worthless. One thing of beauty, it is true, should inspire a man throughout his life, yet the gleam of this single inspiration should illuminate everything else.

No one to feel the other's grief, no one to understand the other's joy! People imagine that they can reach one another, but in reality they only pass one another by. Oh misery for him who realizes this!

All that I have created is born of my understanding of music and my own sorrow: that which is engendered by grief alone seems to please the world least of all.

One step alone divides the sublime from the ridiculous and the greatest wisdom from the grossest stupidity.

Man comes into the world armed with faith, which is far superior to knowledge and understanding: for in order to understand a thing one must first of all believe in it. Faith is that high fundament in which the weaker intellect erects the first pillars of conviction.

Reason is nothing more than analyzed belief.

O imagination! Man's greatest treasure, inexhaustible source at which both art and learning come to drink! O remain with us, though recognized and venerated only by the few, so that we may be safeguarded from so-called Enlightenment, that hideous skeleton without blood or flesh.

Translated by Venetia Savile

To Emperor Franz II (1826)

Your Majesty!
Most gracious Emperor!
With the deepest submission the undersigned humbly begs Your Majesty graciously to bestow upon him the vacant position of Vice-Kapellmeister to the Court, and supports his application with the following qualifications:

(1) The undersigned was born in Vienna, is the son of a schoolteacher, and is 29 years of age.

(2) He enjoyed the privilege of being for five years a Court Chorister at the Imperial and Royal College School.

(3) He received a complete course of instruction in composition from the late Chief Kapellmeister to the Court, Herr Anton Salieri, and is fully qualified, therefore, to fill any post as Kapellmeister.

(4) His name is well known, not only in Vienna but throughout Germany, as a composer of songs and instrumental music.

(5) He has also written and arranged five Masses for both smaller and larger orchestras, and these have already been performed in various churches in Vienna.

(6) Finally, he is at the present time without employment, and hopes in the security of a permanent position to be able to realize at last those high musical aspirations which he has ever kept before him.

Should Your Majesty be graciously pleased to grant this request, the undersigned would strive to the utmost to give full satisfaction.

Your Majesty's most obedient humble servant,

Franz Schubert

Vienna, April 7, 1826

Translated by Venetia Savile

To Franz von Schober (1828)

Vienna, November 12, 1828

Dear Schober,

I am ill. I have had nothing to eat or drink for eleven days now, and can only wander feebly and uncertainly between armchair and bed. Rinna is treating me. If I take any food I cannot retain it at all.

So please be so good as to come to my aid in this desperate condition with something to read. I have read Cooper's *Last of the Mohicans, The Spy, The Pilot,* and *The Pioneers.* If by any chance you have anything else of his, I beg you to leave it for me at the coffeehouse with Frau von Bogner. My brother, who is conscientiousness itself, will bring it over to me without fail. Or indeed anything else.

Your friend,
Schubert

Translated by Venetia Savile

Felix Mendelssohn Bartholdy

To Carl Friedrich Zelter (1830)

Munich, June 22, 1830

Dear Herr Professor,

I have wished to write to you for a long time and once more express my gratitude. But it is difficult for me to say "thanks" in writing; the words seem so cold and formal while what I enjoyed so greatly and want to thank you for, still appears so vividly to me. When you introduced me nine years ago into Goethe's house, you were perfectly aware of how great a happiness your kindness had in store for me. But I could not know that myself at the time, nor could I fully appreciate a gift whose value was not yet clear to me. But now that I have experienced greater delight and comfort with Goethe and his family than ever before, now that I have lived through a number of unforgettable days, when every hour brought nothing but elation, joy, and pride—now at last I know how to appreciate it. Nevertheless, I cannot thank you as I ought. You did not do it in order to be thanked, and so you will excuse my speaking about it, even though my words have not the tone I would like to give them, and are not adequate for their purpose. Well, I am sure you know how I feel.

I have often played to Goethe in the morning hours. He wanted to get an idea of how music has developed and wished to hear the music of different composers in chronological order. He seemed rather wary of Beethoven; but I could not spare him this acquaintance because he had to hear "where sounds had turned to," and so I played for him the first movement of the C Minor Symphony which he liked very much. He was delighted with the overture by Johann Sebastian Bach, the one in D major with the trumpets, which I played on the piano as well as I could; "in the beginning it sounds so distinguished and pompous, one really sees the crowd of smartly attired people walking down the steps of a broad staircase." And I also played the Inventions and quite a few pieces of *The Well-Tempered Clavier*. One day he asked me if I would not care to pay a compliment to craftsmanship and call on the organist who might let me see and hear the organ in the cathedral. I said, yes, of course I would, and the instrument gave me great pleasure. I was told that you, too, had given your expert opinion on the repair work, and that therefore it had been done better than on any repaired organ I know of. Owing to the long narrow space in which it is housed, the pedal-pipe is fitted deep in the rear; nonetheless the full organ sounds ample and strong, the tone does not tremble in the least, and this shows that there must be plenty of wind. The pedal is in perfect proportion to the manual and there is no lack of beautiful, soft voices of various kinds. The organist offered me the choice of hearing something scholarly, or something for "people" (because he said that for people one had to compose only easy and bad music), so I asked for something scholarly. But it was not much to be proud of; he modulated around enough to make one giddy, but nothing unusual came of it; he made a number of entries, but no fugue was forthcoming. When my turn came to play to him, I started with the D Minor Toccata of Sebastian and remarked that this was at the same time scholarly and something for "people" too, at least for some of them; but mind, hardly had I begun to play when the superintendent dispatched his valet upstairs with the message that this playing had to be stopped right away because it was a weekday and he could not study with that much noise going on. Goethe was very much amused by this story.

Here in Munich, the musicians behave exactly like that organist; they believe that good music may be considered a heavensent gift, but just *in abstracte,* and as soon as they sit down to play they produce the stupidest, silliest stuff imaginable, and when people do not like it they pretend that it was still too highbrow. Even the best pianists had no idea that Mozart and Haydn had also composed for the piano; they had just the faintest notion of Beethoven and consider the music of Kalkbrenner, Field, and Hummel classical and scholarly. On the other hand, having played my-self several times, I found the audience so receptive and open-minded that I felt doubly vexed by those frivolities. Recently, at a soirée given by a Countess, who is supposed to lead in fashion, I had an outbreak. The young ladies, quite able to perform adequate pieces very nicely, tried to break their fingers with juggler's tricks and tightrope-walker's feats of Herz's; when I was asked to play, I thought: well, if you get bored it serves you right, and started right out with the C-sharp Minor Sonata of Beethoven. When I finished, I noticed that the impression had been enormous; the ladies were weeping, the gentlemen hotly discussing the importance of the work. I had to write down a number of Beethoven sonatas for the female pianists who wanted to study them. Next morning the Countess summoned her piano teacher and desired from him an edition of good, really good music, by Mozart, Beethoven, and Weber. This story went around in Munich, and the good-natured musicians were very pleased that I had set myself up as the preacher in the desert. Subsequently I gave a long sermon to the leading pianist and re-proached her for having contributed nothing towards the knowl-edge and appreciation of the works of the great masters here and for having just followed the popular trend instead of guiding the taste of the public—and she vowed to improve. Since that time I play only what I really like, however serious, and everybody lis-tens to me with attention.

I am delighted to make so much music here, and though I have little time left to compose and to think, this gay life inspires me with many new ideas and proves to be cheering and refreshing. I have a sacred piece in mind; as soon as I find time to write it down, I shall mail it to you. Goodbye for today, dear Professor Zelter. With the most cordial greetings for you and yours and the best wishes for your health and happiness,

Always your faithful
F.M.B.

Translated by Grisella Selden-Goth and Marion Saerchinger

To the Committee of the Lower Rhine Music Festival (1838)

Leipzig, January 18, 1838

I am deeply grateful for the invitation contained in your letter of the 8th of January. Your kind remembrance is not less prized by me than the prospect of again attending such a pleasant festival, and deriving from it as much enjoyment as that for which I have already to thank the Rhine Music Festivals. I therefore accept your invitation with sincere delight, if God grants health to me and mine, and if we can mutually agree on the selection of the music to the full satisfaction of both parties. The more successful the previous Cologne festival was with regard to the arrangement of the pieces performed, especially in Händel's work with the organ, the more important it seems to me to have at least *one* piece in the program by which this year's festival may be distinguished from others, and by means of which progress may, as far as possible, be manifested. For this purpose I consider it absolutely necessary to have the name of Sebastian Bach in the program, if only for one short piece; for it is certainly high time that at these festivals, on which the name of Händel has shed such luster, another immortal master, and in many points superior to all, should no longer be forgotten. The same scruples which exist in opposition to this must also have existed in former years with regard to the works of Händel, and you are all grateful to those who, disregarding these obstacles, revealed to you such treasures of sublimity and elevation. Earn for yourself, then, similar thanks from the Rhenish friends of music by making a beginning which is indeed difficult (for this I do not deny), and which must be proceeded with cautiously, but which will certainly be attended with the best results and universally imitated by others. When anything of Bach's has been once performed, it will be easy to discover that it is beautiful and to perform it again; but the difficulty is at the beginning. The proposal that I wish to make to you on this subject is to introduce into the Music Festival a short psalm of Bach's (about twenty minutes or half an hour in length), and if you are afraid of doing this on the second day for fear of scaring away the public, which might be alarmed by this arcane name, then do so on the first day and give in addition a rather shorter oratorio by Händel. It is fairly certain that no fewer people will come to hear Händel, for those who do not fear the one will be equally disposed to like the other, and there are still three or four totally unknown and truly admirable oratorios of his that would not occupy more than an hour and a half, or scarcely two hours at most, and would be a welcome novelty to all music lovers. I first became acquainted with these works by the splendid gift of the previous committee, and I shall be very glad if you can derive any benefit from these volumes for this year's festival. With regard to the second day, may I first inquire whether you intend to apply to Cherubini for his grand *Requiem?* It must be translated, and it is entirely for men's voices, but as it will only last an hour or even less, that would not matter much, and according to the universal verdict it is a splendid work. At present, however, the chief object seems to me to be the first point in this letter, and I therefore beg you to arrange for it as soon as possible.

Translated by Lady Wallace

To Marc-André Souchay (1842)

Berlin, October 15, 1842

. . . There is so much talk about music, and yet so little is said. For my part, I believe that words do not suffice for such a purpose, and if I found they did suffice I would finally have nothing more to do with music. People often complain that music is too ambiguous; that what they should think when they hear it is so unclear, whereas everyone understands words. With me it is exactly the reverse, and not only with regard to an entire speech, but also with individual words. These, too, seem to me so ambiguous, so vague, so easily misunderstood in comparison to genuine music, which fills the soul with a thousand things better than words. The thoughts expressed to me by music that I love are not too indefinite to be put into words, but on the contrary, too *definite*. And so I find in every effort to express such thoughts, that something is right but at the same time, that something is lacking in all of them; and so I feel, too, with yours. This, however, is not your fault, but the fault of the words which are incapable of anything better. If you ask me what I was thinking of when I wrote it, I would say: just the song as it stands. And if I happen to have had certain words in mind for one or another of these songs, I would never want to tell them to anyone because the same words never mean the same things to different people. Only the song can say the same thing, can arouse the same feelings in one person as in another, a feeling which is not expressed, however, by the same words.

Resignation, melancholy, the praise of God, a hunting-song, do not conjure up the same thoughts in everybody. Resignation is to the one what melancholy is to the other; the third can form no vivid conception of either. Why, to anyone who is by nature a keen sportsman, a hunting-song and the praise of God would come to pretty much the same thing, and to him the sound of the hunting-horn would actually be the praise of God, while to us it would be nothing but a hunting-song. And however long we might discuss it with him, we would never get any further. Words have many meanings, but music we could both understand correctly. Will you allow this to serve as an answer to your question? At all events, it is the only one I can give, although these, too, are nothing, after all, but ambiguous words!

Translated by Grisella Selden-Goth and Marion Saerchinger

Robert Schumann

To Friedrich Wieck (1829)

Heidelberg, November 6, 1829

I have just put the A Minor Concerto aside, my honored master, and have let down the venetian blinds, lighted a cigar, drawn my chair up to the table, buried my face in my hands, and—hey, presto!—I am at the corner of the Reichsstrasse, going to my music lesson!

Ah, why did I leave Leipzig, where the Olympus of Music was being so delightfully opened to me, yourself being the priest, who with imperceptible force removed the veil from the eyes of your dazed disciple! Here everything has turned out just as I expected. People are, as a rule, very fond of music, but not many have real talent. Occasionally one comes across a few old-fashioned critics, but there is precious little genial activity in matters musical. I detest theory pure and simple, as you know, so I have been living very quietly, improvising a good deal, but not playing much from notes. I have begun many a symphony, but finished nothing, and every now and then have managed to edge in a Schubert waltz between Roman Law and the Pandects, and have often hummed the Trio in my dreams, which brought back the heavenly hour when I first learned the piece with you. On the whole, I think I have not gone either forward or back very much, and of course that is almost equivalent to standing still. Yet I feel that my touch has become more powerful in the *fortes* and more tender and eloquent in the *pianos,* although I may have lost some of my accuracy and execution. Without overestimating my own abilities, I feel modestly conscious of my superiority over all the other Heidelberg pianists. You have no idea how carelessly and roughly they play, and of the noisiness, slap-dash, and terrible feebleness of their style. They have no notion of cultivating "touch," and of bringing a fine tone out of the instrument; and as to regular practice, finger exercises, and scales, they don't seem ever to have heard of anything of the kind. The other day one of them played me the A Minor Concerto. He performed it very correctly and without mistakes, keeping a sort of rhythmical marchtime, and I could conscientiously praise him. But when I played it to him, he had to admit, that though his rendering was quite as correct as mine, yet somehow I made the whole thing *sound* different; and then how in the world did I get such a *violin-like* tone, etc.? I looked at him with a smile, put Herz's finger exercises before him, and told him to play one every day for a week, and then come and try the Concerto again. This he did, and in due time came back enchanted and delighted, and called me his good genius, because my advice had helped him so much. And he actually did play the Concerto ten times better.

I am now working at the last movement of Hummel's Sonata in F-sharp Minor, which is indeed a great epic work of truly titanic dimensions, reflecting a tremendous spirit at once struggling and resigned. This will be the only thing I shall play you at Easter, and will be a test by which you can judge of my improvement. An opposition faction is forming against Thibaut, to which I belong; and after all the delightful hours I have spent with him, you would not believe how much it *grieves* me to observe his narrow-mindedness, and truly pedantic opinions in music, which are such a contrast to his broad-minded views in jurisprudence, and all the fine qualities of his tremendously fiery and *crushing* spirit.

A fortnight ago, I came back from a tour in Switzerland and Italy, a few napoleons out of pocket, but all the richer in knowledge of the world, and full of high and sublime recollections. By Jove, you have no idea of Italian music, for it must be heard under the sky which inspired it, namely, the sky of Italy. How often I thought of you in La Scala at Milan, and how enchanted I was with Rossini, or rather with Pasta, of whom I will say nothing at all, from pure veneration—nay, almost adoration. In the Leipzig concert hall, I have sometimes felt a sort of shiver run through me, when the genius of sound has awed me by his presence; but in Italy I learned to love him, and for one single evening in my life I felt as though I were in the presence of the deity, and allowed for a few moments to gaze reverently upon the unveiled face of the god, and that was at Milan, when I heard Pasta and—Rossini!! Do not smile, master; it is the truth. That was really the only musical treat I had in Italy, for as a rule the music there is simply unbearable, and you have no idea with what a combination of slovenliness and zeal they scrape away at everything.

I will not enter upon my other adventures, however new and interesting many things were to me, but will keep the history of it all for some future time, when we can talk and laugh over them together.

Schubert is still "my only Schubert," especially as he has so much in common with "my only Jean Paul"; and when I am playing his music, I feel as if I were reading one of Jean Paul's novels. The other day I was playing his four-hand Rondo, op. 107, which I consider one of his best compositions; and is there anything to compare with the thunderous calm, the great, self-contained lyrical madness, and the gentle, deep, ethereal melancholy which pervades this truly great and complete work? I can just see Schubert walking up and down his room, wringing his hands as though in despair, while his mind keeps running on

 etc.

He cannot get rid of the idea, and brings back the great pure strain once more at the end, where it seems to breathe its last in a gentle sigh. I remember playing that very Rondo at an evening party at Herr Probst's, but at the finish, both players and listeners stared at one another, rather at a loss to know what to think, or to know what Schubert meant by it all. As far as I remember, I never heard *you* speak of it either; do look it up, and tell me what you think. Altogether, I think nobody's compositions are such a psychological puzzle in the course and connection of their ideas as Schubert's, with their *apparently* logical progressions. Very few composers have succeeded in stamping their individuality upon a mass of tone-pictures in the way he has done, and still fewer have written so much for themselves and their own hearts. What a diary is to those who jot down all their passing emotions, his music-paper was to Schubert. To it he confided all his moods; and his intensely musical soul finds expression in notes, when ordinary mortals use words—at least that is my humble opinion. For years I have been studying the artistic side of music, and was really getting on very well, though I felt that I lacked decided opinions, and was very much wanting in objectivity, so that I sometimes found what others missed, and vice versa. But if you only knew how my mind is always working, and how my symphonies would have reached op. 100, if I had but written them down; and how perfectly at home I feel in the whole orchestra, *and how I could confront my enemies, overcome them, drive them into a corner, and repulse them altogether!* I am not very proud, though more from circumstances than principle (with some people, who deserve it, I put on a certain haughty manner); but sometimes I am so full of music, and so overflowing with melody, that I find it simply impossible to write down anything; and when I am in that kind of mood, if a critic were to say to me: "You had better not write anything, for you effect nothing," I should be bold enough just to laugh in his face, and tell him he knew nothing about the matter. Forgive me my *apparent* frankness. And now I have nothing but favors to ask of you. The first and most pressing is: Please write to me; and the second and still more pressing one, Let it be soon. I swear, your letters quite replace all the Leipzig concerts I have to miss. And so you have had Paganini there, and you heard him four times, did you? Four times! Good heavens, the idea of your hearing him *four times* makes me completely wild! Please write me a full account of all your doings during the last half year, and tell me all about your present pupils, and your daughter Clara, and your two other little ones with their great musical eyes. Perhaps you could lend me the *Musikalische Zeitung* from April to September for a fortnight. Not a soul reads it here, and probably you have finished with the numbers.

I am also going to ask you to send me all Schubert's Waltzes, and put them down to my account. I think there are ten or twelve books of them. Also Moscheles's G Minor Concerto and Hummel's B Minor Concerto without the parts; and further I should like sent *on approval,* so that I can return what I do not like, all Schubert's compositions which have appeared since op. 100, and please do not forget the Quintet, as I want to have a look at it. Likewise any compositions for the piano which have appeared at Leipzig in my absence, and which you think I might like. You know my taste pretty well. I might also have a few new things by Herz and Czerny, as I visit several families here. Thibaut must shut up, with his Handelian operatic airs.

I have really not half done, but must bring this letter to a close. Remember me very kindly to Madame Wieck, to Dr. Carus, to whom I have written, but received no answer; to Herr Probst, who has reason to be angry with me, but whom indeed I like very much; and to Mdlle. Reichold, who is, I trust, engaged to be married.

And now, most honored master of my *mind*, accept the assurance of my most hearty esteem,

R. Schumann

Translated by May Herbert

"Rage Over the Lost Penny" (1835)

It would be hard to conceive of anything more amusing than this little escapade. How I laughed when I played it for the first time! And how astonished I was when, a second time through, I read a footnote telling me that this capriccio, discovered among Beethoven's manuscripts after his death, bore the title: "Rage over the Lost Penny, Vented in a Caprice." . . . O! It's the most adorable, futile rage, like that which seizes you when you can't get a boot off, and you sweat and swear and the boot looks up at you, phlegmatically—and unmoved!

I've got you at last, you Beethoven fanatics! I'd like to vent my feelings about you in quite another fashion, and pummel you with the softest of fists when I see you beside yourselves, your eyes bulging, lost in rapture, and gasping: "Beethoven strives ever for the rapturous, from star to star he flew, free from this earth!"

"I'm really unbuttoned today," was his favorite expression when his spirits were high. And then he would laugh like a lion and let loose about him—for he was unruly in all circumstances.

Well, with this capriccio I shall be unruly with you, my friends. You'll call it common, unworthy of a Beethoven, just like the tune to the ode "To Joy" in the D Minor Symphony, you'll bury it deep under the *Eroica*.

Should there one day be a resurrection of the arts, and Genius hold the scales with the capriccio about the penny balanced against ten of the newest dramatic overtures, well, I tell you, the overtures would flip skyward!

And you composers, young and old, there is one essential thing that you could all learn from it, something you need to be reminded of from time to time: nature, nature, nature!

Translated by Henry Pleasants

Chopin's Piano Concertos (1836)

I

Rejoice, young artists, at the sound of the first voice lifted against you! Welcome it as proof of your talent, and assess the significance of the latter in proportion to the vehemence of the opposition.

Still, it is odd that in the drought years before 1830, when one should have thanked heaven for the meagrest kernel, even the critics, instead of recognizing Chopin, were inclined to shrug him off. Criticism, to be sure, usually brings up the rear, unless it issues from creative heads; one critic, indeed, went so far as to state that Chopin's compositions were barely worth tearing up! Enough of all that! Or should we mention a certain petticoat journal which flirts with us from behind the mask with eyes like daggers, and only because we once observed, laughingly, to one of its correspondents, who had written something about Chopin's *Don Giovanni* Variations, that like a bad verse, he had a couple of feet too many, and that it would seem a kindness to him to cut them off? At least, so we are told. We don't read it, and flatter ourselves that we bear some slight resemblance to Beethoven in that respect!

But should we be thinking of such things today, fresh from Chopin's F Minor Concerto? God forbid! What are an entire year's issues of a musical journal against a concerto by Chopin? What are the ravings of a pedant against those of a poet? What are ten editors' crowns against the Adagio of the Second Concerto? And truly, those in the League of David, we should count you unworthy of any respectful salutation could you not yourselves dare the kind of work about which you write—with certain exceptions, of course, including this Second Concerto, which none of us can presume to approach, unless it be with the lips to kiss the hem!

Away with musical journals! The triumph and ultimate objective of a good one would be to achieve that high estate where people would read it for some higher reason than for want of anything better to do, or to have encouraged such musical productivity that the world would have neither the time nor the desire to read what is written about it! The music critic's noblest destiny is to make himself superfluous! The best way to talk about music is to be quiet about it!

Odd thoughts to be coming from a journalist! But critics should not suppose themselves to be supreme among artists. They live from artists, after all, and the latter could let them starve to death if they chose to. If criticism is good for anything, then only as a tolerable fertilizer for future works; and God's own sun provides enough of that. Again, why write about Chopin? Why not create at first hand, do one's own playing, one's own writing, one's own composing? For the last time, away with the musical journals, this one and all the rest!

Florestan

II

If things were ordered according to that lunatic Florestan, one could call the above a review—and let it stand as an obituary for this periodical. Florestan should remember that we also have an obligation to Chopin, about whom we have heretofore said nothing. We, ourselves, may regard our silence as the ultimate homage, but the rest of the world may interpret it quite differently. If the homage of words is still outstanding (and a thousand hearts have offered him the most beautiful homage of all!), it is due partly to the hesitancy one feels when confronted with a phenomenon one would prefer to approach through the senses; partly to an awareness of one's own inadequacy vis-à-vis the majesty of the subject and the impossibility of encompassing it from every side at once and in all its height and depth; partly to the inner artistic affinity we feel with this composer, and partly, at last, to the fact that Chopin, in his most recent compositions, appears to be striking out upon a higher path, if not a new one, about whose direction and presumable destination we hoped to get some clearer idea before rendering an accounting to our absent allies.

Genius creates empires, whose smaller states are distributed by higher authority among talents. To the latter falls the task of organizing and perfecting details, while genius remains preoccupied with grander productions. Just as Hummel, for example, followed the voice of Mozart, and clothed the master's thoughts in a more brilliant, more buoyant covering, so Chopin follows the voice of Beethoven. Or, to dispense with the metaphor: just as Hummel adapted Mozart's style to the purposes and pleasures of the piano virtuoso, so Chopin introduces the spirit of Beethoven into the concert hall.

He made his entrance, not with an orchestral army, as great geniuses do; he entered with a small following, but his own right down to the last hero. His teachers had been the best—Beethoven, Schubert, and Field. The first, we may assume, developed his spirit in daring, the second his heart in tenderness, and the third his hand in dexterity. Thus he stood, equipped with profound knowledge of his art, confident of his own strength and armed with courage when, in the year 1830, the mighty voice of the people arose in the west. Hundreds of young men were awaiting this moment. But Chopin was one of the first to scale the wall, behind which lay a cowardly restoration, a dwarfish philistinism fast asleep. Blows fell to right and left; the philistines awoke, angrily, and cried: "What impudence!" In the rear of the attackers others shouted: "What splendid courage!"

This was not all that fate ordained to distinguish Chopin from all others. There was also a strong and original nationality—namely, Polish! This was an important element in a favorable coincidence of time and circumstance. Now that the Poles are deep in mourning, their appeal to us artists is even stronger. It is probably just as well that neutral Germany did not immediately appeal to him, and that his genius diverted him straight to one of the world's great capitals, where he could freely compose—and freely rage. For if the mighty autocratic monarch in the north could know that in

Chopin's works, in the simple strains of his mazurkas, there lurks a dangerous enemy, he would place a ban on music. Chopin's works are cannon buried under flowers!

In his origin, in the fate of his country, one may find the explanation of his virtues and also of his failings. Who does not think of him when the talk is of passion, charm, and spontaneity, of fire and nobility? But who, also, does not think of him when the talk is of eccentricity, of sickly idiosyncrasy—yes, even of savagery and hate?

These evidences of extreme nationalism mark all of Chopin's earlier works. But art demands more. The parochial concerns of the homeland had to give way to the interests of the outside world. The physiognomy is no longer too specifically Slavic in his later works, and tends little by little towards that universal ideal pictured for us most congenially by the heavenly Greeks. Thus, following a new path, we may in the end celebrate a reunion with Mozart. We said "little by little," for he should never entirely deny his origin. But the more he distances himself from it, the more significant will he be for the art as a whole.

If we must explain in words the significance which in part he has already achieved, then we should say that he contributes to an insight whose confirmation seems ever more urgent: that progress in our art is possible only with the artist's own progress towards a spiritual aristocracy according to whose statutes a command of the mere craft is not only demanded but is taken for granted as a prerequisite, with admittance denied to all insufficiently talented themselves to do what they require of others; in other words they must have imagination, temperament, and intelligence. All this is required in order to bring about a higher epoch of general musical cultivation, an epoch in which there can be as little doubt about the truly genuine as about the various figures in whom the truly genuine might appear. The term "musical" would be understood to mean that inner, living will and capacity to participate, that active sympathy, that ability quickly to give and to receive! All this in order that the molding of creation and recreation into a society of artists may lead us closer to the higher goals of art!

Eusebius

Translated by Henry Pleasants

To Clara Wieck (1838)

Leipzig, April 13, 1838

How full of music I am now, and always such lovely melodies! Just fancy, since my last letter I have finished another whole book of new things. You and one of your ideas are the principal subject, and I shall call them *Kreisleriana,* and dedicate them to you; yes, to you, and to nobody else; and you will smile so sweetly when you see yourself in them. Even to myself my music now seems wonderfully intricate in spite of its simplicity; its eloquence comes straight from the heart, and everyone is affected when I play before people, as I often do now, and like to do. And when you are standing by me, as I sit at the piano, then we shall both cry like children—I know I shall be quite overcome. . . . That Fantasia of Liszt's was the most wonderful thing I have ever heard you play. Play him the Toccata, and the Études, which he does not know yet, and call his attention to the Paganini Études. The *Children's Scenes* will probably be finished by the time you arrive; I am very fond of them, and make a great impression when I play them, especially upon myself. The next things to be printed are some Fantasias, but to distinguish them from the *Fantasy Pieces* I have called them "Ruins," "Victory Arch and Constellation," and "Poems." It was a long time before I could think of that last word. It strikes me as being a very refined and most characteristic title for a piece of music.

But you must have patience with me sometimes, and often scold me. I have got plenty of faults, though less than I used to have. Our having had to wait so long has had some advantages: we shall have got over a good deal that other people experience after marriage. I have just noticed that marriage [*Ehe*] is a very musical word, and a fifth too:

But to return to my faults; I have got one detestable habit, namely, showing my affection for people I love most, by playing all sorts of tricks on them. For instance, supposing there is a letter which I ought to have answered long ago. You might say, "Dear R., do answer that letter, it has been lying there such a time"—but do you suppose I would do it? No such thing. I would sooner make all sorts of pretty excuses, etc. Then I have got another very saucy trick: I am one of the greatest admirers of beautiful women; I simply delight in them, and revel in praising your sex. So if ever we are walking together through the streets of Vienna, and meet somebody pretty, and I should exclaim, "Oh, Clara, look at that divine creature," or something of that sort, you mustn't be alarmed, or scold.

Now just look at your old Robert. Is he not just the same trifler, joker, and teller of ghost stories? But I can be very serious too, and sometimes for days together; but don't let that alarm you, for it is only when my mind is at work, and I am full of ideas about music and my compositions. I am affected by everything that goes on in the world, and think it all over in my own way, politics, literature, and people, and then I long to express my feelings and find an outlet for them in music. That is why my compositions are sometimes difficult to understand, because they are connected with distant interests; and sometimes striking, because everything extraordinary that happens impresses me, and impels me to express it in music. And that is why so few compositions satisfy me, because, apart from all their faults of construction, they deal in musical sentiment of the lowest order, and in commonplace lyrical effusions. The best of what is done here does not equal my earliest musical efforts. Theirs may be a flower, but mine is a poem, and infinitely more spiritual; theirs is a mere natural impulse, mine the result of poetical consciousness. I do not realize all this while I am composing; it only comes to me afterwards; you, who are at the top of the tree, will understand what I mean. And I cannot talk about it; in fact, I can only speak of music in broken sentences, though I think a great deal about it. In short, you will find me very serious sometimes, and will not know what to make of me. Then, you must not watch me too closely when I am composing; that would drive me to desperation; and for my part, I will promise you, too, only very seldom to listen at your door. Well, we shall indeed lead a life of poetry and blossoms, and we will play and compose together like angels, and bring gladness to mankind. . . .

I have not been to see Mendelssohn very often, he generally comes to me. He is certainly the most eminent man I have met. I have heard people say that he is not sincere with me. I should be very grieved to think so, as I feel that I have become very fond of him, and have let him see it. But one of these days, tell me all you know. At all events, it will make me careful, and I will not waste my affection, when perhaps hard things are said of me behind my back. I know exactly what he is to me in music, and could go on learning from him for years. But he can also learn something from me. If I had grown up under the same circumstances as he did, and had been destined for music from childhood, I should now beat every one of you; I can feel that in the energy of my ideas. Well, everyone's life has something peculiar about it, and I will not complain of mine. My father, a man whom you would have honored if you had only seen him, saw through me very early, and intended me for a musician, but my mother would not allow it. Afterwards, however, she spoke very kindly, and even approvingly of my change of career.

Translated by May Herbert

Schubert's Symphony in C (1840)

A musician visiting Vienna for the first time may well rejoice in the festive street sounds and pause in admiration before St. Stephen's spire. But he will shortly be reminded how near to the city lies a churchyard dearer to him than any other of the city's sights, the place where almost side by side lie two of the greatest men his art has ever produced.

Many young musicians will have wandered as I did out to this churchyard in Währing to lay a wreath upon those graves, or even a mere wild rose such as the one I found planted on the spot where Beethoven finally found repose. Franz Schubert's grave was unadorned. So it was that one of my fondest wishes was fulfilled. I stayed for a long time contemplating the two hallowed graves, almost envying that Count O'Donel—if I have remembered the name correctly—who lies buried between them.

To see a great man face to face for the first time, to grasp his hand, is one of life's most blessed experiences. It had not been my good fortune to encounter either of these artists, whom I admire most among the more recent composers, during his lifetime, and so I would have liked to have at my side during this pilgrimage some person who had been close to at least one of them, preferably one of their brothers. And then it occurred to me as I walked back to the city that Schubert's brother Ferdinand still lived, of whom Schubert thought so highly. I looked him up soon afterwards and found a strong resemblance, judging by the bust that rests by Schubert's grave. He was rather smaller, but sturdily built, his features expressing honesty and music alike. He knew me as an outspoken admirer of his brother, told me much and finally showed me some of his treasures—namely, those of Franz Schubert's compositions still in his hands. The assembled wealth set me to trembling with joy! Where to begin? Where to stop? He showed me, among other things, the scores of a number of symphonies, some still unheard, some examined and put away as too difficult and extravagant.

One must know Vienna, the problems of musical life there, the difficulty of assembling the resources required for the performance of large works, to understand how it could be possible that in the city where Schubert lived and worked little or nothing of his music is heard beyond his songs. Who knows how long the symphony now under discussion might have lain in darkness and dust had I not promptly arranged with Ferdinand to send it to Leipzig and to the management of the Gewandhaus concerts, or to Mendelssohn himself, whose keen eye rarely misses the most modestly budding beauty, much less the radiant full bloom? And so it was. The symphony arrived in Leipzig, was heard, grasped, heard again and almost universally admired. The enterprising firm of Breitkopf & Härtel purchased the work and the rights, and thus we have it now complete with all the parts, with a full score, we hope, soon to follow for the use and enlightenment of the world.

Let me state at the outset: he who doesn't know this symphony knows little of Schubert. In view of what the world has already received from him this may seem hardly credible praise. It is so often said, and to the considerable annoyance of composers, that "after Beethoven one should forgo symphonic ambitions," and it is true that most of those who have disregarded this advice have produced only lifeless mirrorings of Beethovenesque idioms, not to mention those sorry, dull symphonists who have managed a tolerable suggestion of the powdered wigs of Haydn and Mozart but not their heads. One may make an exception for single important orchestral works, but they have been more interesting for the light they have cast on the development of their composers than for any influence they have had on the public or on the evolution of the symphony. Berlioz belongs to France, and is only mentioned from time to time as an interesting foreigner and madman. I had suspected and hoped—and probably many others, too—that Schubert, who had shown such a sure sense of structure, such invention, and such versatility in so many other forms, would also tackle the symphony from the flank and find the spot from which he could get at both it and the public. All this has now most wonderfully come to pass.

It was not his intention, to be sure, to continue Beethoven's Ninth Symphony. Industrious artist that he was, he produced symphony after symphony of his own. That the world is now suddenly confronted with his seventh without having known its predecessors or having been able to follow the progress that led to it is perhaps the only regrettable aspect of its publication and one which could contribute to its being misunderstood. Perhaps, on the other hand, it may lead to the release of the others. The smallest of them will have its Schubertian significance. Indeed, those Viennese who, a few years ago, offered a prize for a "best" symphony need not have gone to such lengths or so far afield to find the laurels they coveted. Fine symphonies were lying piled up sevenfold in Ferdinand Schubert's little study in a Viennese suburb. Here were laurels for the asking. So it goes. If one speaks to a Viennese of —— he'll praise Vienna's Franz Schubert to the skies. But among themselves they have no very high opinion of either of them!

Be that as it may, we may refresh ourselves here in the fullness of the spirit that flows forth from this delightful work. Granted, this Vienna, with its St. Stephen's spire, its lovely women, girded by the Danube with countless ribbons, stretching out to the fertile plain and beyond to ever higher mountain ranges, with all its reminders of the greatest German masters—this Vienna cannot fail to provide rich nourishment for the musician's fantasy. I used to look down upon it from the hilltops and think how Beethoven's restless eye must have strayed out to those distant Alpine ranges, how Mozart must have dreamily followed the course of the Danube, everywhere losing itself in reed and wood, and how Papa

Haydn must have looked up at St. Stephen's, shaking his head in disbelief at the spire's dizzy height. Put the Danube, St. Stephen's, and the distant Alps together and you have something of Vienna. Imagine the soft Catholic fragrance of incense, add the surrounding landscape, and you have something that vibrates strings within us that would never have sounded under any other circumstances. With this symphony of Schubert's, with its bright, blossoming, Romantic life, the city stands before my eyes again, more distinctly than ever before, and I understand once more how, precisely in this surrounding, such works can be born.

I shall not attempt to give the symphony a program. Persons of various ages choose too variously in their imagining of texts and pictures. The eighteen-year-old often hears something earth-shaking in music which suggests to a grown man no more than a local incident. The composer himself may have had nothing else in mind than to get down the best music that was in him. But one likes to believe that the outside world, bright today, dark tomorrow, often penetrates to the spiritual recesses of the poet and musician, and to hear such a symphony as this is to concede that it carries hidden away within it more than mere lovely song, more than mere joy and sorrow expressed in conventional musical terms. It is to concede that it guides us to a new realm. Here, beside sheer musical mastery of the technique of composition is life in every fiber, color in the finest shadings, meaning everywhere, the acutest etching of detail, and all flooded with a Romanticism which we have encountered elsewhere in Franz Schubert. And this heavenly length, like a fat novel in four volumes by Jean Paul—never-ending, and if only that the reader may go on creating in the same vein afterwards. How refreshing is their sense of inexhaustible wealth where with others one always fears the ending, troubled by a presentiment of ultimate disappointment.

One would be at a loss to explain how Schubert suddenly came by this sovereign command of the orchestra were it not known that this symphony was preceded by six others and that it was written in his prime. It is still evidence of an extraordinary talent that he who heard so little of his own instrumental work during his lifetime could achieve such an idiomatic treatment both of individual instruments and of the whole orchestra, securing an effect as of human voices and chorus in discourse. This resemblance to the human voice I have never encountered so deceptively and so strikingly except in much of Beethoven. It is the reverse of Meyerbeer's treatment of the singing voice. The symphony's utter independence of Beethoven's symphonies is another indication of its masculine origin. One sees here how rightly and wisely Schubert's genius manifests itself. Aware of his more modest resources, he avoids the grotesque forms and bold proportions of Beethoven's later works. He gives us something charmingly and yet still very originally formed, never departing too far from the central idea and always returning to it. So it must appear, at least, to one who has heard it and studied it often. The brilliance and novelty of the instrumentation, the breadth and expanse of the form, the striking changes of mood, the whole new world into which we are transported—all this may be confusing to the listener, like any initial view of the unfamiliar. But there remains a lovely aftertaste, like that which we experience at the conclusion of a play about fairies or magic. There is always the feeling that the composer knew exactly what he wanted to say and how to say it, and the assurance that the gist will become clearer with time.

This sense of security is established right at the beginning in the splendid, Romantic introduction, although everything is still veiled in secrecy. Brilliantly novel, too, is the transition to the Allegro; we are aware of no change of tempo, but suddenly without knowing how, we have arrived. To break down the individual movements into their constituent parts would amuse neither ourselves nor the reader. One would have to write out the whole symphony to get an idea of its novel character. Only the second movement, speaking to us in such touching tones, I cannot pass over in silence, especially that passage where a horn is heard as from a distance. It seems to come from another sphere. Here everything listens, as if a heavenly spirit were wandering through the orchestra.

The symphony made an effect here like that of none other since Beethoven's. Artists and art-lovers were united in its praise. From the master who had so carefully prepared it I heard words which I should have liked to pass on to Schubert as the ultimate in joyous tidings. It may be years before the symphony establishes itself in Germany. That it will be forgotten or overlooked one need not fear. It bears within it the seed of eternal youth.

Thus my visit to the grave, which, in turn, led me to a relative of the deceased, brought me a second reward. The first I harvested on the day of the visit when I found on Beethoven's grave a steel pen which I have treasured ever since and which I use on special occasions—such as this!

Translated by Henry Pleasants

To Felix Mendelssohn Bartholdy (1845)

Dresden, October 22, 1845
Wednesday morning

Dear Mendelssohn,

You must now be well in the middle of my symphony. Do you still remember the first rehearsal of it in the year 1841—and the "stopped" trumpets and horns at the beginning? It sounded as if the orchestra had a cold in its head; I can't help laughing when I think of it. And now let me thank you for again thinking about my piece and again taking trouble over it. It is with the greatest pleasure that I think of that first evening's performance. How beautifully it went, better than I have ever heard it since! I might perhaps repeat the experience tomorrow, but I dare not come. I am sorry to say that I have not yet regained my full strength; every divergence from my simple regime upsets me, and induces morbid irritability. That is why I reluctantly stayed away when my wife was with you. I must avoid every form of gaiety. There is nothing for it but to go on hoping, and that I am determined to do.

Clara told me with genuine pleasure how good and kind you had been. You know she is an old admirer of yours, and is happy at your least sign of approval. For her untiring zeal and energy in her art she really deserves everyone's love and encouragement; then, as a woman, she is indeed a gift from heaven. So, you see, she came back from Leipzig quite delighted, frankly admitting that you were the chief cause of her delight. Lately we have been absorbed in your organ sonatas, unfortunately with the piano as substitute; but we should have discovered that they were yours without the name on the cover. They are stamped on every page with that striving after perfection which makes me look to you as my model. Then the poetry and originality of the form! Each sonata is rounded off to a complete picture. Bach's music gives me the impression of himself seated at the organ, but yours brings me a vision of a Cecilia fingering the keys. How charming that that should be your wife's name, too! The fifth and sixth struck me as being the most important. One thing is certain, dear Mendelssohn, no one but you writes harmonies so pure, harmonies ever increasing in purity and spiritual beauty. Have I been praising you again? May I? What, indeed, does the world in general (many so-called musicians included) understand of pure harmony? There is Wagner, who has just finished another opera. He is certainly a clever fellow, full of crazy ideas and audacious to a degree. Society still raves over *Rienzi.* Yet he cannot write or think out four consecutive bars of beautiful, hardly of good music. All these young musicians are weak in harmony, in the art of four-part writing. How can enduring work be produced in that way? And now we can see the whole score in print, fifths, octaves, and all. It is too late now to alter and scratch out, however much he may wish it. The music is no fraction better than *Rienzi,* but duller and more unnatural, if anything. If one says anything of the sort it is always put down to envy, and that is why I only say it to you, knowing you have long been of the same opinion. . . .

Translated by Hannah Bryant

New Paths (1853)

Many years have passed since I have been heard from in the *New Journal for Music,* an arena so rich in memories for me—indeed, almost as many years as I once devoted to editing it—namely, ten. I have often been tempted to speak out, despite strenuous creative activity. A number of important new talents have come along in the meantime, a musical era has appeared to be in the offing, heralded by many rising young artists, even though the latter may be known to a rather small circle. Following their progress with the utmost interest, I felt certain that from such developments would suddenly emerge an individual fated to give expression to the times in the highest and most ideal manner, who would achieve mastery, not step by step, but at once, springing like Minerva fully armed from the head of Jove. And now here he is, a young fellow at whose cradle graces and heroes stood watch. His name is Johannes Brahms.

He comes from Hamburg, where he had been working in quiet obscurity, initiated by an excellent and inspired teacher into the most difficult canons of the art. He was recommended to me by an eminent and famous master. Even in his external appearance he displays those characteristics which proclaim: here is a man of destiny! Seated at the piano, he began to disclose most wondrous regions. It was also most wondrous playing, which made of the piano an orchestra of mourning or jubilant voices. There were sonatas, more like disguised symphonies; songs, whose poetry would be intelligible even to one who didn't know the words, although a profound vocal line flows through them all; a few piano pieces, partly of a demoniac character, charmingly formed; then sonatas for violin and piano, string quartets, etc.—all so different one from another that each seemed to flow from a separate source. And finally it seemed as though he himself, a surging stream incarnate, swept them all together into a single waterfall, sending aloft a peaceful rainbow above the turbulent waves, flanked on the shores by playful butterflies and the voices of nightingales.

When once he lowers his magic wand over the massed resources of chorus and orchestra, we shall have in store for us wonderful insights into the secret of the spiritual world. May the highest genius lend him strength; and well it may, for in him resides a second genius—namely, that of modesty. His contemporaries greet him as he sets off into a world which may bring him pain, but which will surely bring him laurels and palms as well. We welcome him as a staunch combatant.

Every age has a secret society of congenial spirits. Draw the circle tighter, you who belong to one another, that the truth of art may shine ever more clearly, spreading joy and blessings everywhere!

Translated by Henry Pleasants

Otto Nicolai

Some Reflections on Italian Opera in Comparison to German (1837)

Unfortunately, both Germany and Italy exhibit such a great one-sidedness of opinion about each other at this time, such a grave difference of opinion about music, that I must fear the consequences if these lines come to the attention of certain of my countrymen. They think they can demand of me, as a born German, an absolutely libelous statement on Italian music.—I ask these people not to read this little essay. I do not travel about in the world with a preconceived opinion, or wanting to find things just as I always thought they must be—but rather, seeking to take things in as quietly and observantly as possible, to weigh things, select the best, and, if I should possess enough strength, apply them. In short—I try to be unprejudiced.

When I set foot in Italy three years ago—I needn't be ashamed of this confession, particularly when I speak with Germans, for the same thing will happen at some point to anyone trained in the truly German school of art—I felt such a great aversion to Italian opera that I would have preferred to turn right around and come home again! I poured out my disdain in a long essay on this subject and sent it to Herr Ludwig Rellstab in Berlin. Whether it was ever printed, I don't know, and I don't know what has become of it now. I am almost sorry I didn't make a copy of it, so that I could now gauge the extent to which my perspective has changed.—For I confess to you: I now find some beautiful things in Italian opera music. . . . Oh, I can already see how those smart gentlemen will pity me as they state so haughtily and with a learned air: "Too bad about the young man: Italy has spoiled him, for bad examples corrupt good manners!"—However, I console myself and simply respond: Gentlemen, it is very difficult to make a truly correct judgment! I implore you not to be so hasty!—

In music, we Germans could learn a number of things from the Italians, although they undoubtedly could learn more from us. Only a mixture of the two schools will produce something more closely approximating perfection, more absolutely beautiful. Mozart and Gluck knew that!!—Since that time, however, works have changed in form, artistic resources have expanded, demands have grown. But who realizes this today?—Or, if anyone knows it, who acts accordingly? Oh, what a tragic state of affairs! The two nations endowed with the greatest gifts for music, the Italians and the Germans, stand opposed to each other in their artistic achievements like sworn enemies. If only that would at least lead to healthy competition! But no: one despises the other! In Germany, people are at least fair enough to perform the compositions of Italians, and the names Rossini, Donizetti, Bellini, etc. are certainly known. But many German musicians condemn all Italian music as idle nonsense and titillation for the ear, lacking any character; and frequently they are right!—

But these people judge things one-sidedly, never considering the manner in which this music is performed for them, and unfamiliar with the limitations placed upon an opera by the Italian public, for whom this music is, after all, written. In Italy, the situation is far worse: the entire nation believes that only they are capable of producing operatic music and that the *Oltramontani* are barbarians! They won't even try to perform or listen to German vocal music. Italian translations of German operas are absolutely nonexistent, and the names Beethoven, Weber, Spohr, Marschner, etc. are completely unfamiliar to them. What little they do know of German opera music is condemned as unintelligible, unmelodious, unsingable, or as mere academic exercise; and isn't there also some truth to this?—. . .

In all honesty, I must confess that it often seems to me a sad thing to be a composer under current conditions. What am I to think of the basic principles of musical judgment when I see that the things so deeply felt here are viewed there as being ridiculous?

Is it not the very purpose of musical art to produce feelings through sound? However, when something that so perfectly achieves the intended feeling here so entirely misses the mark there—isn't it enough to drive one to despair? Such a small stretch of earth separates these peoples, and their capacities to feel and judge are already so totally different! Isn't it a disheartening thought for a composer that something universally beautiful cannot be created? But certainly it is possible! Indeed, it can arise from a unification of the two schools.—The ideal shimmers in the distant future, but we will scarcely be able to experience it in our lifetime. Perhaps our grandchildren.—

No art is so directly bound up with the character of a nation as music, and this in turn depends upon climate, education, political circumstances, etc.! If there is some learned, impartial person who wants to write on this subject: it is a rich one!—I am not equal to the task, and lay claim only to being a good musician, not a man of letters.

"The Italian goes to the theater to enjoy himself." The German certainly does this too: but he finds his enjoyment in something other than the Italian. I recall having read in Rochlitz (in his writings *For Friends of Music*) that true enjoyment of music can only occur once our intellectual faculties are engaged. That is truly German! The Italian, on the other hand, already views this as a form of labor; he doesn't wish to employ his ability to think, but rather his ear, and this, to be sure, in a pleasant way.

The composers of both countries write music in accordance with these demands; and for this reason the more philosophical, learned, intellectually profound compositions are written in Germany, while the lighter, more sensuously appealing ones are written in Italy. Now, it is certainly not to be denied that it is more noble, worthy, and honorable to the human spirit to bring forth products like those of the Germans. At the same time, one should bear in mind that music entails a certain something that cannot be subordinated to human reason—something inexplicable, supernatural. Who would seek to explain to me why it is that a simple, beautiful sound, a single resounding chord, produces upon the listener's soul an effect that, in turn, is dependent upon and modified by the current state of the soul?

I am not yet speaking about words, which can be combined with sound in the human voice and can, in a sense, explain it; rather, I speak only about the essential element of the art of music—sound. And I am tempted to assert that Italian opera music is more concerned with this specifically musical element, with sound, whereas German opera has more to do with the associated words and their meanings. . . .

In everything involving the external disposition, organization of the company, public order, stage machinery, etc., the Italian theater is infinitely far behind the German. It is almost impossible to build a good opera ensemble in Italy. This can be explained by the way the theater is organized. The house belongs either to a wealthy person in the city, or to some corporation, or even to the reigning prince. In any case, it is then rented to a theater entrepreneur, called the impresario, with the stipulation that a certain number of operas, normally three, and one or two ballets be staged. Now, this entrepreneur brings together from the most diverse regions the artists needed for the brief season—after which they disperse again in all directions, even though they've hardly begun to know and understand each other fully. It is the same thing with the orchestra: artists from different cities are brought together for the current season, and in this way, of course, no unity can be achieved.

As a rule, a season comprises about sixty performances. If we divide that number by three or four operas, then each one must be given at least fifteen to twenty times, which is precisely what happens. Given the unfortunate situation that one of the operas displeases the audience and is booed down, the one given previously must be run across the boards again and may, depending on the circumstances, be presented up to thirty times that season.

Given such a tired routine, how could the interest and attention of the public be kept alive? Thus they go to the theater in the evening because their social circle gathers there once during the opera season. Every family of any standing has its own loge, to which one is invited and where one makes social calls as though it were the family's private residence. People talk, play cards, laugh, joke around, and pay little attention to the music. However, at premieres they are attentive, and on such evenings few visits are made to the loges.

How different, how infinitely superior and more worthy of art is the state of German opera! Indeed, if only the German system, with its order, precision, discipline, diligence, and endurance, could be transplanted to Italy! But that wouldn't work, for even if one were to populate all of Italy with Germans, in a short time they would become even worse than the Italians now living there. The climate determines the character of the people! Where the lemon trees blossom and wine costs almost nothing—there people look upon thinking as something laborious!

The situation can therefore scarcely be rectified. It would have to be accomplished by those German who, blessed with talent and already equipped with German training, would for a time (but not too long, for too much would be unhealthy!) study Italian vocal music in Italy, and then return home to the fatherland to put these studies to proper use.

Translated by Michael Gilbert

Franz Liszt

To Robert Schumann (1838)

My dear Monsieur Schumann,

I shall not attempt to tell you how grateful and touched I am by your friendly letter. Mademoiselle Wieck, whom I have been so happy as to meet here, will express to you better than I can all the sympathy, all the admiring affection I have for you. I have been such a nomad recently that the pieces you were kind enough to address to me at Milan only reached me on the eve of my departure from Venice about a fortnight ago; and since then we have been talking so much of you, day and night, that it hardly occurred to me to write to you. Today, however, to my great astonishment, I get a fresh token of your friendly remembrance, and I certainly will not delay thanking you many times for it, so I have just left a charming party of very pretty women in order to write these few lines to you. But the truth is you need hardly thank me for this little sacrifice, for it is a great pleasure to me to be able to have a little chat with you.

The *Carnaval* and the *Fantasy Pieces* have interested me excessively. I play them really with delight, and God knows that I can't say as much of many things. To speak frankly and freely, it is absolutely only Chopin's compositions and yours that have a powerful interest for me.

The rest do not deserve the honor of being mentioned . . . at least, with a few exceptions,—to be conciliatory, like *Eusebius.*

In six weeks to two months I shall send you my twelve Studies and a half-dozen "fantasy pieces" (*Impressions et Poèmes*)—I con-

148

sider them less bad than others of my making. I shall be happy to think that they do not displease you.

May I confess to you that I was not very much struck with Henselt's Studies, and that I found them not up to their reputation? I don't know whether you share my opinion, but they appear to me, on the whole, very *careless*. They are pretty to listen to, they are very pretty to look at, the effect is excellent, the edition (thanks to our friend Hofmeister) is most carefully done; but, all counted, I question whether H. is anything but a distinguished mediocrity. For the rest, he is very young, and will doubtless develop. Let us, at least, hope so.

I am extremely sorry that I cannot come and pay you a little visit at Leipzig at present. It is one of my keenest desires to make your personal acquaintance and to pass some days with you. But as that is not possible now, let us, at least, try not to be entirely separated, and let us combat, as far as we can, the laziness about writing, which is, I think, equally in us both.

In a fortnight I am returning to Venice. I shall be back in Milan at the time of the coronation (towards the end of August). Next winter I expect to spend in Rome, if the cholera or some other plague does not stop it. I will not induce you to come to Italy. Your sympathies would be too deeply wounded there. If they have even heard that Beethoven and Weber ever existed, it is as much as they have done.

Will you not have what you have sent me printed? Haslinger would have it gladly, I think, and it would be a great pleasure to me to see my name associated with yours.

If I might make a request, I would ask you to write some trios, or a quintet or septet. It seems to me that you would do that admirably, and for a long time nothing remarkable in that line has been published. If ever you determine to do so, let me know at once, as I should be anxious to have the honor of making them known to the public.

Adieu, my dear Monsieur Schumann; keep me always in affectionate remembrance, and accept once more my warm sympathy and devotion.

F. Liszt

Translated by Constance Bache

To Countess Marie d'Agoult (1840)

London, June 1840

"I can't do anything else at this moment and probably always but live completely alone." That's what you had to tell me! Six years of the most absolute devotion have brought you only to this result. . . . And thus many of your words! Yesterday (to recall only one day) the whole way from Ascot to Richmond you did not utter a single word that was not an offense, an outrage. But what good is it to return to such sad things, to count up one by one all the wounds in our hearts? Perhaps you will add these words to those you will no longer admit. My words have changed so much. You say so, at any rate.

Midnight

Love is not justice. Love is not duty. It is not pleasure, either, but it mysteriously contains all these things. There are a thousand ways of experiencing it, a thousand ways of practicing it, but for those whose heart is utterly and infinitely thirsty, there is one, eternally one, without beginning or end. If it is manifested anywhere on earth, it is above all in this complete trust of one in the other, in this supreme conviction of our angelic nature, inaccessible to any taint, impenetrable to everything outside of it. So let us not argue about words (or even about things), let us not bargain, let us not measure. If love is still at the bottom of our hearts, all has been said; if it has disappeared, there is nothing more to say.

Adieu, I feel extremely tired. I'd like to talk with you longer, but the memory of your words constrains and chills me. Good night. Sleep well. A thousand ideas bother and irritate me. Shall I be able to talk to you? I don't know, but perhaps this time again my words will win you over? Adieu, I do not despair.

Translator anon.

Visit to Beethoven (ca. 1875)

I was about eleven years old when my respected teacher Czerny took me to see Beethoven. Already a long time before, he had told Beethoven about me and asked him to give me a hearing some day.

However, Beethoven had such an aversion to infant prodigies that he persistently refused to see me. At last Czerny, indefatigable, persuaded him, so that, impatiently, he said: "Well, bring the rascal to me, in God's name!" It was about ten o'clock in the morning when we entered the two small rooms in the Schwarzspanierhaus, where Beethoven was living at the time, myself very shy, Czerny kind and encouraging. Beethoven was sitting at a long, narrow table near the window, working. For a time he scrutinized us grimly, exchanged a few hurried words with Czerny and remained silent when my good teacher called me to the piano. The first thing I played was a short piece by Ries. When I had finished, Beethoven asked me whether I could play a fugue by Bach. I chose the Fugue in C Minor from *The Well-Tempered Clavier*. "Could you also transpose this fugue at once into another key?" Beethoven asked me. Fortunately, I could. After the final chord, I looked up. The Master's darkly glowing gaze was fixed upon me penetratingly. Yet suddenly a benevolent smile broke up his gloomy features, Beethoven came quite close, bent over me, laid his hand on my head, and repeatedly stroked my hair. "Devil of a fellow!" he whispered, "such a young rascal!" I suddenly plucked up courage. "May I play something of yours now?" I asked cheekily. Beethoven nodded with a smile. I played the first movement of the C Major Concerto. When I had ended, Beethoven seized both my hands, kissed me on the forehead, and said gently: "Off with you! You're a happy fellow, for you'll give happiness and joy to many other people. There is nothing better or greater than that!"

This event in my life has remained my greatest pride, the palladium for my whole artistic career. I speak of it only very rarely and only to my intimate friends.

Translated by Michael Hamburger

Richard Wagner

From "A Pilgrimage to Beethoven" (1840)

. . . Nor was Beethoven's outward appearance calculated to put me at my ease. His clothes were untidy and informal; he wore a red woollen stomach-band; his long, dark gray hair was dishevelled; his expression gloomy and unfriendly. We sat down at a table covered with paper and pens.

An uncomfortable silence reigned. Evidently it irritated Beethoven to find himself receiving two visitors instead of one.

At last in a hoarse voice he addressed me: "You come from L—?"

I was about to reply when he interrupted me by picking up a sheet of paper and pencil, which lay to hand. "Use these," he said. "I cannot hear."

Of course I knew all about Beethoven's deafness and had prepared myself. But it smote my heart to hear that hoarse, broken voice say: "I cannot hear." To be poor and joyless, one's only solace one's sovereignty in the realm of sound, and have to say: "I cannot hear." In a flash I understood why Beethoven looked as he did: why the deeply careworn cheek, the somber angry glance, the tightly drawn defiant mouth. . . .

Confused, hardly knowing what I was doing, I wrote down an apology, together with a brief explanation of the circumstances that had compelled me to appear accompanied by the Englishman. When he had read this Beethoven turned to the latter, sitting opposite dumb and contented, and asked him somewhat angrily what he could do for him.

"I have the honor. . ." began the Englishman.

Beethoven interrupted him hastily. "I do not understand you. I cannot hear, and neither can I speak very much. Write down what it is you want."

The Englishman reflected calmly for a moment. Then he drew out of his pocket an elegant-looking piece of music manuscript and said to me: "Good. Write down that I request Herr Beethoven to look over my composition, and if anything should displease him be so kind as to mark the passage with a cross."

I wrote down every word, thinking that now at last I might get rid of him. And so indeed it proved. After he had read the request Beethoven with a curious smile put the Englishman's composition on the table, gave him a curt nod, and said: "I will send it to you." The gentleman appeared perfectly satisfied. He rose to his feet, made one of his most elegant bows, and excused himself.

I gave a mighty sigh of relief. He had actually gone.

Now at last I could feel I was really within the sanctuary. Even the gloom in Beethoven's face began to lift. After looking at me calmly for a moment, he addressed me thus:

"So that Briton has been plaguing you, has he?. . . Then take comfort from me. I've been plagued to death by these Englishmen who come here to stare at a poor composer as though he were some rare wild animal. I'm very sorry I took you for one. . . . You said in your letter that you were satisfied with my compositions. I'm glad to hear it; these days I don't reckon very much on people liking my things."

As I listened to these simple, intimate words I lost my painful shyness. With a thrill of joy I wrote down that I was very far from being the only one whom his works filled with enthusiasm, and that it was my great longing that he would give my native city, for example, the joy of welcoming him: he would soon be convinced of the enormous impression his works had made on the entire public.

"I can well believe that my works go down better in North Germany," Beethoven replied. "The Viennese here are a great disappointment. The trash they listen to every day makes it impossible for them to bring their minds to bear on anything serious." By way of contradicting him, I told of the performance of *Fidelio* I had attended yesterday, which the Viennese had applauded with the greatest enthusiasm.

"Hmph, *Fidelio*," growled the master. "There's nothing more to all that hand-clapping than mere vanity, you can take it from me: the people think it was their advice I was following when I made all those revisions. Now they want to repay me for my trouble and so they cry 'bravo.' . . . They're a good-natured, uncultivated folk; I prefer them to the really clever people. . . . Did you like *Fidelio*?"

I described my impressions of yesterday's performance, remarking that the revisions seemed to me to have gloriously enhanced the total effect.

"A tiresome labor!" Beethoven growled. He continued: "I am no opera composer—that is to say, there isn't a single theater in the world for which I'd willingly write another opera. If I were to write one after my own heart people would run away. All that stuff operas are patched together out of nowadays—arias, duets, terzettos, and what have you—I'd get rid of and put in its place what no singer would want to sing and no public to hear. Glittering lies, boring sugary trash: that's all they understand. Anyone who composed a true musical drama would be written off as a fool. And so he would be if he tried to get it performed, instead of being content to keep it for himself."

"And how would you go to work on such a musical drama?" I asked excitedly.

"As Shakespeare did when he wrote his plays!" was the reply, delivered with something like violence. "Those who make it their business to supply the kind of vocal trumpery, with which any mediocrity can win himself an ovation, would be better employed dressmaking in Paris than composing dramas. . . . I'm not made for that kind of sport. I know all the pundits say that I only understand how to write for instruments and that I'll never be at home in vocal music. If by vocal music they mean operatic music, then they're quite right. Heaven forbid that I should ever feel at home there!"

At this point I ventured to ask whether Beethoven really believed that anyone who knew his "Adelaide" would dare to dispute his mastery in the realm of song.

After a short pause the master replied: "When all is said, 'Adelaide' and such things are trifles, which your professional singer takes up because they enable him to display his virtuosity. But why shouldn't vocal music be considered as great and serious as instrumental music? Why shouldn't it receive the same respect from the frivolous singer-folk as a symphony does from an orchestra? The human voice, a far nobler and more beautiful organ than any orchestral instrument, is *there,* a fact of life. Why should it be handled any less independently? What new results might not be achieved? Develop the very thing which sets the voice apart and you throw open fresh possibilities of combination. Instruments represent the primal organs of creation and nature; their expression can never be clearly defined and formulated, since they convey the primal feelings as they first issued forth from the chaos of the creation, perhaps even before there was any human heart to hear and feel. The genius of the voice is completely different: this represents the human heart, the separate individual sensibility, limited, but clear and definite. Imagine, now, these two elements brought together and united! Imagine the instruments that convey the primal feelings—those raw wild feelings encompassing the infinite—united with the voice that represents the limited, but clear, definite sensibility of the human heart. That second element, the voice, would have a beneficial effect upon the instruments' expression of the struggle of primal feeling in that it would set it within the framework of a definite, unifying course; on the other hand, the human heart itself, represented by the voice, would be infinitely strengthened and expanded by gathering to itself those primal feelings: for now its former vague awareness of the highest would be transformed into a God-like consciousness."

Here Beethoven paused for a few moments as though exhausted. "Of course there would be grave difficulties to overcome," he continued with a sigh. "Voices must have words, and where is poetry to be found worthy of such a union? The poem would be overshadowed: words are too feeble an instrument for such a task. . . . You will soon be hearing a new composition of mine, a symphony with choruses, which will bring home what I've just been saying. Words had to be found, and the task of finding them was a great problem. In the end I decided to use our Schiller's beautiful ode 'To Joy'—a very noble uplifting poem, of course, yet a very long way from expressing what in this case no poem in the world could possibly utter."

The happiness I felt at receiving out of Beethoven's own mouth these clues to the understanding of his gigantic last symphony, which he had just completed and which nobody knew—this happiness is something which even now I find impossible to picture. I expressed my deep gratitude for the privilege and my delighted surprise at the news of another great composition. My eyes filled with tears—I could have knelt before him.

Beethoven seemed to notice my emotion; with a kind of sad, mocking smile he said: "You will be able to defend my new work when it comes out. Remember me, when all the pundits think I've gone mad, or at any rate declare that I have. But you, Herr R—, have seen that a madman I am not—though I have good cause to be. People think I ought to write what *they* consider good and beautiful; they forget that a poor devil, deaf as a post, might have his own ideas, and that I can only compose as I feel. . . . If I cannot think and feel their beautiful things," he added ironically, "well, that precisely is my misfortune."

So saying he rose and strode across the room with short swift steps. Deeply moved though I was, I too stood up: I could feel myself trembling in every limb. It was impossible for me to continue the conversation either by gestures or by writing. Moreover I felt that the moment had come when my visit should be brought to an end. Merely to write down a few heartfelt words of thanks and farewell seemed inadequate; better to take my hat, go up to Beethoven, and let him read in my eyes what I was feeling.

He seemed to understand. "You are going?" he asked. "But you'll be staying on in Vienna yet awhile?"

I wrote down that the sole purpose of my journey had been to make his acquaintance, and that now that I had been granted the great privilege of this interview I intended to start my journey home tomorrow.

"You said in your letter how you earned the money to come here," he replied with a laugh. "You should stay on in Vienna and write galops—this is just the place for them."

I declared that the occupation was a thing of the past: never again would I find an object to make it worth my while.

"Don't be too sure!" he rejoined. "I'd do a lot better as a composer of galops; as things are, old fool that I am, I shall always be badly off. . . . Have a good journey," he continued, "and remember me. Whenever you are in trouble think of me and be comforted."

I was about to take my leave when he called me back. "Wait a minute! There's that musical Englishman to be dealt with. Let's see where the crosses have to go!" He picked up the Briton's manuscript and smiling quickly looked it over. Then he carefully gathered up the pages, folded a sheet of paper over them, seized a thick pen and drew over the folder a single colossal cross. "Here's the fellow's masterpiece!" he said, handing me the package. "Give it to him from me. . . . He's a donkey—not that I don't envy him his long ears! . . . Good-bye, my dear fellow—think fondly of me."

Upon my return to the inn I saw the Englishman's servant packing his master's trunk. He too had achieved his goal, and I had to admit that he too had shown a great deal of determination. I hurried up to my room and made my preparations for my return journey tomorrow. At the sight of that cross on the folder containing his composition I laughed aloud—all the same it was a souvenir of Beethoven, and as such I grudged it the evil genius of my pilgrimage. My decision was quickly taken. I unfolded the sheet, took out my packet of galops and inserted them in place of the Englishman's composition. This latter I then sent to the Englishman, together with a note, in which I reported that Beethoven had declared he had not known where to put a cross and that he envied him.

As I was departing from the inn there was my old fatal companion sitting in his coach. "My best wishes!" he called. "You have done me a great service. I am very pleased to have made Herr Beethoven's acquaintance. . . . Would you like to drive with me to Italy?"

"Why are you going there?" I asked.

"I want to make Signor Rossini's acquaintance; he is a very famous composer."

"Good luck to you!" I called back. "As for me, to have met Beethoven is enough for one lifetime."

We parted. I threw a last lingering look at Beethoven's house and turned northwards, my heart uplifted and ennobled.

Translated by Robert L. Jacobs and Geoffrey Skelton

The Artist and the Public (1840)

When I am on my own and my mind is full of musical noises which at last fuse into a melody revealing to me the essence of my being, so that my heart beats violently and my unseeing eyes shed heavenly tears of rapture, then I often tell myself what an utter fool I am not to be content to stay alone with this marvelous experience, what an utter fool to go rushing out with it to that horrible amorphous mass, the public. As though the right to exercise my talent depended upon its completely meaningless approval! As though that solitary glorious exercise were not worth a hundred times more than its loudest acclaim! . . . Why do artists, in whom the divine fire burns, quit their private sanctuaries and run breathless through the city's filthy streets eagerly looking for bored, dull-witted people upon whom to force the offering of an ineffable joy? The exertions, the excitements, the disappointments they endure before they even reach the stage of being able to make the offering! The tricks and stratagems they spend a good part of their lives devising in order to bring to the public something it can never understand! Do they do it because they are afraid that one fine day the historic development of music might come to a standstill? Perhaps precisely today, when all the talk is of stereotyped schools and styles, they feel that to tear up the precious pages of their hearts' histories might snap the bonds which have hitherto magically united kindred spirits across the centuries?

Something strange and incomprehensible seems to be at work; those who feel themselves subject to it cannot but regard its power as fatal. One's first thought is that the case is simply that of the genius's urge to communicate: what rings loud within him must be made to ring out to the whole world! Indeed it is held that the genius is duty bound to give pleasure to mankind—though who imposed the duty God alone knows! Certainly the genius himself is not conscious of it—least of all when his genius is operating. True, he is not expected to be; but when his works are finished and ready, then surely he should feel bound to pay for the enormous advantage he has over his fellow men by giving them the benefit of his creations. But the fact of the matter is that of all people the genius is the least responsive to the call of duty; he can do nothing with it in his art, and neither, I believe, does it govern his dealings with the world. In whatever he does, however foolish, he remains true to his nature as genius, and indeed I believe that his compulsion to find a public is governed rather by some equivocal motive of which he is not fully conscious, yet which is serious enough to expose even the greatest artist to contempt. . . . In any case the compulsion is hard to understand. Bitter experience teaches the genius that it draws him into an inferior world, with which he can only come to terms by adopting an inferior guise. Would not everybody run away if the genius were to expose himself as he really is in his god-like nakedness? Perhaps it is his instinct to do just this; for were he not fortified by a conviction of his utter chastity, how could he, in the act of creation, be consumed by an almost lascivious delight in himself? Yet his first contact with the world obliges him to disguise himself. For there the rule runs: the public must be amused: therefore whatever he has to offer he must bring in the guise of an amusement. It could, I suppose, be said that the genius who forces himself to obey this rule is prompted by a sense of duty, since duty in the nature of the case involves self-denial. But what sense of duty requires that a man should sacrifice his honor or a woman her modesty? On the contrary, duty demands that men and women should be prepared to sacrifice every personal advantage for their sake. But more precious than honor to a man or modesty to a woman is genius to its possessor. For it is his very self. If you injure that self in the slightest particle of its being—a being containing honor and modesty to their highest possible degree—then nothing is left of the genius, absolutely nothing.

It cannot be a sense of duty, then, which drives the genius to accept the terrible self-denial which presenting himself to the public involves. Some secret demonic force must be at work. This privileged being, blessed with unique powers, goes begging. Cap in hand, he seeks the favors of bored, satiated pleasure-lovers, empty-headed snobs, ignorant know-it-alls, malicious envious corrupt reviewers, and God knows what else that goes to form the public opinion of the day. And the humiliations the poor man has to bear! The martyred saint can smile: his soul is beyond the reach of torture; the wounded warrior dragging his body through the stormy night can smile: his honor and his courage are not smirched; the woman suffering shame and disgrace for the sake of love can smile: her love and her honor are transfigured and shine the more brightly. But the genius who exposes himself to contempt because he has to pretend that he wants to *please?* The world can count itself fortunate that *his* sufferings are comparatively unknown!

No, these sufferings are not undergone out of a sense of duty;

whoever thinks so is drawing his idea of duty from a different source: the need to earn one's daily bread, to maintain one's family. These are important motives—but they do not affect the genius. They impel the laborer, the craftsman. They may impel the genius to do the work of a craftsman; but it is not they which drive him to create and then to seek a market for his creations. But precisely this is the subject under discussion, namely, how explain the demonic compulsion which drives the genius to hawk his most precious possession?

Certainly the mysterious interweaving of a multitude of factors is involved: the whole mind of your highly gifted artist—the whole mind, hovering between heaven and hell—would have to be comprehended before the mystery could be solved. No doubt the paramount factor, the one which alone sustains him in his darkest hours, is a god-like impulse to communicate his own inner bliss to the hearts of all men. This impulse is nourished by the genius's belief in himself, which is stronger than any other man's—and which is responsible for the pride that proves to be his undoing when he is dealing with the miserable realities of life. Feeling, as he does, free in himself, he desires to be free in life, to have nothing to do with its necessities, to be borne along lighthearted, without a care in the world. Were his genius recognized he would achieve this, and so he works for recognition. Thereby he creates the impression of being ambitious, but this is not so: what he is striving for is not honor for its own sake, but for the freedom which is the fruit of honor. Unfortunately all the time he is mixing with people who are merely ambitious or who are content to enjoy freedom without honor. How to distinguish himself from them? In the rough-and-tumble he is constantly being mistaken for someone that he is not. How uncommonly clever he needs to be, how carefully he needs to watch every step in order to keep on the right path and not create a false impression. But clever in that sense is precisely what the genius is not: faced with all the meannesses of everyday life the only thing he can do with his genius is to let it drive him into a perpetual state of self-contradiction: tricked and fooled at every turn, he finds himself abusing his enormous gifts and letting them run to waste. . . . And yet all he really desires is freedom to rejoice the world with his works. The desire seems to him so natural that he cannot understand why it should not be granted: surely the issue is simply that his genius should be given the opportunity to manifest itself? He keeps on feeling that surely he must succeed, if not tomorrow, then the day after. Just as though there were no such thing as death. And Bach, Mozart, Beethoven, Weber? . . . Yet surely it must happen some time? . . . What a misery it all is!

And in the meantime to make oneself appear ridiculous!

When he looks at himself as we are now looking at him, in the end he too cannot help laughing. And this laughter is perhaps his greatest danger, since it is just this which gives him the strength to keep on going back into the mad dance. His laughter, though, is very different from the mockery of those who laugh at him. Its basis is pride. He sees himself as he really is, and in the infamous *quid pro quo* in which he is engaged, this self-recognition is the source of an overflowing gaiety, of which he alone is capable. So he is saved by his levity—only to be led thereby into still worse disasters. It is then that he allows himself to sup with the devil— giving himself the right because he knows, however many lies he may tell, that his truthfulness will never be sullied; for his sufferings, every nail of them, have made him feel that truthfulness is his very soul. There is a curious consolation, too, in the knowledge that nobody believes his lies, that his deceptions are always seen through. Who would take him for a funny fellow? . . . Why then does he seek to give the impression of being one? Because the world leaves him no other way of attaining freedom—freedom, from the point of view of the world, meaning one thing only, namely, money. To have his genius recognized he must make money: that is the object of the whole mad exercise. And so he thinks: "God, if I were only somebody like Meyerbeer!" Only the other day Berlioz was imagining what he would do if he had five hundred francs to spend. He would not squander it on some ballade not worth five sous, as some unfortunates do; instead, he would engage the finest orchestra in the world and have it perform the *Eroica* Symphony for him amid the ruins of Troy. . . . One sees to what heights the fantasy of impecunious genius can rise! . . . Not that such things are impossible. Miracles can happen—one happened to Berlioz himself when that wonderful miser, Paganini, honored him with a substantial present. But that is only the beginning. Such a sign appears to everyone at some time; call it a bribe from hell, for it means that from now on you are an object of envy. "Why, now you have *more* than you deserve!" The world will cease to offer you even its sympathy!

Lucky the genius upon whom good fortune has never smiled! . . . In any case, genius is such a huge thing, what can good fortune add to it?

So he says to himself, smiling—and then he laughs, his strength renewed, as he hears within a stirring and surging of new sounds, brighter and more glorious than ever. A work such as even he had never foreseen is growing and thriving in the quietness of his solitude. This is it! This will set the world on fire! Off the maniac rushes down the familiar path as though it were all new and fresh and lovely. He splashes into the mud. He collides with a splendidly attired lackey—whom he mistakes for a general and greets respectfully. He bumps into a sack of gold, shouldered by a no less important looking bank official, and gets a bloody nose. These are all good signs! So he goes rushing and stumbling—until at last he finds himself standing once again in the temple of his shame! And everything is back again where it was before, for as the poet has said: "Every fault committed upon this earth avenges itself."

Yet perhaps all this is a blessing in disguise, perhaps some good genius, probably his own, sees to it that his wishes are never fulfilled. For were he to be made welcome in that curious temple it could only be as the result of a colossal misunderstanding—and what torments of hell could be compared to the agony of the gradual day-by-day clarification of that misunderstanding? It has been taken for granted that you would be reasonable, that you would be prepared to make compromises. You urgently want a *succès*, do you not? Well, here it is guaranteed. You have only to make this and that slight adjustment: there is the singer, there the dancer, there the great virtuoso—go and arrange things with them. There they are standing by that wonderfully curtained doorway through which you have to pass in order to reach the great public. Don't you know that everyone who has trodden that blessed path has had to bring his little sacrifice? How the devil do you suppose that the great Opéra would have survived if it had spent its time bothering about trifles?

Can you tell a lie? . . .

No, I cannot! . . .

Then you will be ruined and treated with contempt, as the atheists are in England. No respectable person will have anything more to do with you! . . .

Nothing for it then but to keep on hoping that your guardian angel will spare you *that* fate—and to keep on being merry and lighthearted—and to keep on patiently toiling. So all may come right in the end.

Best of all—keep on dreaming!

Translated by Robert L. Jacobs and Geoffrey Skelton

To Karl Gaillard (1844)

Dresden, January 30, 1844

Dear Sir,

. . . Those, therefore, who know me only by my *Flying Dutchman* usually hold it against me that I write the texts of my operas, inferring from the difficulties I have encountered in this plot that I am not equal to the subject. Those who know my *Rienzi* judge differently, and claim on the contrary I could not have found a more felicitous book than this which I made myself. I really do not pride myself on my abilities as a poet, and I confess that it is only out of necessity, and because no good books have been offered to me, that I have set out to invent them myself. But I couldn't possibly compose a text alien to me for the following reason: My way is not to select any plot I like, put it into verse, and then ponder about how to add suitable music: if I should proceed in this way I would subject myself to the inconvenience of having to inspire myself twice, which is impossible. The way I produce is different: the only subject which can appeal to me is one which presents practical as well as musical possibilities. Before starting to write a verse, or even to outline a scene, I must first feel intoxicated by the musical aroma of my subject, all the tones, all the characteristic motifs are in my head, so that when the verses are finished and the scenes ordered, the opera proper is also finished for me and the musical treatment in detail is rather a calm and considered afterwork which the moment of real creation has preceded. Furthermore, only subjects should be chosen which are suited only for musical treatment: I would never choose a plot which could just as well be used by a good playwright for a spoken drama. As a musician I am free to choose subjects, to invent situations and contrasts, which are quite outside of the province of the poet-dramatist. Here we arrive at the point where opera and drama part completely and where each can quietly pursue its own course. While nowadays it is the task of the dramatist to purify and to spiritualize the material interests of our time, it falls to the poet and composer of opera to conjure up the holy spirit of poetry, which has come down to us from the legends and sagas of past ages. For music offers the means for synthesis which the poet alone, especially in the drama, cannot command. This is the way to raise the opera to a higher level from a debasement that has come about because we have expected composers to treat commonplaces, intrigues, etc., subjects which spoken drama and modern comedy are far more successful in presenting.

I have chosen for my next opera the beautiful and characteristic saga of the knight Tannhäuser, who dwelt in the Venusberg and then went to Rome on a pilgrimage to seek absolution! I linked that saga with the singers' contest at the Wartburg where Tannhäuser takes the place of Heinrich von Ofterdingen—by this combination I achieve a richer dramatic life. It will be obvious that only a musician could treat such a subject. . . .

Yours very truly,
Richard Wagner

Translated by Hans Abraham et al.

From "Opera and Drama" (1851)

Let us now clearly bring into focus the form of the drama with which we are here concerned, in order that we may hold it up to recognition, with all its necessary and constantly renewed changes, as being by its very nature the only complete and unified one. But we also have to consider what makes this unity possible.

The unified artistic form can only be conceived as a manifestation of a unified content. A unified content can only be recognized by its being given an artistic expression that directly communicates with our feelings. A content which makes a two-fold expression necessary—an expression, that is, which forces the author to turn alternately to reason and feeling—must likewise be divided and ambiguous.

Every artistic intention originally craves a unified form; for only to the degree that it approaches this form can any manifestation become an artistic one. Division inevitably commences at the point where the intention can no longer be fully conveyed by the means of expression at one's disposal. As it is the instinctive desire of every artistic intention to speak to the feelings, a divisive expression will be one that is incapable of doing so. But an expression must speak to our feelings if it is to convey its full meaning.

The poet proper finds this total involvement of the feelings impossible in his medium of expression; and what he cannot convey to the feelings he is obliged to communicate to reason, so as to be fully able to clarify his aims. He is thus forced to let the mind think what he is unable to make the heart feel; and when the decisive moment is reached, he can only realize his intentions by means of sententious utterances, or as intention in its naked form. Thus he shifts, of sheer necessity, the content of that intention to an unartistic level.

While the work of the poet thus appears as an unrealized poetic intention, the work of the composer of absolute music must be regarded as one altogether lacking in poetic intent; for although feelings may well be aroused by purely musical means, they cannot by such means be fixed as to their actual nature.

The limited range of expression at the poet's disposal forces him to divide his contents into those related to feeling and those related to reason, which causes feeling to be restless and dissatisfied and reason to reflect vainly on the restlessness of feeling. The musician faces the same dilemma as the poet, since he compels reason to assign a meaning to the expression which strongly arouses the feelings, without leading from this extreme commotion to a resting point. The poet furnishes this content in the form of sententious statements, while the musician, in order to create the semblance of some intention not actually present, prefaces his composition by a title. Both are thus compelled to turn from feeling to reason: the poet in order to define an incompletely determined emotion, the musician in order to apologize for having aroused a feeling to no purpose.

Should we, accordingly, wish to name the kind of expression

whose unity renders a unity of content possible, we must define it as that which is able to convey the most comprehensive intention of the poetic mind most suitably to the feelings. Now an expression of this kind is one in which the poetic intention inheres in each situation but, at the same time, is concealed in each from the feeling by being realized.

This complete realization of the poetic intention would not be possible even in the case of vocal music were it not for the presence of a second musical medium that coexists with it. Thus whenever vocal music, as the most direct refuge of the poetic intention, is forced to lower its own expression so deeply—for the sake of the unbreakable tie between this intention and ordinary life—as barely to cover it with a musical veil that is nearly transparent, the equilibrium of the unified emotional expression can be successfully sustained.

We have seen that the orchestra is the agent which constantly completes the unity of expression and which, whenever the vocal expression of the dramatic characters lowers itself in order to define the dramatic situation more clearly—and that to the extent of demonstrating its relation to the expression of ordinary life in a rational manner—balances the abated expression of the dramatic character. It does so by means of its ability to evoke past and future in such a way that the feelings that have been aroused continue on their level of elevation and are not forced also to descend to the level of purely rational activity. The same height of feeling, from which no descent, but only ascent, is possible, is determined by the same height of expression and, through it, by the sameness, i.e., the unity of content.

We must also bear in mind that the orchestral passages in which this levelling of the elements of expression occurs are never to be determined by the arbitrary will of the musician as a sort of decorative embellishment, but solely by the poetic intention. If these passages express anything that is either inconsistent with, or superfluous to, the dramatic situation, the unity of expression is disturbed by a deviation from content. The purely musical embellishment of abated or foreshadowed situations (such as those which have found favor in opera in the form of the so-called *ritornello*, in interludes, and even in orchestral accompaniments) radically destroys all unity of expression and affects our sense of hearing no longer as a means of expression but rather as expression itself.

These situations, too, must be strictly guided by the poetic intention, and that in such a way as to focus our feelings, by way of anticipation or remembrance, always and exclusively upon the characters and their dramatic context. These anticipatory or reminiscent orchestral passages should be felt as the completion of a message which the character now before our eyes is either unable or unwilling to transmit.

Through the orchestra these melodic passages, which are in themselves suited to maintain the emotion on the same level of intensity, become, in a way, so many signposts for the feelings throughout the drama's complex structure. Through them we gain access to the innermost secrets of the poetic intention and participate in its realization. Between them (as the vehicles of anticipation and retrospection) there stands verse melody, the active and passive individuality, which is conditioned by the emotional context consisting of the moments in which the character's own feelings or those of others, whether previously felt or still to be experienced, are manifested. These passages, which meaningfully complete the emotional expression, are relegated to the background as soon as the character proceeds to the full expression of the verse melody. Then it is that the orchestra merely continues to support the verse melody by exercising its explanatory power, so as to be able, whenever the glowing tints of the verse melody's expression fade away into melodious prose phrases, to complement the general expression of feeling once more by anticipatory reminiscences, as well as to effect, as it were, the necessary transitions of feeling, by means of our own interest that has been kept alive throughout.

These melodic passages—in which presentiment is remembered while remembrance turns into presentiment—have sprung naturally from the principal dramatic motives which constitute the condensed and intensified leitmotifs of an action that is equally condensed and intensified. The poet uses these motifs as pillars of his dramatic structure, using them not in helter-skelter profusion but so sparingly as to enable him to arrange them plastically and conspicuously.

In these leitmotifs, which are no sententious utterances but plastically developed emotional situations, the poetic intention becomes most clearly intelligible, since it is realized in the receptivity of feeling. The musician who realizes the poet's intentions has to arrange these motifs (condensed into melodic passages) in such perfect agreement with these intentions that the most unified musical form results as a natural consequence of the perfectly natural mutual repetition—a form hitherto arbitrarily invented by the composer, but which can only be properly unified, i.e., made intelligible, when corresponding with the design of the poet.

In opera, up to now, the composer did not even try to achieve unity of form for his entire work, each single number having its independently filled-out form and being related to the other closed numbers of the opera only in point of external structure, but possessing no actual affinity based on subject matter. Incoherence was thus peculiar to operatic music. Only the single number, within its self-appointed limits, possessed any formal coherence, which, having been brought about by the requirements of absolute music, was upheld by custom and foisted upon the poet as a burden. What was coherent in this form was a theme composed beforehand and alternating with a second theme, the repetitions being introduced arbitrarily and for purely musical reasons.

Change, repetition, shortening or lengthening of the theme constituted the only motion of the instrumental compositions on a larger scale (the symphonic movement) conditioned by them and striving to acquire unity of form by means of the fusion and repetition of themes justified, as far as possible, before the feeling. The justification of this return, however, always rests on the mere assumption of an underlying content, and only the poetic intention is able to render the justification possible, because it urgently demands this justification as a necessary condition of intelligibility.

In their return, which is so naturally guided by relationships similar to those observed in the use of rhyme, the principal motifs of the dramatic action, having now attained to the condition of a distinct melodic phrase that fully realizes the underlying intentions, are gathered into a unified artistic form extending, as a binding medium, not merely over individual parts but over the drama as a whole. In this way not only these melodic passages, which elucidate each other and thus create a unity, but also the emotional and phenomenal motifs to which they refer are transmitted to the feeling. In this context, the perfectly unified form has been accomplished, and, through it, a unified content is manifested or, better still, rendered possible.

In summarizing once again everything that is relevant to the problem in question, we designate as the most perfect unified form of art that in which the widest range of human experiences—as content—is conveyed to the feelings in so completely intelligible a manner that the manifestation of this content at every point of the action first arouses and then satisfies the emotions. The content must, accordingly, be closely linked to the expression, while the expression must continuously evoke the content in its full scope. For that which is not present to the senses is grasped by thought alone, while feeling comprehends only that which is brought before it.

In this unity, which results from an expression that renders everything present and embraces the content according to the structural correlation of its parts, the problem of the unity of time and place is also solved in the most conclusive manner.

Space and time, as abstractions of the real and corporeal qualities of action, only attracted the attention of our playwrights because a unified expression capable of completely realizing the desired poetic content was not within their reach. Space and time are imaginary qualities ascribed to real, corporeal phenomena which, being isolated, immediately lose their impact. The body of these abstractions is the real and sensuous element of action manifested in a definite spatial environment and in a progression of movement dependent thereupon.

To base the unity of the drama on unity of time and space is to base it on nothing: for space and time in themselves are nothing. They turn into something only when negated by something real, a human action and the context out of which it grows. This human action must constitute that which is unified, i.e. coherent, in itself. Its temporal extension depends on the possibility of rendering its context intelligible, its spatial extension on the possibility of an appropriate setting. For its sole desire is to communicate with the feeling. The greatest condensation of space and time may result in the unfolding of an action that is utterly disunited and incoherent, as may easily be gauged from contemporary plays in which the unities are observed.

Unity of action, on the other hand, depends on the intelligibility of the context itself, which can be obtained by one means only: by neither space nor time, but by expression. If, in the foregoing, we have shown this expression to be a unified one, i.e., one whose parts are interconnected and constantly evoke the total context, we have also re-entered into the possession of that which had been separated by time and space but which is now again reunited and ever-present where intelligibility requires it. Its necessary presence lies not in time and space but in the impression which time and space make upon us. The conditions which resulted from the lack of this expression (connected, as they were, with time and space) have been annulled by the acquisition of this expression; and time and space have been annihilated by the reality of the drama.

Thus the real drama is no longer subject to any external influences but is something organically being and becoming which, prompted by its own internal conditions, develops and forms itself by the one required contact with the external world, namely the necessity of making its manifestation (a manifestation of its being and becoming) understood. This intelligible formation, however, benefits from the fact that from a deep-seated urge it gives rise to the expression of its content that renders everything possible.

Translated by Ulrich Weisstein

From His Diary (1865)

Vienna, October 24

Oh Cosima! All the things I now know about!—Florence, Rome, Naples, Sicily, Spain—all is a matter of indifference to me, they will be nothing to me without you, and only by virtue of your being included in it all!—Oh foolishness still to try to seek salvation outside harbor when to run to harbor was the final salvation!—How easy death is: for *me* almost all is dead already. Am *I* the ghost, or is the world? Again I've grabbed at broken glass: the merest glimpse of this Vienna, and then tell myself it was here I once wanted to build my harbor! I'll give something, my love, not to see Paris again either: I'll have to feel hideously ashamed to tell myself there that there too I once wanted to be at home—always with the glass-grabbing sensation!—Oh!—

My love, my love! Things really have gone nice and differently with us. There were a couple of stars that came together in constellation only every leap year: then they looked at each other in amazement, and did not know what next. Not a word they said—they set, shone here and there, floated in broken glass—ether—and so it had to be. Then came death: they wanted to die. The spasm let go, the crazy orbits reached out no more. As the sail, when the mad wind eases, trembles, falters, and flutters, so I hung upon your lips—ready for death! And we knew all. And now the orbits are changed.—Now the eternal leap year has been won. And now—you grow ever more beautiful to me!—Everything I have lived away so quickly: nothing has held, no illusion. With us everything was willing. You are coming ever more beautifully to life again, so that less and less can I understand how I wandered distant from you for so long. Oh Cosima! Certainly you cannot see, looking at me, how I love you, how I respect and honor myself because you love me! Now I expect you will look shrewdly at me and laugh?—

No, imagine me now here in Vienna. I've been out, once, quite briefly, and now I've sworn only to drive out on my errands. I am now so hideously ashamed at having once run around here looking as if I fancied I'd make something out of it for myself, if not even find something in it. Fine nonsense!—Besides, certainly now after three years, the people here have become much more brutish.—No—my propylaea—quiet, peace—my Parsifal and—and—and—high above, deep inside—who then? Probably you?—Ask!—Franz has just come and only just brought me your letter which you gave him—: yesterday, after our arrival, he was quite giddy with Vienna, and forgot it. My love, I thank you!—You do, don't you? Love me?—

Yesterday evening Standhartner was with me: we've put a lot in order. Today it's off with him to the dentist—it's that monster who will now decide my existence—that is to say, in Vienna.—This evening at Fröbel's.—Yesterday settled business. Received Porges III. Am being clever and awaiting chances.—

Oh heavens, now into my house—and never again any further

than to the Nymphenburg and the English Garden! And write pages
and pages, no "learned papers"—that goes without saying, for then
I get a telling off—always music, nothing but music!

My love! I've slept well. How about you? And Isolde?—

Now I shall telegraph to you so that you have something for the
witching hour. Dear Cosima! Cosima! Cosima!——And once
more—Cosima!—Shall I now be angry with your begetter—that
won't do? But that's what he's out for! The devil!—Adieu!—

Translated by George Bird

To Friedrich Nietzsche (1870)

Dear Friend!

It is a wonderful comfort to be able to exchange letters of this
kind! I have no one with whom I can discuss things so seriously
as with you—the *only one* excepted. God knows what I should do
without you two! When, after a period of deep dejection, I come
back to my work, I am often thrown into a mood of sheer good
humor, simply because I cannot comprehend it and am therefore
obliged to laugh about it. At such times, the reason for all this comes
to me like a flash, but to attempt to analyze this feeling and endeavor to express it in terms of "Socratic wisdom" would require
an unlimited amount of time and the elimination of all other claims
upon me. Division of labor is a good thing. You, for example, could
assume a large part, in fact half of my objectives, and (perhaps!)
thereby be fulfilling your *own* destiny. Only think what a poor
showing I have made as a philologist, and what a fortunate thing
it is that you are on about the same terms with music. Had you
decided to become a musician, you would have been, more or less,
that which I should have become had I persistently clung to philology. As matters now stand, philology exerts a great influence over
me, in fact, as an adjunct of prime importance, it even directs me
in my capacity as a musician. On the other hand, you remain a
philologist and allow your life to be directed by music. What I am
now saying is meant very seriously. In fact, it was you yourself
who gave me the idea of the unworthy circle in which a philologist
by profession is doomed to revolve at the present time, and you

have assuredly learned from me something of all the mathematical rubbish among which an absolute musician (even under the most favorable circumstances) is obliged to fritter away his time. Now you have an opportunity of proving the utility of philology, by helping me to bring about the grand "renaissance" in which Plato will embrace Homer, and Homer, imbued with Plato's spirit, will become more than ever before the truly supreme Homer.

These are just random thoughts which occur to me, but never so hopefully as since I have taken so strong a liking to you, and never so clearly—and (as you see) never so clamoring for expression—as since you read us your "Centaurs." Therefore, do not doubt the impression created upon me by your work. A very serious and profound wish has been awakened in me, the nature of which will also be clear to you, for should you not cherish the same wish, you will never be able to carry it into fulfillment.

But we must talk this all over. Therefore—I think—in short, you must come to Tribschen next Saturday. Your sleeping room, the Gallerie, is ready, and [as Goethe's Faust says to Mephistopheles:] "you can exit by the chimney whenever you like"—in other words: good-bye!

With all my heart,
Yours,
R.W.

Translated by Caroline V. Kerr

Anton Bruckner

To Baron Hans von Wolzogen (1884)

Esteemed Baron:

It was around the beginning of September in 1873 (Crown Prince Friedrich was then in Bayreuth) when I asked the Master's permission to show him my Second in C Minor and my Third in D Minor. The recently deceased man refused because of lack of time (building the theater) and said he was unable to look at any scores and had even been forced to put aside the *Nibelungs*.

When I replied: "Master, I have no right to steal even fifteen minutes of your time," but thought that, with his keen penetration, a mere glance at the themes would suffice to know how matters stood, the Master slapped me on the back, told me to come along, led me into the salon, and looked at the Second Symphony. "Very fine," he said, although he thought it was too tame (they had scared me so much in Vienna at first), and then he took up the Third (in D Minor) saying: "Look, look, what's this?" and he went through the entire seventh section (he was especially struck by the trumpet); then he said: "Leave this work here with me and I shall examine it more carefully after dinner" (it was twelve o'clock). I thought to myself: do I dare utter the request that Wagner provokes in me? Very timidly, my heart throbbing, I said to the Master whom I loved so ardently: "Master! there is something in my heart that I do not trust myself to say."

"Out with it," said the Master, "you know how much I like you." I expressed my request but only on condition that it would be agreeable to the Master, for I did not wish to desecrate his illustrious name. The Master said: "You are invited to Wahnfried at five o'clock in the evening; you will find me there, and after I have examined your D Minor Symphony more closely, *we shall talk about this matter.*"

At five o'clock I was at the theater they were building at Wahnfried. The Master of Masters hurried over to me, held out his arms, and warmly embraced me. "Dear friend," he said, "the dedication is all settled; this work of yours will give me *uncommonly great* pleasure." Then I had the good fortune to sit with the Master for two and a half hours, during which he talked about musical relationships in Vienna, brought me beer, and led me into the garden and showed me his *grave!!!* Afterwards he, or rather I, the lucky one, was permitted to accompany him into one of the houses. The next day he sent me his wishes for a good journey, adding "the way the trumpet begins the theme!"

In Vienna and Bayreuth he often asked me whether the symphony had been performed yet, saying: "Play it, play it." In 1882 the Master, who was then already suffering, took my hand and said: "Rely on me. I myself will play your symphony and all your works." I said: "Oh, Master!" to which he replied: "Have you been to *Parsifal*? How did you like it?" While he held my hand, I bent down on my knee, kissing and pressing his noble hand to my mouth, and said: "O Master, I worship you!" The Master replied: "Calm yourself, Bruckner; good night!" Those were his last words to me.

The next day the Master, who was sitting behind me at *Parsifal,* rebuked me once because I was applauding too violently.

Esteemed Baron, I beg you to guard this with the greatest care. It is my most precious legacy—*until up there!!!*

Esteemed Baron, your most grateful,
A. Bruckner

My stomach!!!

Translator anon.

Johannes Brahms

To Clara Schumann (1855)

Sunday, August 12

My beloved Friend,

I have been diligently playing and reading the whole day and thinking of you the whole time, and now I will quietly tell you all about it. I am always thinking of you. For a long while I have not thought of anyone so tenderly and incessantly as I have of you, and today I began to hope quite early for a letter from you in the evening, which would give me all news of the dear ones in Hamburg.

My swollen mouth has got worse. This morning I kept a fig in my mouth and bound it round with wool. But as it only got more inflamed towards midday, I tore it all off in anger. It is too much of a bore to have to go about all muffled up.

Fräulein von Meysenbug has written me a letter smothered in sugar. I am now her highly respected and genial master. What funny ideas people get into their heads when a young man writes something out of the way. Many a young man probably wishes he had the wings of an eagle, and may even imagine that he has them. Then he falls among books and music and soon sticks fast in the mire and forgets how to fly. Fortunately I do not often fear that such a fate will overtake me. But I frequently feel sad that I no longer seem to know how to compose or how to create. I wish this time would soon be over and I could become freer and more full of courage. I could fall sick with longing for a new fresh strain. Just fancy, I sometimes feel convinced that I shall fall quite ill and then become twice as healthy as before. At other times I imagine that I have been sick and that I am now recovering. How unhappy I should be perhaps if I had not got you. You teach me every day afresh that one does not derive vitality (= vital creative power) from books, but only out of one's own soul. One must not absorb, one must express. You must always remain at my side as my guardian angel, and then I shall certainly become what I should and can become. I am not reading all this rigmarole through again. Forgive me, and allow yourself to be heartily embraced by your

Johannes

The children are all well. Bertha is very melancholy and my new pupil has up to the present proved a dolt.

Translator anon.

To Marie Lipsius

Vienna, May 27, 1885

Dear Miss:

Indeed, I do have the courage to request that you leave the letters in question unprinted. I know and confess that I never write other than reluctantly, hastily, and casually; but I am ashamed when an example like yours comes before my eyes.

It takes a kind of courage to write to an unfamiliar, educated, and kind man as casually as I did in this particular case.

To agree, however, that such letters be printed, to explicitly consent to that—that would take something other than courage!

If you will allow me to state here expressly that no one could do me a greater disservice than to print my letters—then I will gladly make an exception with this one.

You can also include it in your book all the more readily, since it will clarify to your readers that I, not you, am to blame for any deficiency in it; and since I have resisted drawing any conclusion concerning the remaining content and value of your book from your intention to include my letters.

There are, as I know not only from "Schiller and Goethe" but also from most pleasant personal experience, enough people who write letters well and with pleasure.

But all the same there are also those of my nature, and one should read and interpret their letters, if the writers are otherwise deserving of this, cautiously and indulgently.

For example, I keep with pleasure a letter from Beethoven as a sacred relic; however, I am shocked when I consider all the things such a letter is supposed to mean and explain!

I feel the same way about works left to us by earlier composers.

How ardently have I at all times pursued such traces, have studied and frequently copied them. How dear to me, for example, were—in the case of Haydn and Franz Schubert—those untold, bounteous demonstrations of diligence and genius.

I always wished that one might copy such valuable and instructive treasures for larger libraries, so that they would be accessible to anyone seriously interested in them.—But I will not pursue here how different my feelings are when I see such cherished treasures printed—or myself see to it that this is at least done as correctly as possible.

In the one case, as in the other, things are misunderstood, misinterpreted to a totally unbelievable degree; and whether such publication is necessary and good, or superfluous and even harmful—I don't know!

At the risk that you might consider the beginning of this letter to be hypocritical,

I sign, respectfully,

J. Brahms

Translated by Michael Gilbert

To Clara Schumann (1888)

Thun, July 24

I was delighted by the very sight of your letter. "So much written by her own hand," thought I, "must mean that her rheumatism is better, and we ought to be pleased." Nevertheless I delayed answering your dear letter, for I had something on my heart and in my thoughts which I found it hard to tell you. But after all it cannot be helped. So summon up all your goodness of heart and your friendly feelings for me and listen, and then be kind and say "Yes." I feel the deepest concern for everything connected with you, as well as for all the anxieties and cares that cannot be excluded from a life so full as yours has been—but of which you have certainly had too great a share.

I do not take an exaggerated view of those smaller cares which are financial, but it annoys me that you should have such cares when all the time I am rolling in money that is no use to me and out of which I get no particular pleasure. But I cannot and do not wish to live any differently. It would be quite useless to give my relations more than I already give them, and when my heart bids me to do so I can help others to any extent and do them good without feeling it. After my death, however, there will be no obligations to fulfill and no particular wishes. In short, the position is a simple one. All these days I have been turning over in my mind how in the world I could set about sending you a certain sum, whether I should do so as a rich artistic friend by means of an anonymous letter, or whether I should make a belated contribution to the Schumann Fund. But I should be unable to do either without drawing somebody so far into my confidence that he would be bound to guess the truth. If, however, you take me as I should like you to be—then the second stage of the transaction would be quite simple and you would allow me without further ado to disburden myself of some of my superfluous wealth in order this year to contribute towards your expenses for the grandchildren the sum of about 10,000 marks.

Simrock has again taken a whole heap of choral pieces, quartets, and songs. But I shall not even notice the handsome fee that all this means. It simply slips silently and uselessly into the Reichsbank. Now just think how much pleasure these works and the fee would give me if you were just to send me a good clear "Yes"! But as there are two sides to every question, I may tell you that the event of an unfavorable reply I have made up my mind to instruct Simrock to pay the sum into the Schumann Fund. I shall deal with the rest of your letter in a few days. For the present I will only say that with regard to the Wieck affair I am in favor of the most complete silence. I should think the book would be so bad that it will hardly see the light of day. I cannot imagine what would have to be done to me to provoke me to make a public protest.

Apparently dear Frau Röntgen is just dead. Julius was with me a little while ago when a telegram came summoning him to Leipzig. As I say I shall write more later on. All I ask for today is that you will send me a friendly card and on it the one happy word for your then most happy

Johannes

Translator anon.

Gustav Mahler

To the Members of the Budapest Opera House (1888)

Budapest, [October 10,] 1888

Ladies and Gentlemen,

Today I have the honor of assuming the leading position in an establishment that is in every respect fitted to be a home for and an ornament to this country's art.—First of all I should like to thank our revered chief, the Secretary of State, Herr von Beniczky, for the confidence he has shown in me by conferring upon me an office at once so responsible and so eminent, and I hereby pledge to devote myself to my duties wholeheartedly and single-mindedly. I also wish to address a few words to you, ladies and gentlemen.

It is with pride and pleasure that I see gathered around me a throng of artists whom any general might be proud to lead to victory. It must fill each one of us with pride to belong to an establishment promoted so benevolently and munificently by that noble patron of the arts, His Majesty the King, an establishment towards which the highest representatives of the kingdom have always been open-handed, one that forms—and which should form—the focal point of Hungary's artistic endeavors and at the same time is the pride of the nation.—Yet what stringent demands we must make on ourselves in our awareness of our duty to maintain and enhance the significance of such an establishment.—

Ladies and gentlemen, let ᵥs vow to dedicate ourselves wholeheartedly and with utter devotion to the proud task that falls to us! *To perform our tasks with the utmost rigor*, with complete absorption in and devotion to the work as a whole—let that be the motto inscribed on our banner.

Do not expect either promises or acts from me in the immediate future. Nor shall I present you with a program today.

Let us first get to know one another and collect ourselves for the difficult work that lies ahead of us.

If I promise one thing today, it is that I shall set an example in being eager to work and always sincere in intention.

Let us set to work—each one to his task! Then our labor will be crowned with success.

I conclude now in the joyful hope that as true artists you all agree with what I have said and will support me in the difficult task ahead of us.

Gustav Mahler

Translated by Eithne Wilkins and Ernst Kaiser

To Arthur Seidl (1897)

Hamburg, February 17, 1897

My dear Dr. Seidl,

I was overjoyed and greatly stimulated by your kind and deeply thoughtful letter. It is extraordinary how you have been able to explain me to myself in a number of ways. You have defined my aims, as distinct from those of Strauss, quite accurately. You are right in saying that my "music *generates* a program as a final imaginative elucidation, whereas with Strauss the program is a set task."—I believe that there you have touched on the great conundrums of our age, at the same time enunciating the *either-or* of things.—Whenever I plan a large musical structure, I always come to a point where I have to resort to "the word" as a vehicle for my musical idea.—It must have been pretty much the same for Beethoven in his Ninth, except that the right materials were not yet available in his day.—For Schiller's poem is, in the last resort, inadequate; it cannot express the wholly new, unique idea he had in mind. Incidentally, I recall R. Wagner's somewhere saying the same thing quite baldly. In the last movement of my Second I simply had to go through the whole of world literature, including the

Bible, in search of the right word, the "Open Sesame"—and in the end had no choice but to find my own words for my thoughts and feelings.

The way in which I was inspired to do this is deeply significant and characteristic of the nature of artistic creation.—

I had long contemplated bringing in the choir in the last movement, and only the fear that it would be taken as a formal imitation of Beethoven made me hesitate again and again. Then Bülow died, and I went to the memorial service.—The mood in which I sat and pondered on the departed was utterly in the spirit of what I was working on at the time.—Then the choir, up in the organ-loft, intoned Klopstock's *Resurrection* chorale.—It flashed on me like lightning, and everywhere became plain and clear in my mind! It was the flash that all creative artists wait for—"conceiving by the Holy Ghost"!

What I then *experienced* had now to be expressed in sound. And yet—if I had not already borne the work within me—how could I have had that experience? There were thousands of others sitting there in the church at the time!—It is always the same with me: *only when I experience something* do I compose, and only when composing do I experience!—I know you will understand this without my enlarging on it. After all, a musician's nature can hardly be expressed in words. It would be easier to say what is *different* about him than about others.—But what this difference is he himself would perhaps be least able to say. So it is the same too with his *aims*! He moves towards them like a sleepwalker—he does not know what road he is taking (perhaps past yawning abysses), but he heads towards the distant light, whether it be the ever-radiant star or a seductive will-o'-the-wisp! I was very pleased by what you said about "productive" criticism. I have always sensed that in you—in everything I have heard or read about you.

Happy the artist who has such a "critic" as an ally!—I cannot but regard our having met as a rare stroke of luck. I hope you do not take this as flattery or *quid pro quo!* The fact that you cannot come to Berlin is a drop of salt in my cup of joy. I say "cup of joy" because I am still unaccustomed to "being performed." You cannot imagine how often I have been seized with agony of mind when putting score upon score into my drawer, no one taking the slightest notice of the work I was producing (despite frantic efforts on my part).—I shall never cease to be thankful to *Strauss* for getting things going, and in what a truly high-minded way! Let no one suggest that I might regard myself as a "rival" (as unfortunately happens so often nowadays).—I must repeat that I cannot regard two such people as "rivals." Apart from the fact that my works would doubtless have earned me a reputation as a freak if Strauss's successes had not paved the way for me, I number it among my greatest joys that I found among my contemporaries such a comrade-in-arms, such a comrade in creation. Schopenhauer somewhere uses the image of two miners digging a shaft from opposite ends and then meeting underground. This seems fittingly to characterize my relationship to Strauss.—How lonely I should feel and how hopeless my efforts would seem if I could not divine future victory from these "signs and wonders." When you refer to us, in a way so flattering to me, as the "opposite poles" of the new magnetic field, you express a view I have for a long time held in secret, and only when you come to know the scores I have written since my Second will you realize, I think, how profoundly intuitive your way of putting it is.—Forgive the sloppiness of this letter. I am writing in a great hurry in the midst of preparations for a tour of several weeks, which will take me to Moscow, Petersburg, Munich, Budapest, etc. The fear of not being able to reply to your kind letter for weeks compels me to dash off these hasty lines. Finally, my warmest gratitude for the touching care with which you have collected notices of my appearance in Dresden. As yet, nothing definite can be said about *Vienna* and the directorial crisis there. *Between ourselves*—this crisis cannot be resolved until the *autumn*, and the choice now seems to lie between *Mottl* and my humble self.

Candidly, I do not know whether I really want to be offered the post, which might perhaps *divert* me from my essential aims. But I am really fatalistic about that, for the present not giving the matter a thought, simply waiting to see what happens.

With kindest regards, and once again many thanks—not for what you have done for me, but for what *you are* to me: it is an enrichment of my whole life and work.

In sincere friendship,
Gustav Mahler

Translated by Eithne Wilkins and Ernst Kaiser

To Alma Mahler (1907)

Hotel Bristol, Berlin, January 1907

My dear, good Almschili,

I went to the Strausses' yesterday afternoon. *She* greeted me with: "Sh!—sh! Richard's asleep," and pulled me into her (very untidy) boudoir, where her old mother was sitting over coffee, and let loose a flood of nonsense about all the financial and sexual events of the last two years, rapidly interjecting questions about "a thousand and one" things without waiting for the answers. She would not hear of my going, told me Richard had had an exhausting rehearsal yesterday morning in Leipzig, had then returned to Berlin to conduct *Götterdämmerung* at night, and today, being reduced to pulp, had lain down to sleep in the afternoon, while she kept strictest watch. I was quite touched. Suddenly she leaped up: "But now to wake the brute." Before I could stop her, she dragged me by both hands into his room, and roused him with a stentorian shout: "Get up. Gustav's here." I was "Gustav" for an hour, and after that Director. Strauss got up with a patient smile, and the torrent of nonsense was resumed as a trio. Then we had tea and they took me back to the hotel in their automobile after it had been arranged that I should lunch with them on Sunday. There I found two front-row stalls for *Salome;* so I took Berliner with me.—The performance (orchestra and singers excellent—scenically utter tripe) and Stoll again made an extraordinary impression on me. It is emphatically a work of genius, very powerful, and decidedly one of the most important works of our day. A Vulcan lives and labors under a heap of slag, a subterranean fire—not merely a firework! It is exactly the same with Strauss's whole personality. That is why it is so difficult in his case to sift the chaff from the grain. But I have an immense respect for the whole phenomenon he presents, and it has been confirmed afresh. This is an immense pleasure to me, for it puts me entirely at one with him. Blech conducted excellently yesterday. Strauss conducts on Saturday and I am going again! Destinn was magnificent! John the Baptist (Berger) quite good. The rest moderate. Orchestra splendid. This evening Berliner and I are going to see Frau Wolff. I promise you, my dear, I shall not fall in love with her. She is not the girl you dreamed of. Anyway, I dreamed of you last night. Your hair was done as it was when you were a girl, and I thought you so charming!

Almschili, do do your hair one day as you used in those days. I like it so much better than this modern Jewish fashion. Now, at twelve, I am going to rehearse with the singer. I fear I may have a shock. These last three days I have been sleeping until ten, and for an hour, too, in the afternoon. It suits me very well and probably these idle ways do me good. I kiss you, my dear heart! Have you nothing to say of the children? Many greetings to Mamerl too and tell her to be good. Karl too.

Your old
Gustl

I met Messchaert yesterday at the Opera. He was charming and very enthusiastic about my works.

Translated by Basil Creighton

To the Members of the Court Opera Company (1907)

Vienna, December 7, 1907

The hour has come that brings our work together to an end. Departing from the place of work that had become so dear to me, I herewith bid you farewell.

What I leave behind me is not such as I dreamed, something whole, something complete in itself, but fragments, things unfinished, as is man's lot.

It is not for me to judge what my activity has meant to those to whom it was dedicated. But at such a moment I may say of myself: I have always tried to do my best, always aimed high. My endeavors could not always be crowned with success. No one is so exposed to "the resistance of the material"—"the malice of inanimate objects"—as the executant artist. But I have always exerted myself to the limit, subordinating myself to the cause and my inclinations to duty. Never sparing myself, I have been able to demand that others too should give all that was in their power to give.

In the thick of the skirmish, in the heat of the moment, neither you nor I have remained unscathed or been immune from error. But whenever a work was accomplished, a task fulfilled, we forgot all the toil and effort, feeling richly rewarded—even when the world failed to accord us its approval. We have all made progress, and with us the Opera House for the sake of which we have striven.

My heartfelt thanks now go out to all of you who have supported me, aided me, struggled on with me, in my difficult, often thankless task. To all of you my sincerest wishes for your further journey through life and for the prosperity of the Court Opera, the future destinies of which I shall always follow with the keenest sympathy.

Gustav Mahler

Translated by Eithne Wilkins and Ernst Kaiser

Hugo Wolf

Opera Etiquette (1884)

June 15, 1884

Fidelio—with Frau Sucher and Herr Vogl as guest artists. Two loquacious neighbors ruined the overture for me by their inconsiderate behavior. They were of that infamous category of public nuisance (Kapellmeister Kreisler called them people with the souls of servants) that chatter during the performance, rattle their fans, let their gaze wander absently, greet their friends, wave to acquaintances, noisily lift and lower their folding seats, snap their operaglass cases open and shut, beat time with their feet, drum with their fingers, and commit more similar mischief. One of these creatures, during the playing of the great *Leonore* Overture, uttered to her companion (how characteristic of such miserable people!) the following remarkable words: "Look at this audience! So quiet and attentive. You'd think they were in a concert hall!"

I was dumbfounded by this shameless naiveté. There we have it! The perfectly natural and obviously appropriate deportment of a civilized audience—a situation where not even a cannibal would be other than attentive and still as a mouse the minute the first strains of the overture resound through the hall—regarded as curious and abnormal! Is what we hear in an opera house any less music than what is played in a concert hall? Does the quality of music depend upon the nature of the place in which it is listened to? Has anyone ever heard such hair-raising nonsense? Is the music of Mozart, Wagner, Gluck not music at all because it is produced in a theater? Are the absolute musical compositions of these masters there only to transport the bored, dirty, heedless creatures, fluttering from loge to parterre and from parterre to loge, on the golden surface of blossoming tone? An ignominious office even for the prudish muse of our symphony composers, riding the pack donkey or the camel. But to see the true, pure, and unique muse of our dramatic composers, Gluck, Mozart, Weber, Marschner, and Wagner, sacrificed to the cold scorn and the contemptuous stupidity of those people who betray themselves as inferiors in the theater and concert hall could turn a dove into a tiger from anger and pain. What is one to make of my estimable neighbor's clever words? That one goes to the theater to hear music? Good heavens, no. Anything but that! The best, the most sensitive, the most intelligent among these wretches go to the opera house to revel in an effective stage set, the pretty voice of a singer, the voluptuous hips of a ballerina. They have an eye for everything immaterial that takes place upon the stage. Only toward the music do they adopt a threatening attitude.

To a second category belong all those operagoers who attend the opera only in order to inspect continuously, both during the overture and even when the curtain is up, the boxholders, the newest fashions, the ladies' dresses, etc. These people preserve the most impervious indifference to the most obvious, the most effective happenings on the stage. For them the main thing is not the singer, male or female, but the virtuoso manipulation of the opera glass. The superlative category of such creatures, however, is composed of those who come for no other reason than to be seen. They always arrive after the overture, conduct themselves noisily, like ill-bred youngsters, as they enter. They happily make a racket with their seats and with the inevitable opera-glass case, and then begin—a conversation! This is conducted in a lively manner, and, despite its gaiety, one can detect the basic subject—business. The bull and bear markets alternate in their conversation no less than *forte* and *piano* in the orchestra. Figures occur frequently. If ladies are involved, there will be amiable discussion of familial matters. How the cook knows how to prepare roast goose in a special way, how clever, how talented, how promising (!) their delightful children are, how little Elsa, despite the fact that she is just five, plays all of Mendelssohn's *Songs Without Words* from memory, how little Siegmund, or even Siegfried, is writing poems, and what a joy it is to experience such things. Etc. Etc. Too much, too much, I say with Tannhäuser.

Translated by Henry Pleasants

A Monologue Recalled by Hugo Wolf (1884)

November 1, 1884

One thoroughly unpleasant night, not long ago, I spied a stranger standing before a kiosk, trying earnestly by the gaslight to decipher the Philharmonic prospectus. I stepped a little closer and heard a monologue, now quiet, now agitated, which seemed to contain so much truth that, upon returning to my lodging, I wrote it all down, determined, on some suitable occasion, to publish it. I do so herewith:

"Philharmonic concerts"—so he began—"probably the same old hackneyed stuff. Let's see, Bach, Mozart, Beethoven, Haydn—good, good.—The public loves classical music. It is very cultivated, very serious, very upright, very severe! Beethoven, Mozart, Haydn are actually already too familiar, too melodious, too intelligible. But Bach! Only a violin concerto this time, to be sure, but even if there are no double fugues, no twelve-voiced canons, one can still be sure of some masterly counterpoint"—here he mimicked derisively the public's rapture. "Ah, Bach! Yes, of course. That's music! Everything granite, bronze, everywhere deep, elemental, great, exalted, genius!" Then in his natural voice: "Goodness me! I do believe that the Philharmonic audience would rather flounder in the Pontine marshes than hear compositions of this esteemed master if they did not adorn the programs of the Philharmonic. But what does one not suffer for fashion? Bach has become fashionable with the Philharmonic audience, and it is thought good form to tick off all the Bach cantatas with one's fingers and, in the middle of a Mendelssohn *Song Without Words,* to exclaim: 'Very nice, charming, but why don't you play the *St. Matthew Passion,* or the *St. John,* or the *Christmas Oratorio,* or the *Well-Tempered Clavier?*'

" 'I'll play you the Italian Concerto.'

" 'That's nothing. Play the B Minor Mass from memory, or at least from the score.'

" 'Good heavens, the man is cultivated!'—

"Innocent soul!—Don't believe a word of it. Play your *Songs Without Words,* for your Bach enthusiast is already scared stiff that you may inadvertently lay out a dozen Bach cantatas on the music rack. He would as soon swallow vitriol as listen to a cantata from beginning to end.

"How many make the detour via Bach's complete works, which they 'would like to hear,' in order to pull up at last at [Johann Strauss's] *The Merry War,* or, if all goes well, at Chopin's Waltz in D-flat. Yes, what all of Bach's profundity cannot achieve, fashion brings to pass. It is the intermediary between this composer and our public. And, since Bach's authority, fortunately, comes to the latter's assistance, one may safely assume that its applause is sincere, i.e. that it originates in a firm belief in Bach's enormous classicism!

"Brahms? Goodness! He gives old Bach a run for his money when it comes to classicism. Herr von Bülow, to be sure, modestly terms our shrewd symphonist merely Ludwig II, thus denying him the ultimate classicism, since he presumes to acknowledge in Herr Brahms a perpetuator of Beethoven when Ludwig I, in his last period, cannot be called a classicist in any strict sense of the term. Can it be, perhaps, that Herr von Bülow errs? Was it, perhaps, not at all his intention to injure his friend Brahms by so thoughtless a word, and thus to have underestimated his classicism?

"What else do we have here? Schumann, Schubert, Mendelssohn—Dvořák? But not a symphony, for God's sake? No! Slavonic Rhapsody—in God's name!"—Let the amiable reader not be surprised at the double invocation. One grows pious in adversity, and to hear a piece by Dvořák seems to my stranger to represent a misfortune.—"Robert Fuchs? Aha, another serenade? No, a symphony. Robert Volkmann—probably a symphony? No, a serenade. Next year it will be the other way around: symphony by Volkmann, serenade by Fuchs. Oh, well, we must have variety, and the Philharmonic knows all about that! *Penthesilea* by Goldmark—a splendid subject for musical development; but the composer's talent is not commensurate with the greatness of the material. Only a Makart could have caught Penthesilea in colors, only a Liszt or a Berlioz in music. No one else could do it. But is that all the prospectus has to offer?

"Ha! Richard Wagner: 'A *Faust* Overture.' We always enjoy hearing that. But why not the 'Siegfried Idyll'? Why not the new

Venusberg music, which we are also denied in the opera? Why not excerpts from *Der Ring des Nibelungen?* or *Parsifal?* Why? Why?

"But what? And how? Do my eyes deceive me? Berlioz? *Symphonie fantastique?* No, really? That's absolutely impossible—and yet, there it is, plain as can be: *Symphonie fantastique* by Hector Berlioz. No, the courage of the Philharmonic has something Spartan about it. They dare to shock their subscribers with such a thing. Oh! It's hilarious how the classical public trembles at the prospect, how the pure at heart among them lower their pious gaze because at the end comes a witches' sabbath, how the serious-minded condemn the mad substance, how the pedants rage at the free form, the free harmonies, the free fantasy, and the composer's other freedoms!

"Needless anxiety! Needless rage! Exaggerated agitation. The Philharmonic can easily speak of the devil, because it lies in its power to let him in. 'Honorable public,' I would like to say, 'he will not show up. Console yourselves. You will not have to hear the *Symphonie fantastique.* I could almost promise it. So, be calm.'

"The gentlemen of the Philharmonic are far too polite to concern themselves with what might be in their subscribers' interest, and far too contented to permit themselves any honorable agitation for their own sake, even if it were to displease a cultivated public. Otherwise, they would have to include a symphonic poem by Liszt in each of their concerts, and get it through their heads, at last, that among twelve symphonic poems, with which Liszt has earned first place after Beethoven in the field of purely instrumental music, the choice must not be restricted to 'Les Préludes' and 'Mazeppa.'

"If the Philharmonic Society were truly animated by an artistic spirit, its objective should be to educate an audience, to cultivate it. This can be achieved successfully only by ruthless measures. Nothing serious, nothing great, nothing significant will be gained with concessions here, concessions there. This is as true of art as of life. And with the Philharmonic everything favors a ruthless policy. It has, to begin with, no competition, standing quite alone of its kind. Herr Kretschmann's Orchestra Society is hardly to be compared with it. Things are different in Paris, Berlin, London, and even Leipzig. There one can speak of competition, but in Vienna. . . . Secondly, the public flocks to the Philharmonic not only because it has no other way of satisfying its hunger for music, but also because fashion dictates that one be seen there. Whoever can produce a season ticket to the Philharmonic concerts is to the unfortunates who cannot as are fat people, with their substantial shadows, to the tragic Schlemiels who, casting no shadow at all, have no right to existence. Not to speak of the Founder tickets, whose owners are so proud of their property that our planet would long ago have collapsed under the weight of their prodigious complacency were such complacency not, fortunately, distributed among all the other planets. A concert institution, however, that regularly finds subscribers is also relieved of financial anxieties. What prevents the Philharmonic, then, from proceeding more artistically in the building of its programs than has heretofore been the case? Are there solid reasons for its inartistic policies? I think not. Had I a decisive voice in the selection of programs, I would say: We shall play something of Liszt or Berlioz in every concert, as these are two masters whose greatness and significance the public has yet to grasp. Should the public protest at first, so what? Time will take care of that. The public's indifference toward these masters will turn to attentiveness, its frivolity into reverence, its astonishment into comprehension and then into admiration, love, and enthusiasm. You will be praised for having achieved through your determination that which your calling requires: to lend your resonant organ to all that represents progress in art, that announces itself as truly new, substantial, and pathbreaking, that raises itself above the common and mediocre, and strives toward the ultimate, shrinking before no difficulty, and holding out to the last man when it is a matter of serving a worthy cause!"

Thus, in short, and approximately, the monologue of that nocturnal enthusiast whose views may well strike a sympathetic chord in many a reader of these lines.

Translated by Henry Pleasants

Bruckner on Two Pianos (1884)

December 28, 1884

Bruckner? Bruckner? Who is he? Where does he live? What can he do?

Such questions may be heard in Vienna today, and even from regular subscribers to the concerts of the Philharmonic Orchestra and the Society of Friends of Music. If you meet someone to whom the name is not wholly unfamiliar, he will actually recall that Bruckner is a professor of music theory at our Academy. Another might add that he is an organ virtuoso—and fix the first half-educated informant with a triumphant look. A third will believe, a fourth may know, a fifth will assert, and a sixth will swear that Bruckner is also a composer, nothing special, to be sure, not a classical composer. A connoisseur will shake his noble head skeptically, observing that he has no sense of form. A dilettante bemoans the confusion of musical ideas in his compositions. Another remarks his faulty instrumentation, and the critics find it all abominable, and let's hear no more about it!

One other remains to be heard from—the conductor. He, in fact, has good words for this composer's works, and brings his influence to bear in their behalf despite the critics' slanderous opposition. He proposes to perform them. To whom does he make this proposition? To his subordinates, the orchestra. And here his trouble begins. If the tribunes of the orchestra veto the conductor's decision, the conductor may move heaven and earth—to no avail. Dictatorial power is not his to wield. He must abide by the orchestra's verdict.

(What can be expected from such a procedure is obvious, especially when these orchestra tribunes are as little able to grasp the deeper substance of a composition as they are capable of admirable accomplishment on their instruments. It does not follow that because a man is a good soldier he has the makings of a field commander. An orchestra musician can blow or fiddle a heavenly solo and still be far, far, very far from conceiving an expressively played solo within the context of the whole piece.)

Thus vanishes the last hope, and Bruckner, this Titan in conflict with the gods, must be content with trying to communicate his music to the public from the piano. It's a miserable business, but better than not being heard at all. And when our unlucky fellow has the good luck to find such enthusiastic interpreters as Löwe and Schalk, then we must count him at least partially compensated for the unjust procedure of our fashionable musical institutions.

I have just spoken of Herr Bruckner as a Titan in conflict with the gods. I could not, in truth, think of a more appropriate metaphor with which to characterize this composer, combining as it does both praise and disparagement in equal portions: raw natural forces against the predominance of the intellect. Translated into the terminology of art, it reveals an extraordinary native artistic endowment in all its freshness, incompatible with the musical sensibility, the intelligence, the manifestations of a level of cultivation, characteristic of our time. These are the principal elements in the work of this composer, and they find themselves, unfortunately, at loggerheads. Had Bruckner ever succeeded in achieving their reconciliation, he would have become, without doubt, a great figure approaching the significance of Liszt.

It is a certain want of intelligence that makes Bruckner's symphonies, for all their originality, grandeur, power, imagination, and invention, so difficult to grasp. There is always and everywhere the will, the colossal strivings—but no satisfaction, no artistic resolution. Hence the formlessness of his works, the apparent extravagance of the exposition. Bruckner wrestles with the idea, but he lacks the courage to come to the point and then, fully in the clear as to his intentions, get on with it.

Thus he wavers, rooted halfway between Beethoven and the new advances of the moderns, the latter represented most successfully and vividly in Liszt's symphonic poems, unable to decide for the one or the other. That is his misfortune. I do not hesitate, however, to describe Bruckner's symphonies as the most important symphonic creations to have been written since Beethoven. They are the works of a floundered genius, like the colossal writings of Grabbe. Common to the works of both Bruckner and Grabbe are the bold, grandiose conceptions—and the confusion and shapelessness of the execution. As in Grabbe the luxuriance of his fantasy, and the genius betrayed in the flight of his thought, remind us of Shakespeare, so in all of Bruckner's symphonies we detect in the grandiose themes and their thoughtful elaboration the language of Beethoven.

It would certainly be rewarding, then, to give this inspired evangelist more attention than has been accorded him hitherto. It is a truly shocking sight to see this extraordinary man barred from the concert hall. Among living composers (excepting Liszt, of course) he has the first and greatest claim to be performed and admired.

Translated by Henry Pleasants

Brahms's Symphony No. 4 (1886)

January 24, 1886

A lucky thing for the famous sculptor Thorvaldsen that his good genie gave him the happy notion of sculpting a scene from the life of Alexander the Great. The prospects for this artist's enduring celebrity might otherwise not have been bright. But now that he has had the unearned distinction of having inspired the famous Kopi, i.e. the composer Johannes Brahms, to write a new symphony, he is assured of immorality for all eternity.

Unfortunately, no information has been forthcoming from reliable sources as to what kind of sculptures may have imposed upon Herr Brahms the awesome obligation of writing three symphonies. If we were to indulge in idle speculation, inclining greatly to the assumption that Friedländer's old disabled veterans constitute an essential element of those symphonies—at least as far as freshness of invention and variety of expression are concerned—one might see in it no more than an honest endeavor to get on the track of those providential external influences and impressions which, in Schumann's opinion, are not to be despised. The fact remains, if we are to give credence to Kalbeck's assurances, that the immediate cause of the first suspicious symptoms of that cold artistic fever that has so troubled Herr Brahms for some fifteen or twenty years, and to which, as with his previous three symphonies, a fourth has now fallen victim, was the chance impression made upon him by Thorvaldsen's "Alexander."

The Fourth Symphony, in E minor—"But stop! Already the choice of tonality belongs to the distinguishing characteristics; for, curiously, neither Mozart, Beethoven, or Schubert, nor even Mendelssohn or Schumann, ever wrote a symphony in E minor." Now in the name of the garden spider, that's a colossal discovery! What an original, profound artist Herr Brahms must be when he can compose symphonies not only in C, D, and F, as Beethoven could, but even, unprecedently, in E minor! Heavens! I begin to stand in awe of Herr Brahms's uncanny genius. Ben Akiba's notorious pronouncement that there's nothing new under the sun must now be regarded as an old wives' tale, and merit no more than a compassionate smile. But what an accumulation of wisdom is not required for such a discovery!

When Richard Wagner, discussing Beethoven's Ninth, expressed doubt about the development of new art forms in the symphonic field, it was Franz Liszt's works that relieved his anxiety. But it never occurred to him that something strikingly new could emerge, anchored in the traditional form, simply through the clever choice of tonality. Yes, indeed, there's nothing new under the sun; only a symphony in E minor. It is to Herr Hanslick's undying credit to have called attention to this fact with appropriate emphasis. Ben Akiba's awesome assertion, so discomfiting and discouraging to all who would be original, is suddenly gone without a trace, as if it had been only a breath of air. A new field is now opened to all modern composers, and a grateful field, too, the cultivation of which requires nothing more than the denial of all those disciplines without which, unfortunately, not even a Beethoven could write a symphony. Equipped with a good nose for tonalities not previously employed by major composers in their symphonies—what further need for the melody of graphic representation and similar nonsense? Whoever now, and in the future, writes symphonies in the tonalities of A-flat minor, E-flat minor, F-sharp minor, C-sharp minor, and B-flat minor, which those fine masters forgot to exploit in their symphonies, will not have to wait for his hair to grow long before knowing whether he is original or not. He is, even if he remains a baldpate for the rest of his days. But to leave nothing to chance, try the following tonalities: B-sharp major, A-sharp minor, C-flat minor. Even C-flat major is not to be despised. But if some genius of the future wants to pile Pelion on Ossa and storm Olympus, he would be well advised to turn to more complex tonalties such as E-double-flat minor, G-double-sharp major, and the like. Since Herr Hanslick is, as everyone knows, a very objective critic, as amply demonstrated on the one hand by his reviews of Richard Wagner, and on the other hand by his reviews of Brahms, he will have no choice but to remark the extraordinary in this procedure with increasing emphasis and seriousness, the more emphatically and the more seriously in the same degree that the tonality of E-sharp minor is more complicated than E minor, and F-double-sharp major more complicated than E-sharp minor, and so on.

Conspicuous is the crab-like progress in Brahms's output. It has, to be sure, never reached beyond the level of mediocrity, but such nothingness, emptiness, and hypocrisy as prevails throughout the E

Minor Symphony has not appeared in any previous work of Brahms in so alarming a manner. The art of composing without ideas has decidedly found in Brahms its worthiest representative. Just like the good Lord, Herr Brahms is a master at making something from nothing. (This opinion is shared even by Herr Klabeck—ah, pardon! Herr Klobeck, I mean Herr Kalbek. Anyway, why should I not be permitted a typographical slip? After all, Herr Hanslick "first" started it with his "austere frost.")

In this sense, at least, one may call Brahms's art divine. Certainly it is not human, unless one chooses to recognize in the composer's musical impotence, and in his vain struggle against it, a trace of human weakness, and sense therein, perhaps, some human feeling. In truth, all four of Brahms's symphonies speak the language of mute despair. Therein, too, may lie the cause of the ghastly monotony in the last larger works of this composer. Herr Brahms attempts, indeed, to bring life to his symphonies by contrasts. He is not very successful at it, unfortunately, for to the fundamental tone of these symphonies, deriving from "can't do," he can offer only "wish I could" as a contrast, which comes to the same thing. But to let the dead-tired fantasy run the gauntlet between "can't do" and "wish I could" through four movements is, in the end, no joke. Nor does the audience have much to improve its spirits, what with little crumbs of melody, limping rhythms, and arid harmonies, the sum total of Brahms's riches. How easily, however, might both be assisted if Herr Brahms could bring himself to have done with his self-laceration. Enough of this awful business. May Herr Brahms be content to have found in his E Minor Symphony not only a tonality in which, heretofore, tolerable fare was produced only in smaller forms, but also the language giving most eloquent expression to his despondency: the language of the most intensive musical importance. . . .

Translated by Henry Pleasants

Richard Strauss

Is There an Avant-Garde in Music? (1907)

I have a great aversion to providing some sort of program for the aesthetic observations and critical essays on music to be published in this weekly.

I dislike programs as such. To one reader they promise too much. Another they are apt to influence far roo much. A third maintains that a program upsets the functioning of his own imagination. A fourth prefers not thinking at all to following the lines of other people's ideas. A fifth makes some other excuse—in short, programs are unfashionable. Now I am usually credited with a good nose for sensational matters and, as certain clever contemporaries have long since found out, I spend my day speculating like a kind of musical tailor how best to satisfy next year's fashions; it was for this reason that I first intended to launch the musical part of this periodical without any editorial blessing (which would have been the most modern thing to do), the more so since by doing this, I hoped to indulge my insuperable aversion to literary labor.

The publishers, however, refused to let it go at that. "If you are prepared to act as editor at all, Herr Strauss, it is just not good enough for you merely to play the 'Spiritus Rector' behind the scenes. You simply must introduce our new periodical *Morgen* with a short but significant statement since you are, after all, the 'Leader of the Moderns' and the 'Head of the Avant-Garde.' "

Now I hate such statements from the bottom of my heart. In spite of one's good intentions, one cannot avoid speaking more or less *pro domo,* and my principle is that one should allow actions and works to speak on one's behalf, but not words. The most daring words of artists have never caused as much confusion as the paper proclamations of their adversaries who endeavor to fight against the works with words. I therefore leave such proclamations now and in the future to those who have no desire to lead a life devoid of slogans, or who are deluded enough to believe that they are capable of halting the natural course of progress with dogmatic prohibitions, such as the opponents of futurist music or such Wagnerians as, sinning against the spirit of their master, have become no less petrified than the Mozartians around Franz Lachner, the Mendelssohnians around Carl Reinecke, or the Lisztians behind Draeseke.

In short, I refused stubbornly, but those alluring phrases, "Leader of the Moderns" and "Head of the Avant-Garde" which are now so studiously and thoughtlessly bruited about, refused to be driven from my mind and I began to meditate in particular upon the "avant-garde."

Meditation is always unpleasant, but this time, at any rate, it had the good effect of making me wonder whether there was such a thing as an "avant-garde." After continued thought, I could only answer this question with a definite no.

When all is said and done, the genuine narrow Wagnerians consisted of an association of like-minded disciples, whose aim it was to explain and propagate the ideas of their master, to remove errors and misunderstandings, to agitate the indifferent section of the public, confirm the judgment of the well-wishers, and repudiate that of the opponents. But it was not these partisans who achieved what progress has been made: the finally decisive driving force, which has brought victory to a Richard Wagner, as to all other great original artists, is the multitude of naïvely receptive listeners: always the most reliable means of progress in art. As compared with the fact, demonstrated time and again by history, that a great artist is instinctively recognized by the great public as a natural genius, even if its judgment of details is not at all clear-headed, the machinations of a narrow group of experts whom one might describe as an "avant-garde" are not of decisive importance. The main thing is the compelling contact between the creative genius and the mass of listeners willing to appreciate progress, who far exceed the limits of any possible "avant-garde." We must not allow ourselves to be confused by the fact that this same great public frequently welcomes easily digestible stuff, commonplaces, and even banalities, perhaps for a while more enthusiastically, than what is artistically significant, new, and in advance of its time. The public, after all, has two souls, but a third is conspicuous by its absence: it appreciates least of all that art which is neither immediately comprehensible nor eminently forceful. This is the reason for the agonies of disappointment suffered by so many serious musicians whom not even their opponents would accuse of being banal, and of whom not even their friends could say that they were capable of captivating the masses.

Carl Maria von Weber once said of the great public, "The individual is an ass and yet the whole is the voice of God." And indeed, the soul of this myriad-headed multitude assembled in a concert hall or theater for the enjoyment of art will, as a rule, instinctively appraise correctly what it hears provided that busybody critics or professional rivals refrain from inoculating it with preconceived ideas to prejudice its innocence.

Alexander Ritter once told me a good example of the curious confusion wrought in the critical faculties of an audience by external influences.

When, approximately fifty years ago, Franz Liszt first conducted three concerts consisting of his own orchestral works in Dresden, the performance of these symphonic poems, then heard for the first time, and to be so much maligned later, provoked the completely unbiased audience to tremendous enthusiasm. The papers wrote, the morning after, that Liszt was not a composer at all, and the very same people who had given free rein to their splendid enthusiasm the night before grew ashamed of their excitement. None admitted to having applauded and everyone had a thousand reservations after the event.

But whatever is great can only be impeded in its victorious progress for a little while at the most, and can never be finally halted by the men behind the scenes: thus it was that the great public—the voice of God—enabled even Franz Liszt to conquer malice and stupidity, just as its enthusiasm enabled Richard Wagner in 1876 to defeat decisively all his critics, ill-wishers, and detractors.

But although there is not, and need not be, such a thing as an "avant-garde," in the proper meaning of the word, it is necessary to protect the natural sound judgment of the unprejudiced against the onslaught of those who are forever reactionary, and who labor unceasingly out of ignorance, inability, complacency, or self-interest to stifle the public's innate flair for progress.

After 1876 people honestly believed that the enthusiasm of the great public had silenced the hue and cry of the enemy sufficiently to ensure that only behind the walls of the conservatories, where the public could not penetrate, would they attempt to instill their venom against the audacious revolutionary into the innocent souls of harmless students of music. People were beginning to hope that everyone in the musical world would, in future, be allowed to work out his own salvation, writing music as he pleased, according to his talent.

This hope proved false.

Professional musicians, anxiously concerned as they are for their own position, artistically impotent, possessing only a certain musical technique culled from some artistic epoch of the past, stubbornly and violently opposed to all expansion of means of expression and artistic form, and critics whose views of art are based on the petrified aesthetics of the past, are once again stirring abroad as a united "reactionary party" endeavoring more than ever to make things difficult for those who wish to go forward.

Now I find it impossible to call a man a reactionary just because he prefers Beethoven's *Eroica* to a feeble modern symphonic poem, or because he says he would prefer to see *Der Freischütz* twelve times in succession rather than some worthless modern opera. To this extent, I am a reactionary myself; but the reactionaries I cannot bear are those who demand that Biblical subjects should be taboo because Richard Wagner took his subjects from the Teutonic legends (here I am, of course, speaking *pro domo*), and those who maintain that it is vulgar to use the valve trumpet as a melodic instrument for the sole reason that Beethoven was forced to let his natural trumpets tackle tonic and dominant only. In short, all those who, armed with great tablets of the law, endeavor to say nay, with their *anathema sit*, to everyone who has the ability and the intention to create something new.

It was Richard Wagner who said, "I should like to give my *Siegfried* just once before an audience of appreciative listeners assembled from the four corners of the world and then I'd burn the score."

Thank goodness, we say today, that he didn't do it! *Siegfried*s are unfortunately so rare that we cannot afford to be prodigal with such precious gifts. But the idea behind this noble intention of the great master, namely that even a perfect work of art should only be considered as one stage in a great organic development, that it should be planted as seed in the souls of our descendants, to inspire and assist in the birth of even higher and more perfect creations, this wonderful idea we will honor, laboring unceasingly in the continuous perfecting of our art, and never forgetting, over and above the love and admiration we owe to the masters of the past who have found perfection, that art is subject to the selfsame laws as ever-changing life.

Not for us, therefore, the application of dogmatic aesthetics to works which should be judged by their own standards; not for us the tablets of the law that have long since been shattered by the great masters; not for us the high priests who dare stand in the path of a vigorous evolution; not for us all those things whose existence is justified solely by the fact that they existed yesterday. But let us, in this periodical *Der Morgen,* extend a welcoming hand and promise protection and assistance to everyone who has too much respect for the great masters to desecrate and vulgarize their work by cheap imitation, be it out of complacency, for the sake of earning a living, or to satisfy an ambition which is not, in the last analysis, born of art.

Welcome to all those who "strive unstintingly" and may the reactionary party perish!

Translated by L. J. Lawrence

To Hugo von Hofmannsthal (1913)

December 15, 1913

Dear Herr von Hofmannsthal!

The highly talented musician Wolf-Ferrari, in conjunction with the equally highly talented librettist Herr Batka, has written an opera called *The Lover as Doctor,* taken from Molière's *Le Médecin malgré lui.* This opera was produced in Dresden a few days ago, with our *Ariadne* costumes, and had an overwhelming success—

the press welcomed it as *"the* long-expected musical comedy of our time"! How many comic operas in the last five years have been welcomed as *"the* musical comedy of our time"—with the one exception of *Der Rosenkavalier,* which was given here three days ago for the eighty-ninth time, and not a seat to be had in the house!

In a Dresden paper I read that the Wolf-Ferrari-cum-Batka work is the real "renaissance of Molière" through the medium of music—a thing which I, thanks to your "clumsiness," was unable to achieve in *Ariadne!* The fellow has evidently heard something about Nietzsche's *Birth of Tragedy through the Medium of Music,* and now he will have Molière born again through Wolf-Ferrari. My dear friend, must we take all this nonsense lying down? Ought one not rather to protest in some form or other? Or must I go on waiting patiently till people come to see for themselves how carefully and conscientiously you have pondered over the subject before carrying it through—with what nicety we have selected everything from Molière's play that lends itself to music, how our comedy gradually brings us into the very heart of music and leads us on to heights of which no reincarnation of Molière could have any conception! Is it not enough to make one swear when one reads how the public was vastly entertained for a whole evening by the ravishing musical comedy of Messrs Wolf-Farrari and Batka, while in the case of our short abridgment of Molière—in which you have left really nothing that is not amusing and characteristic—the same public was so bored to death that it would not even wait for the opera?

Must we put up with this sort of thing forever? Have you no one among your friends who could say a few plain, far-reaching words that might quash once and for all this legend of "the tedious *Bourgeois*"? This story, which has spread all over the world, gaining, as it goes, by elaboration and innuendo, sprang from the trifling fact that at the original production in Stuttgart, in consequence of two intervals of fifty minutes each (for which the royal visitors were to blame), the public was made to wait three hours before the eagerly expected opera of the composer Strauss began—and their impatience was put down to their boredom at Molière and Hofmannsthal's comedy.

And not a single one of the scribblers has taken the trouble to examine for himself this catch-phrase about the "dreary, unending play of Molière" that in Stuttgart lasted, with intervals, for three hours—although now, whenever it is given, it plays just one hour.

During our Strauss week, the good Princess Marie von Meiningen was here on a visit and heard all my operas (with the exception of *Salome*) for the first time. After reading the text of *Der Rosenkavalier* she wrote me saying she found it tedious; after the performance of Friday she confessed to me that, to her astonishment, she now found the text enchanting! This lady had the courage and the decency to revise, after the performance, the judgment she had previously given—which of the critics would do as much? I should like to see what these people would say if they had to criticize the book, say, of *Die Meistersinger* or *Parsifal* without knowing it was by Richard Wagner; I wager ninety percent would declare it unspeakably tedious, and quite unsuitable for composition.

After all, we must recognize the value of the sort of work we have done in *Ariadne,* and I will allow no one to belittle it; for this reason I am opposed to any revision, or separation of the opera from the comedy. Negotiations are now in progress for the production of *Ariadne* (in English) in America next year, just as we wrote it, and in a small theater.

Once more I ask you, have you no one who can secure a wider publicity for the work by some weighty and influential utterance about it—the style of the whole, and the value of Molière's share in it? The perpetual nonsense one has to listen to on this subject gets on my nerves after a time. I shall get Dr. Bie to come out this afternoon before the performance and talk this matter over with him, for if one allows wrong impressions to go too long uncorrected, they end by being taken for the truth.

With best regards, yours truly,
Dr. Richard Strauss

Translated by Paul England

On Inspiration in Music (ca. 1940)

The melodic idea which suddenly falls upon me out of the blue, which emerges without the prompting of an external sensual stimulant or of some spiritual emotion—the latter, by the way, can be a direct cause more than anything else, as I have often experienced

after excitements of a completely different nature entirely uncon-
nected with art—appears in the imagination immediately, unconsciously, uninfluenced by reason. It is the greatest gift of the divinity and cannot be compared with anything else.

What is inspiration? Generally speaking we understand by musical inspiration the invention of a motif, a melody which occurs
to one suddenly, unsolicited by the intellect, especially immediately after awakening in the early morning or in dreams—Sachs's
words in *Die Meistersinger:* "Man's truest intuition is revealed to
him in dreams." Am I to believe that my imagination has been at
work all night independently of consciousness and without recollection in the Platonic sense?

My own experience has been this: If I am held up at a certain
point in my composition at night and cannot see a profitable way
of continuing in spite of much deliberation, I close the lid of the
piano or the cover of my manuscript book and go to bed, and when
I wake up in the morning—lo and behold! I have found the continuation. By what mental or physical process is this brought about?

To judge from my own experience of creative work, a motif or
a melodic phrase of two or four bars occurs to me immediately. I
put this down on paper and then expand it straight away into a
phrase of eight, sixteen, or thirty-two bars which is not of course
left unaltered, but after a longer or shorter period of "rest" is slowly
fashioned into its final form, which must hold its own against the
severest and most detached self-criticism. Now this operation is
carried out in such a manner that what is most important is to
wait for the moment when the imagination is willing and ready to
serve me further. But this state of preparation is usually produced
and stimulated at leisure, after continued thought, and even, as I
remarked above, by spiritual excitement (even indignation and annoyance). These mental processes do not belong solely to the sphere
of innate talent but also to those of self-criticism and self-educa-
tion. Goethe is supposed to have said, "Genius is industry," but
even industry and joy in one's work are innate and not just the
results of training. A perfect work of art is achieved only when, as
in the case of our great masters, content and form are blended to
perfection.

Translated by L. J. Lawrence

Ferruccio Busoni

Rules for Practicing the Piano (1898)

1. Practice the passage with the most difficult fingering; when you have mastered that, play it with the easiest.
2. If a passage offers some particular technical difficulty, go through all similar passages you can remember in other pieces; in this way you will bring system into the kind of playing in question.
3. Always combine technical practice with the study of the interpretation; the difficulty, often, does not lie in the notes but in the dynamic shading prescribed.
4. Never be carried away by temperament, for that dissipates strength and where it occurs there will always be a blemish, like a dirty spot which can never be washed out of a material.
5. Don't set your mind on overcoming the difficulties in pieces which have been unsuccessful because you have previously practiced them badly; it is generally a useless task. But if meanwhile you have quite changed your way of playing, then begin the study of the old piece from the beginning as if you did not know it.
6. Study everything as if there were nothing more difficult; try to interpret studies for the young from the standpoint of the virtuoso. You will be astonished to find how difficult it is to play a Czerny or Cramer or even a Clementi.
7. Bach is the foundation of piano playing, Liszt the summit. The two make Beethoven possible.

8. Take it for granted from the beginning that everything is possible on the piano, even where it seems impossible to you and even when it really is so.

9. Attend to your technical equipment so that you are prepared and armed for every possible event; then when you study a new piece, you can focus all your power on the intellectual content; you will not be held up by the technical problems.

10. Never play carelessly, even when there is nobody listening, or the occasion seems unimportant.

11. Never leave a passage which has been unsuccessful without repeating it; if you cannot do it immediately because of the presence of others then do it subsequently.

12. If possible allow no day to pass without touching your piano.

. . . What do you think of these "Maxims for Practice"? They are formed from my own experience.

Translated by Rosamund Ley

Mozart (1906)

I write down the following notes at this time when every musician turns his thoughts to Mozart. Subjective and hardly exhaustive though they may be, they help to portray the characteristics of the more or less definite picture which all cultured people have in themselves of the personality of the "divine Master." I send the notes to you in the simple form in which they arose.

I think of Mozart thus:

Up to now he is the most complete manifestation of musical gifts. Every genuine musician looks up to him, happy and disarmed.

His short life and his fertility lift his perfection to the rank of the phenomenal.

His never-clouded beauty disconcerts.

His sense of form is also supernatural.

His art is like a sculptor's masterpiece—presenting from every side a finished picture.

He has the instinct of an animal, setting himself tasks to tax his strength to the utmost limits, but no further.

He dares nothing foolhardy.

He finds without seeking and does not seek what is unfindable—perhaps what would be unfindable to him.

His resources are extraordinarily abundant, but he never uses them all.

He can say very much, but he never says too much.

His is passionate, but keeps to the forms of chivalry.

He bears all characters in himself, but only as presenter and portrayer.

He gives the solution with the riddle.

His proportions are astoundingly correct, but they can be measured and verified.

He controls light and shadow, but his light does not pain and his darkness still shows clear outlines.

Even in the most tragic situations he still has a witticism ready, in the most cheerful he is able to draw a thoughtful furrow in his brow.

He is universal through his dexterity.

He can continue to draw from every glass because he has never drunk to the bottom of one.

He stands so high that he sees further than all and sees everything, therefore, somewhat diminished.

His palace is immeasurably big, but he never steps outside its walls.

Through its windows he sees nature; the window frame is also her frame.

Joy is his most outstanding feature; his smile decks with flowers even what is most unpleasant.

His smile is not that of a diplomat or actor, but of a pure spirit—and yet man of the world.

His spirit is not pure out of ignorance.

He has not remained simple and not become cunning.

He is full of temperament without nervousness.

Idealist without losing touch with the earth, realist without ugliness.

He is a commoner as well as an aristocrat, but never a boor or a demagogue.

He is a friend of order: miracle and sorcery preserve their sixteen and thirty-two bars.

He is religious in so far as religion is identical with harmony.

In him the antique and rococo combine in perfect ways without resulting in a new architecture.

Architecture is next of kin to his art.

He is not demoniacal and not supernatural, his realism is of this earth.

He is the complete and round number, the perfect sum, a conclusion and no beginning.

He is young as a boy and wise as an old man—never old-fashioned and never modern, carried to the grave and always alive.

His smile, which was so human, still shines on us transfigured.

Translated by Rosamund Ley

Hans Pfitzner

To Bruno Walter (1946)

October 5, 1946

Dear Bruno,

Your letter of the 16th of September took two and a half weeks to arrive in my hands from New York. If my answer is to reach you on time—from the 20th of October to the 8th of November—at the London address you provided, I have to write immediately, which I'm doing on the last piece of good letter paper I have.

You're right: at a time when the world lies convulsed, we shouldn't touch on "divisive" issues. In my own defense for having used the words "fictitious atrocity story" concerning the Cossmann case—I don't have a copy of the letter and therefore no longer know in what sense it arose—it should be said that one doesn't weigh every word when writing to an old friend. Further, I would never have felt my remark to be "divisive" or having been made between "divided" people since, as different as our views may be, we are not in divided camps to the extent that we acknowledge the truth as truth, regardless of what it may look like. "I stand accused and must rise to my own defense," so please bear with my rather wide-ranging remarks.

As painful as it is, I have to believe that the stories of atrocities in the concentration camps in the Second World War were not made up, at least not largely so. But in the First World War there were in fact not just isolated atrocity fictions but instead a devilishly conceived system of lies about chopped-off children's hands etc., all to serve the purpose of defaming everything German before the

211

world, outlawing it and holding it up as the scourge "of humanity." You know that as well as I do.

But this sort of thing has to have consequences; it would be naive to think this might not be the case. It is impossible to martyr and humiliate a people the way this happened to Germany during and after the First World War without matching results, which arise in accordance with the law of causality.

And thus the Second World War came about; it cannot be considered or judged without the First. And as always happens in such times, there sprang up a proletarian "Prometheus Unbound"—with all the trimmings!—following a necessity that I would call "meta-causal."

I don't intend to write a political tract or deal at length with Hitler, but I must say one thing: to make the entire German people responsible for his deeds and misdeeds, to identify him with Germany (as even some Germans are shameless enough to do, such as Thomas Mann and Hermann Hesse), is as vapid and false intellectually as it is vile morally. Just imagine the French people being treated this way by the enemy powers after the fall of Napoleon!

But we Germans are now the whipping boys for atrocities that no decent person can fail to abhor. You speak of a "horror surpassing anything fantasy can imagine." This fantasy could be aided if they would show films—as they do for the concentration camp atrocities—of what has been going on since the collapse every single day in East Prussia and everywhere else the Russians have arrived: the rape of women from age seventeen to seventy in such a bestial way that it truly "surpasses everything that fantasy can imagine." Ten men for one woman. . . . And the way the American culture/bombs and humanity/phosphorus canisters have mauled Germany the beautiful—this you haven't seen. . . . As to what I personally have experienced by way of atrocities, mortal danger, and losses, I will keep silent.

But Americans and Russians now sit as judges of the Germans in the name of humanity and sentence brave military commanders who did their duty during the war to ignominious death!

Just as there are character traits in individuals that are innate, eternal, metaphysical, and others that are "added" by temporal circumstances to make up the empirical character, so it is with entire peoples. And that leads me to wonder:

Which deeds of the Germans belong to their eternal, "intelligible" (to use Kant's term) character, and which arise not from an innate singularity (an excellent word!), come not from the inside, but are instead elicited by an outside stimulus?

To summarize: If I ask, what is Germany? it's in the sense of: What is Germany's Platonic idea? Is it the "sacred heart of nations," or is it a band of malicious criminals who number in the millions?

The Platonic idea, the eternal primal image of a thing, cannot include conflicting or contradictory qualities, cannot be anything in process, shifting, or fluctuating, anything merely temporary to be cast aside. Germany is not to be separated from certain judgments that have been attached to it over the course of time, some arising spontaneously, some coined by poets. "The land of poets and philosophers," the "sacred heart of nations" (Hölderlin), "And the world will someday be cured by the German essence" (Geibel).

Opposed to all these and similar statements of people who loved Germany is the negative pole of foreign hatred that cannot be explained any further and serves to prove nothing other than the unique position, the absolutely exceptional quality, the loneliness of Germany. The grounds for this hatred cannot be adduced, it is simply there and otherwise well known in the life of individuals, where it often suffices for a person to be a little "different" from "everyone" to be hated. The canary among the sparrows. It consists of a mixture of fear, envy, spite over superficialities. Premonition of the inconceivable.

But however quick to censure this hatred may be, however much pleasure it takes in disparagement: throughout the centuries the German people in its entirety has never been reproached with cruelty; it is not a fundamental part of the German character. Anyone who perpetrates cruelty in cold blood *is not a German* but an exception, such as always exists in a people of eighty million and under extraordinary circumstances.

Well, be that as it may, I am bound by destiny to this people, and it hasn't always been easy to belong to it, "to be loyal in its womb." Neither in the Wilhelminian era, nor in the succeeding "System" Germany, nor in Nazi Germany was I recognized and treated for what I was and could have been to it. Now, in the evening of my life, I sit ignored, forbidden, "unwanted," suppressed in an old-age home. Sincerely, I do not begrudge your triumphal tour through Teuton-free Europe, practicing your—our!—art to your heart's content.

I, however, will remain faithful to this country despite everything, to the land of Luther, which gave birth to the B Minor Mass and *Faust;* which produced *Der Freischütz* and Eichendorff, the *Pastorale* and *Die Meistersinger,* in which the *Critiques of Reason* and *The World as Will and Imagination* were conceived—to this land I will remain faithful until my last breath.

Hans Pfitzner

Translated by James Steakley

Arnold Schönberg

New Music (1923)

I am not really clear what the principles of the new music are (assuming they can be stated in any sort of unified way—and that does not have to be so, nor has it in fact often been so). These young composers need not necessarily have any new principles. Certain dislikes, certain enthusiasms, many ideas, much imagination, and ability—there you have a better framework than any principles, however splendid. Nothing collapses so completely as renovation through bad growth. And, on the other hand, all revolutions simply bring reaction out into the open and can threaten what took years to grow. I was never *revolutionary*. *The only revolutionary* in our time was Strauss!

The first thing to be done in music—purely technically, for the spiritual is incalculable—seems to me the following:

1. To put an end, practically and theoretically, to the apparent (surely only apparent?) extremeness and lack of restraint present in twelve-tone composition, and to look for its laws. Or better, to find the form in which the laws of earlier art can be applied to the new. Five tones have been drawn into composition in a way not called upon before—*that is all,* and it does not call for any new laws.

2. The path to be taken here seems to me the following: not to look for harmonies, since there are no rules for those, no values, no laws of construction, no assessment. Rather, to write parts. From the way these sound, harmonies will later be abstracted.

3. Gradually one will try to apply this more inclusive sound-

215

material to the old forms. Here there will surely be certain modifications at first, and probably later too. But I am convinced, and have evidence, that *nothing essential changes in all this!*

4. As a reaction against the musical epoch that has just run its course, an epoch which carried to the limit the pathos of subjective feeling, one may expect a more un-pathetic kind of music. Whether it will choose a mode of expression (and perhaps also of vision) that turns against pathos (irony, satire, blasphemy, comment, etc.); whether it will find some other way out, to one side, perhaps placing humor, harmlessness, indifference, or sheer sensuality in the foreground; and whether this foreground is everything, or merely conceals the background—who can recount all the possibilities there are?

In any case, this seems to me the most important thing of all: apart from possible new ideas (new!), it will be more a matter of relatively novel presentations of relatively novel ideas. Five more tones are available; perhaps slightly greater exactness will be possible—or, on the other hand, perhaps it will be necessary to feel one's way for a while.

I hear that the young call their music, "psychological" music. This supposedly means its effect is to be purely on the nerves. But the only changes needed for that would not be in the music, but in the nerves. One cuts them off from the rest of the personality, and henceforth the oldest and newest music alike will merely tinkle in the ears—nobody will have to think about an artist any more. That is easy enough, but I find it correspondingly difficult to think how to produce the necessary music. Imagine the x rays it will need to use, if its own effect is to be limited to the lower half of the mind. Or, since the complete personality turns away these rays, are they supposed to stop short in monstrous disorder? What sort of parts must one write to achieve this?

I can understand that when a young man says such things, he has something in mind—or, to be more accurate, he feels something. And perhaps the feeling does him so much good that he does not have to care what text he speaks to its melody—that what he says is a matter of indifference to him. If I remember rightly, I too used to be the same once; it was fairly long ago, so I need not be ashamed. For, just as the talented young will some day overcome all that, so (without presuming) have I. Nowadays I make a point of keeping my ideas at a decent distance from the feelings accompanying them.

To say it without more ado: if I understand aright, the young demand that their listeners are no longer to take a musical impression for anything more than it is. They want the sound that goes in at one ear to do nothing, before it goes out at the other, but stimulate the brain or spinal cord at a more or less definite point. (I trust I reproduce this in its full severity.) And it is of their listeners (I repeat) that they demand this—for only the latter are in a position to localize the impression, and even that only if they succeed in making themselves into a body that is, up to a point, nonconductive for music. This is certainly not impossible; joking apart (if without charity), it is not impossible, as one sees from the popular saying that certain dance music goes where it belongs—to the feet. However, whether it goes only there, or merely goes there first, is not stated. Certainly "Forest Murmurs" and the *Moonlight* Sonata do not go to the feet—not, at least, as their principal target. It is less hard to imagine someone on whom the waltzes from *Die Meistersinger* and the "Alla danza tedesca" from Beethoven's B-flat String Quartet have such a narrowly "psychological" effect—but one may not feel obliged to view it as a virtue worth mentioning.

Translated by Leo Black

My Public (1930)

Called upon to say something about my public, I have to confess: I do not believe I have one.

At the start of my career, when to the annoyance of my opponents a noticeable part of the audience did not hiss but applauded, and when the hissers did not succeed in carrying the day against the majority, although hisses sound more striking than applause, then these opponents of mine alleged that those bestowing their approval were my friends and had only applauded out of friendship and not because they liked the piece. My poor friends: as true as few. They were indeed thought depraved enough to be my friends and yet not so depraved as to enjoy my music.

Whether I then had a public—that I cannot judge.

But after the upheaval, there were in every major city those certain few hundred young people with just no idea what to do with themselves. They therefore tried hard to put it on record that they had a philosophy—by supporting all lost causes. About then, when that great variable, their philosophy, included even me—blameless party that I was—optimists asserted that I now had a public. I challenged this; I did not see how people could suddenly have come to understand me overnight. (My works had not, after all, become any more stupid or shallow overnight.) The rapid decline of the radicals—still not knowing what to do with themselves but finding other things to meddle with—justified my view: I had not written anything shallow.

There are many reasons why the great public makes little contact with me. Above all: the generals, who today still occupy the music directorates, are mostly moving along lines that my line does not fit, or else they are afraid to put before the public something they do not themselves understand. Some of them (even though when they admit it they politely look regretful) really regard not understanding me as a virtue. Granted even that is their greatest virtue, I still had to feel surprised the first time a Viennese conductor made it known to me that he could not perform my Chamber Symphony because he did not understand it. I was amused, though; why did he have to pick on me in this sudden burst of wanting to understand, and not on the classical works he blithely conducted year in, year out? But seriously, I must say that it is, after all, no honor for a musician not to understand a score, but a matter for shame—many even of my opponents will admit this today, as regards my Chamber Symphony.

Apart from these conductors, those who get between me and the public are the many musicians who do not conduct but know other ways to mislead. I have seen countless times that, as regards the main point, it was not the public who hissed: it was a small but active "expert" minority. The public's behavior is either friendly or indifferent, unless they are intimidated because their spiritual leaders are protesting. As a whole they are always rather inclined to enjoy something they have devoted time and money to. They come less to judge than to enjoy, and can to some extent sense whether the person appearing before them is entitled to do so. What they are not interested in doing is using their more or less correct judgment in order to display themselves in a better light. This is partly because no single member stands to gain or lose anything (he will either be outnumbered or be swallowed up in the majority); and partly because among the public there are, after all, people who count for something, even without first having to shine by their artistic judgments, and who, without losing prestige, may keep their impressions to themselves, unassessed. One may keep anything to oneself, except expert judgment—for what is expert judgment unless one shows it off? For this reason, I also take it to have been the expert judges, not the art-lovers, who received my *Pierrot lunaire* with such hostility when I performed it in Italy. I was indeed honored that Puccini, not an expert judge but a practical expert, already ill, made a six-hour journey to get to know my work, and afterwards said some very friendly things to me; that was good, strange though my music may have remained to him. But, on the other hand, it was characteristic that the loudest disturber of the concert was identified as the director of a conservatory. He it was, too, who proved unable to the end to bridle his truly Mediterranean temperament—who could not refrain from exclaiming: "If there had been just one single honest triad in the whole piece!" Obviously his teaching activities gave him too little opportunity to hear such honest triads, and he had come hoping to find them in my *Pierrot*. Am I to blame for his disappointment?

I have to think it possible that the Italian public did not know what to make of my music. But the image of a concert where there was hissing—in twenty-five years I have seen it so often that I may be believed—was always as follows: in the front third of the hall, roughly, there was little applause and little hissing; most people sat unconcerned, many stood looking around in amazement or amusement toward the parts of the hall farther back, where things were livelier. There the applauders were in the majority—there were fewer unconcerned, and a few hissers. But the most noise, both applause and hisses, always came from the standing space at the back and from the galleries. It was there that the people instructed or influenced by the expert judges went into battle against those who were impressed.

And yet I never had the impression that the number of people hissing was particularly great. It never sounded full, like a chord of solid applause entering with precision, but more like an ad-hoc group of ill-assorted soloists, the extent of whose ensemble was limited to the fact that their noises told one the direction they were approaching from.

That was how I saw the public, and in no other way, except when, as today with my older works, they applauded. But besides a number of very pleasant letters I receive now and then, I also know the public from another side. Perhaps I may end by relating a few pleasing little experiences. When just drafted to a reserve company during the war, I, the conscript, who had had many a bad time, once found myself treated with striking mildness by a newly arrived sergeant. When he addressed me after we had drilled, I hoped I was going to be praised for my progress in all things military. There followed a blow to my soldierly keenness; surprisingly, the tribute was to my music. The sergeant, a tailor's assistant in civil life, had recognized me, knew my career, many of my works, and so gave me still more pleasure than by praising my drill (even though I was not a little proud of that!). There were two other such meetings in Vienna: once when I had missed a train and had to spend the night in a hotel, and again when a taxi was taking me to a hotel. I was recognized the first time by the *night porter*, the other time by the *taxi driver*, from the name on the label of my luggage. Both assured me enthusiastically that they had heard the *Gurrelieder*. Another time, in a hotel in Amsterdam, a *hired man* addressed me, saying that he was a long-standing admirer of my art; he had sung in the choir in the *Gurrelieder* when I conducted them in Leipzig. But the prettiest story last: a short while back, again in a hotel, the *elevator operator* asked me whether it was I who had written *Pierrot lunaire*. For he had heard it before the war (about 1912), at the first performance, and still had the sound of it in his ears, particularly of one piece where red jewels were mentioned ("rote fürstliche Rubine"). And he had heard at the time that musicians had no idea what to make of the piece—the sort of thing that was quite easy to understand nowadays.

It strikes me that I need not alter what I believe about the semi-ignorant, the expert judges; I may continue to think they lack all power of intuition.

But whether I am really so unacceptable to the public as the expert judges always assert, and whether it is really so scared of my music—that often seems to me highly doubtful.

Translated by Leo Black

To William S. Schlamm (1945)

Los Angeles, June 26, 1945

Dear Mr. Schlamm:

That, and why, I am glad about your invitation: to become a charter contributor of the New Magazine: that, and why, I agree with almost everything in your exposé I can show with one basic principle of my thinking:

I believe in the right of the smallest minority.

Because democracy often acts in a manner resembling dangerously something like a "dictatorship of the (very often extremely small) majority," it is impossible, in spite of the freedom of the press, to publish ideas which do not fit into the frame of one of the greater parties; ideas, whose truth might manifest itself only in five, ten, thirty, [one] hundred years; perhaps only at a time, when, to their author, they have become already obsolete!

I am very anxious to know the topics you expect to receive from me, to discuss these and my own, if possible, in a personal meeting.

As a composer, of course, I write ordinarily much about the theory, technique, aesthetics, and ethics of composing. Thus, for example, I have recently started an extensive essay which I plan calling "Theory of Performance" (*Aufführungslehre*). In many respects polemical, predominantly it will establish aesthetic (and ethical) categories, principles and yardsticks in a field which to my knowledge has not yet been tilled. It discusses, for instance, the problem whether, when, and why a composition needs a performer; whether interpretation (rendition: *Auffassung*) is desirable or inevitable; I will explain theoretically and technically the way to produce various musical characters (dolce, grazioso, pathétique, scherzando, etc.); explain tempo and its modifications—and many other pertinent subjects. This might, I am afraid, grow to become a book—!

There is a smaller essay I have started, perhaps to be called "Form in Music Serves for Comprehensibility," denying form the effect of beauty.

I have started a smaller essay explaining that, and why audiences, misled by critics, overestimate performers at the expense of the creators.

I plan rewriting an essay on copyright, stating the injustice of this law, which allows the theft of a creator's property, after a certain period: a period which in most cases deprives a creator of the right to bequeath his heirs his property; and which is especially cruel in cases when recognition has been denied to an author during his lifetime.

I intend writing on the question whether today's musicologists cultivate science as they do not much more but explore in a sterile manner the musical past. In contrast to that, the theory of musical composition is not only the grammar, syntax, and philology of the musical language, but, most important, teaches functional organization.

If it is art, it is not for the masses.

"If it is for the masses it is not art" is a topic which is rather similar to a word of yourself on p. 7.

"Neuen Wein in alte Schläuche" (how can one translate this?) ["New wine in old vessels"] is one of my "favored dislikes."

I hope I have now answered all your questions.

I am looking forward to your kind reply, so that I might know your reaction to the subject I could name.

I am,

With kindest regards, yours sincerely,
Arnold Schoenberg

Written in English

To Josef Rufer (1947)

Los Angeles, December 18, 1947
. . . It's frightful that the Russians should be causing such difficulties. They would do better to put their own house in order, instead of disturbing world peace, in so far as there is such a thing.

I am no communist, as you know, and have never hoped for any good from communism. But I did think the leaders of that party had more common sense, more political sense, than to throw their weight about like this.—Have you read anything about Eisler and his brother? Do you know anything about the views he had in his Berlin days? I shouldn't like to damage him any more than he has already damaged himself here. But it's really too stupid of grown-up men, musicians, artists, who honestly ought to have something better to do, to go in for theories about reforming the world, especially when one can see from history where it all leads. I hope that all in all they won't take him too seriously here. Certainly I never took him seriously, I always regarded those tirades as a form of showing off. If I had any say in the matter I'd turn him over my knee like a silly boy and give him twenty-five of the best and make him promise never to open his mouth again but to stick to scribbling music. That he has a gift for, and the rest he should leave to others. If he wants to appear "important," let him compose important music. . . .

Arnold Schönberg

Translated by Eithne Wilkins and Ernst Kaiser

My Attitude toward Politics (1950)

I am at least as conservative as Edison and Ford have been. But I am, unfortunately, not quite as progressive as they were in their own fields.

In my early twenties, I had friends who introduced me to Marxian theories. When I thereafter had jobs as *Chormeister*—director of men's choruses—they called me "Genosse"—comrade, and at this time, when the Social Democrats fought for an extension of the right of suffrage, I was strongly in sympathy with some of their aims.

But before I was twenty-five, I had already discovered the difference between me and a laborer; I then found out that I was a bourgeois and turned away from all political contacts.

I was much too busy with my own development as a composer, and, I am sure, I could never have acquired the technical and aesthetic power I developed had I spent any space of time to politics. I never made speeches, nor propaganda, nor did I try to convert people.

When the First World War began, I was proud to be called to arms and as a soldier I did my whole duty enthusiastically as a true believer in the house of Hapsburg, in its wisdom of 800 years in the art of government and in the consistency of a monarch's lifetime, as compared with the short lifetime of every republic. In other words, I became a monarchist. Also at this time and after the unfortunate ending of the war and for many years thereafter, I considered myself as a monarchist, but also then did not participate in any action. I was then and thereafter only a quiet believer in this form of government, though the chances for a restoration were at zero.

Evidently when I came to America such considerations were superfluous. My viewpoint since then has been one of gratitude for having found a refuge. And I decided that I, as only a naturalized citizen, had no right to participate in the politics of the natives. In other words, I had to stand by and to be still. This, I have always considered to be the rule of my life. But I was never a communist.

Written in English

Anton Webern

The Path to Twelve-Note Composition (1932)

I didn't invent the title you've seen. It's Schönberg's. This year I was to talk in Mondsee on this subject, so I had a brief correspondence with Schönberg about what such a lecture should be called. He suggested "The path to twelve-note composition."

We must know, above all, what it means: "twelve-note composition." Have you ever looked at a work of that kind? It's my belief that ever since music has been written, all the great composers have instinctively had this before them as a goal. But I don't want to trust you with these secrets straight away—and they really are secrets! Secret keys. Such keys have probably existed in all ages, and people have unconsciously had more or less of an idea of them.

Today I want to deal generally with these things. So what has in fact been achieved by this method of composition? What territory, what doors have been opened with this secret key? To be very general, it's a matter of creating a means to express the greatest possible unity in music. There we have a word we could discuss all day. Perhaps, after all, it's important to talk about these things— I mean things so general that everyone can understand them, even those who only want to sit and listen passively. For I don't know what the future has in store. . . .

Unity is surely the indispensable thing if meaning is to exist. Unity, to be very general, is the establishment of the utmost relatedness between all component parts. So in music, as in all other human utterances, the aim is to make as clear as possible the relationships

225

between the parts of the unity; in short, to show how one thing leads to another.

Turning now to music, it's to some extent historical. What is this "twelve-note composition?" And what preceded it? This music has been given the dreadful name "atonal music." Schönberg gets a lot of fun out of this, since "atonal" means "without notes"; but that's meaningless. What's meant is music in no definite key. What has been given up? The key has disappeared!

Let's try to find unity! Until now, tonality has been one of the most important means of establishing unity. It's the only one of the old achievements that has disappeared; everything else is still there. Now we shall try to probe deeper into this story.

So: what is music? Music is language. A human being wants to express ideas in this language, but not ideas that can be translated into concepts—*musical* ideas. Schönberg went through every dictionary to find a definition of an "idea," but he never found one. What is a musical idea? [Webern here whistles the folk song "Kommt ein Vogerl geflogen."] That's a musical idea! Indeed, man only exists insofar as he expresses himself. Music does it in musical ideas. I want to say something, and obviously I try to express it so that others understand it. Schönberg uses the wonderful word "comprehensibility" (it constantly occurs in Goethe!). Comprehensibility is the highest law of all. Unity must be there. There must be means of ensuring it. All the things familiar to us from primitive life must also be used in works of art. Men have looked for means to give a musical idea the most comprehensible shape possible. Throughout several centuries one of these means was tonality, since the seventeenth century. Since Bach, major has been distinguished from minor. This stage was preceded by the church modes, that's to say seven keys in a way, of which only the two keys, like genders, finally remained. These two have produced something that's above gender, our new system of twelve notes.

Returning to tonality: it was an unprecedented means of shaping form, of producing unity. What did this unity consist of? Of the fact that a piece was written in a certain key. It was the principal key, which was selected, and it was natural for the composer to be anxious to demonstrate this key very explicitly. A piece had a keynote: it was maintained, it was left and returned to. It constantly reappeared, and this made it predominant. There was a main key in the exposition, in the development, in the recapitulation, etc. To crystallize out this main key more definitely, there were codas, in which the main key kept reappearing. I have to keep picking out these things because I'm discussing something that's disappeared. Something had to come and restore order.

There are two paths that led unavoidably to twelve-note composition; it wasn't merely the fact that tonality disappeared and one needed something new to cling to. No! Besides that, there was another very important thing! But for the moment I can't hope to say in one word what it is. Canonic, contrapuntal forms, thematic development can produce many relationships between things, and that's where we must look for the further element in twelve-note composition, by looking back at its predecessors.

The most splendid example of this is Johann Sebastian Bach, who wrote *The Art of the Fugue* at the end of his life. This work contains a wealth of relationships of a wholly abstract kind; it's the most abstract music known to us. (Perhaps we are all on the way to writing as abstractly.) Although there's still tonality here, there are things that look forward to the most important point about twelve-note composition: a substitute for tonality.

What I'm telling you here is really my life-story. This whole upheaval started just when I began to compose. The matter became really relevant during the time when I was Schönberg's pupil. Since then a quarter of a century has already gone by, though.

If we want to find historically how tonality suddenly vanished, and what started it, until finally, one day, Schönberg saw by pure intuition how to restore order, then it was about 1908 when Schönberg's piano pieces op. 11 appeared. Those were the first "atonal" pieces; the first of Schönberg's twelve-note works appeared in 1922. From 1908 to 1922 was the interregnum: fourteen years, nearly a decade and a half, this stage lasted. But already in the spring of 1917—Schönberg lived in the Gloriettegasse at the time, and I lived quite near—I went to see him one fine morning, to tell him I had read in some newspaper where a few groceries were to be had. In fact I disturbed him with this, and he explained to me that he was "on the way to something quite new." He didn't tell me more at the time, and I racked my brains—"For goodness' sake, whatever can it be?" (The first beginnings of this music are to be found in the music of *Jacob's Ladder*.)

I'm sure it will be very useful to discuss the last stage of tonal music. We find the first breach in sonata movements, where the main key often has some other key forced into it like a wedge. This means the main key is at times pushed to one side. And then at the cadence. What is a cadence? The attempt to seal off a key against everything that could prejudice it. But composers wanted to give the cadence an ever more individual shape, and this finally led to the breakup of the main key. At first one still landed in the home key at the end, but gradually one went so far that finally there was no longer any feeling that it was necessary really to return to the main key. At first one did think, "Here I am at home—now I'm going out—I look around me—I can wander off as far as I like while I'm about it—until I'm back home at last!" The fact that cadences were shaped ever more richly, that instead of chords of the sub-dominant, dominant, and tonic, one increasingly used substitutes for them, and then altered even those—it led to the breakup of tonality. The substitutes got steadily more independent. It was possible to go into another tonality here and there. (When one moved from the white to the black keys, one wondered, "Do I really have to come down again?") The substitutes became so predominant that the need to return to the main key disappeared. All the works that Schönberg, Berg, and I wrote before 1908 belong to this stage of tonality.

"Where has one to go, and does one in fact have to return to the relationships implied by traditional harmony?"—thinking over points like these, we had the feeling, "We don't need these relationships any more, our ear is satisfied without tonality too." The time was simply ripe for the disappearance of tonality. Naturally this was a fierce struggle; inhibitions of the most frightful kind had to be overcome, the panic fear, "Is that possible, then?" So it came about that gradually a piece was written, firmly and consciously, that wasn't in a definite key any more.

You're listening to someone who went through all these things and fought them out. All these experiences tumbled over one another, they happened to us unselfconsciously and intuitively. And never in the history of music has there been such resistance as there was to these things.

Naturally it's nonsense to advance "social objections." Why don't people understand that? Our push forward *had* to be made, it was a push forward such as never was before. In fact we have to break new ground with each work: each work is something different, something new. Look at Schönberg! Max Reger certainly developed, too, as a man develops between his fifteenth year and his fortieth, but stylistically there were no changes; he could reel off fifty works in the same style. We find it downright impossible to repeat anything. Schönberg said, and this is highly revealing, "Suppose I'd written an opera in the style of the *Gurrelieder*?"

How do people hope to follow this? Obviously it's very difficult. Beethoven and Wagner were also important revolutionaries, they were misunderstood too, because they brought about enormous changes in style.

I've tried to make this stage really clear to you and to convince you that just as a ripe fruit falls from the tree, music has quite simply given up the formal principle of tonality.

Translated by Leo Black

Alban Berg

The Teacher (1912)

Genius functions didactically from the very start. Its discourse is instruction, its action is exemplary, its works are revelations. It embodies the teacher, the prophet, the messiah; and the spirit of language, which comprehends the essence of genius better than does the spirit of those who abuse language, grants the creative artist the title "master" and says of him that he creates a "school." This realization alone could convince our era of Arnold Schönberg's predestination for the teaching profession, if it were at all aware of the importance of this artist and human being. It is only natural that our era has no idea of this, for if it possessed the capacity to perceive, or had a sense for something so opposed to the essence of our age, like all that comes before its time: then there would be no difference between that era and eternity. And yet, only a prior recognition of the artist's predisposition to the vocation of teaching in general enables one to judge properly Schönberg's way of teaching in particular. Inseparable from his artistry and eminent humanity, this uniquely justified way of teaching is even further advanced by his pronounced will to the vocation, which, like every great artistic will—be it devoted to its own creative work, performance, criticism, or, finally, the field of teaching—must bring forth the greatest achievements. Fully appreciating this wonder, produced under such conditions and circumstances, would mean solving the puzzle of original genius and seeking to fathom the secrets of divinity, an undertaking which must founder on the impossibility of measuring the immeasurable, delimiting the limitless. It must forever remain a mere attempt, resembling the vain hope of portraying the beauty, abundance, and sublimity of the waves of the sea. Yielding to its infinite currents, the fortunate swimmer is carried out upon its highest waves toward eternity, leaving behind with ease and pride those who are dashed to pieces on the submerged rocks of their own mental-spiritual barrenness, or who remain behind in the safe harbor of their own temporality.

Translated by Michael Gilbert

Postscript Concerning *Wozzeck* (1927)

It is now ten years since I started to compose *Wozzeck;* already so much has been written about it that I can hardly say anything without plagiarizing my critics. I should like, however, to correct an error that arose in 1925 soon after it was produced and that has spread widely since.

I have never entertained the idea of reforming the structure of opera through *Wozzeck.* Neither when I started nor when I completed the work did I consider it a model for further efforts by any other composer. I never assumed or expected that *Wozzeck* should become the basis of a school.

I simply wanted to compose good music; to develop musically the contents of Georg Büchner's immortal drama; to translate his poetic language into music. Other than that, when I decided to write an opera, my only intention, as related to the technique of composition, was to give the theater what belongs to the theater. The music was to be so formed that at each moment it would fulfill its duty of serving the action. Even more, the music should be prepared to furnish whatever the action needed for transformation into reality on the stage. The function of a composer is to solve the problems of an ideal stage director. On the other hand this objective should not prejudice the development of the music as an entity, absolute, and purely musical. No externals should interfere with its individual existence.

That I accomplished these purposes by a use of musical forms more or less ancient (considered by critics as one of the most important of my ostensible reforms of the opera) was a natural consequence of my method. It was first necessary to make a selection from Büchner's twenty-five loosely constructed, partly fragmentary scenes for the libretto. Repetitions not lending themselves to musical variation were avoided. Finally, the scenes were brought together, arranged, and grouped in acts. The problem therefore became more musical than literary, and had to be solved by the laws of musical structure rather than by the rules of dramaturgy.

It was impossible to shape the fifteen scenes I selected in different manners so that each would retain its musical coherence and individuality and at the same time follow the customary method of development appropriate to the literary content. No matter how rich structurally, no matter how aptly it might fit the dramatic events, after a number of scenes so composed the music would inevitably create monotony. The effect would become boring with a series of a dozen or more formally composed entr'actes which offered nothing but this type of illustrative music, and boredom, of course, is the last thing one should experience in the theater.

I obeyed the necessity of giving each scene and each accompanying piece of entr'acte music—prelude, postlude, connecting link or interlude—an unmistakable aspect, a rounded off and finished character. It was imperative to use everything essential for the creation of individualizing characteristics on the one hand, and coherence on the other. Hence the much discussed utilization of both old and new musical forms and their application in an absolute music.

The appearance of these forms in opera was to some degree unusual, even new. Nevertheless novelty, pathbreaking, was not my conscious intention. I must reject the claim of being a reformer of the opera through such innovations, although I do not wish to depreciate my work thereby, since others who do not know it so well can do that much better.

What I do consider my particular accomplishment is this. No one in the audience, no matter how aware he may be of the musical forms contained in the framework of the opera, of the precision and logic with which it has been worked out, no one, from the moment the curtain parts until it closes for the last time, pays any attention to the various fugues, inventions, suites, sonata movements, variations, and passacaglias about which so much has been written. No one gives heed to anything but the vast social implications of the work which by far transcend the personal destiny of Wozzeck. This, I believe, is my achievement.

Translated by Willi Reich

On the Hundredth Anniversary of Franz Schubert's Death (1928)

How fundamentally my attitude toward the music of Franz Schubert differs from the prevailing one is already evident in the fact that I suffer a hernia every time his name is mentioned in the same breath with that of Johann Strauss. One encounters this juxtaposition above all in Vienna, but also anywhere else this "city of music" is considered to be a part of heaven, which—as everyone knows—is bedecked with violins for which Schubert and Johann Strauss wrote their immortal melodies.

If this be granted—and I'm even willing to concede that the "Unfinished Symphony" could only have been produced along "the beautiful blue Danube"—doesn't it constitute an obvious sin against the Holy Spirit to be incapable of discerning the infinite distance separating the music of the one—who died in closest proximity to Beethoven—from that of the other, who never, even in the most favored moments of his life, entirely broke away from the people?

But perhaps this lack of artistic judgment isn't so surprising at a time like this, when even such people as we ourselves don't know whether to opt for a Three-Penny Opera or a Ten Thousand Dollar Symphony.

In any event, it is only right and proper—that is to say, it serves us right and doesn't cost very much—to commemorate festively the year in which Franz Schubert has been dead for a century, and in which Berté would have turned seventy. My congratulations!

Translated by Michael Gilbert

On Mahler's Ninth Symphony (1936)

. . . I have once again played through Mahler's Ninth. The first movement is the most magnificent of all the music that Mahler wrote. It is the expression of an unprecedented love for the earth, of a yearning to live upon it in peace, to enjoy it—nature—to the utmost, unto its most profound depths, for now—before death comes. For it is coming ineluctably. This entire movement is guided by the premonition of death. Again and again this foreboding is announced. In it culminate all the reveries *of this earth* (thus the passages which build and always erupt like new ebullitions following the most tender moments)—most powerfully, of course, at the tremendous point at which this *premonition* of death becomes *certainty,* where in the midst of the "greatest power" of a most painful lust for life, death announces itself "with greatest force"—to that end the frightening viola and violin solo and these knightly sounds: death in armor. Against this there can be no further rebellion.—What now happens suggests resignation to me—always with the thought of the hereafter, which appears in the "misterioso" passage (pages 44–45) as if in very thin air—*yet higher* than the mountains—indeed, as if in rarefied space. And once again, for the last time, Mahler turns his attention to the earth—no longer to the battles and deeds *which he, as it were, brushes away from himself*—(as already in *The Song of the Earth,* with its chromatically descending morendo runs)—but rather, *entirely* and *exclusively* to nature. For as long as the earth still offers him something of its treasures, he wants to enjoy it: he desires, far from all tribulations, to create a home in the free, thin air of the Semmering, in order to inhale this air, this purest air of the earth, with ever deeper breaths—ever deeper draughts, so that this heart, this most magnificent heart that ever beat among the likes of man, *expands*—expands *ever further*—before it must cease to beat———

Translated by Michael Gilbert

Paul Dessau

America (ca. 1970)

In the U.S.A. I did one film of my own; otherwise I worked for other people. This was called "nigger work" there. One of the composers didn't finish something and said to me: "Do two or three sequences for me of the twenty-five that I have to turn in." So I did two or three sequences and got about fifty dollars per sequence. I did this, for example, with Waxman. He was one of the many Hollywood composers.

At that time I also gave piano lessons for three dollars an hour. Over here there's still a picture with a little girl. She later became a movie star and a celebrity. I also taught in a settlement house, a type of home for children whose parents were poor and unable to look after their children because of their jobs. Later I worked at a real school in New York, where the traditional repertoire was taught.

That was the period when I became acquainted with Arnold Schönberg. In Los Angeles, where I went on Brecht's advice, I helped Schönberg read his lectures. That was a funny story. Schönberg's eyes were very weak; he really couldn't see very well, and that hindered him in the presentation of his lectures. He was supposed to deliver lectures in Chicago and urgently needed the honorarium. The pension which he received amounted to only a few dollars per month and after all, he had a family of five, didn't he? Two sons and a daughter, that's five people—I mean, he simply couldn't live on it. So it came about that he said: "I can't give these lectures." At that time I was working at Warner Brothers as a "nigger," writing out scores for Waxman, and had my own office. Without a secretary but with a typewriter, and that was a huge old thing—like a machine gun. It just stood there and I didn't use it. I only noticed that it had extraordinarily large letters. When Schönberg then said to me that he wasn't able to read his lectures because the type was too small, I said: "Herr Schönberg, by chance I've discovered in my studio at Warner Brothers a typewriter with very large letters." "Oh," he said, "that's just nonsense," but nevertheless he let me try it out.

In the morning I came into my studio; the door across the hall stood wide open—in America the office doors were always open, which was very pleasant since you didn't need to knock but simply walked right in—and two attractive young women were lying there on the sofa. I went by and said: "What a life you lead here! What are you doing?" "Nothing at all. Right now we have a break." My small office was just across the way and I said, "Come on over here, I have something for you." I then gave them the essays by Schönberg. They typed up nice clean copies for me, and in return for this I gave them piano lessons. That was "barter"—as they said there—a real swap, right? They type, I give them piano lessons. And that's the way things worked out. We became friends—they were two nice young women—and I was able to bring Schönberg the copies. He was satisfied, and in return for this I received manuscripts from him, music with dedications, and so forth.

As a result he was able to hold his lectures in Chicago. That was a vital necessity for the man—and also for those who heard him speak!

One was a lecture of approximately one and one-half hours in length, in which he gave an excellent analysis of his work, with musical examples—a kind of introduction to his work in general, which was certainly much less widely known then than it is today. For our musicians' ears his "Variations" are really no problem at all any more, and it would be important for us to also do something like that sometime. But it takes a Schönberg to prepare such a lecture. Those were the "Variations" in whose introduction the notes "B-A-C-H" [i.e., B♭-A-C-B] appear. Schönberg always said: "If you have a major work in mind, you must first call upon your guardian spirit." He loved Bach, his "guardian spirit," and he could afford to invoke him.

Translated by Michael Gilbert

Theodor W. Adorno (ca. 1970)

I came into contact with Adorno in America through Eisler. Eisler was just writing the book on film music with him. My contact was casual. I've always been a one-sided and deliberate person in contrast to Hanns, who was far more adept in these matters. I became acquainted with Adorno, and I must say that you could learn a great deal from him. Granted, I know only a few people who have such a degree of education and knowledge. When I ran into him later, I often found him boring. He would speak, and I always had to think of Hindemith's comment—in strong Mainz dialect: "He's too smart for his own good." I always claim that this was one of Hindemith's best remarks. It's not entirely true, but I also felt somewhat the same way: these priestly airs, this measured delivery. Each word weighed as if it were gold. I never went to a lecture again.

Translated by Carol Poore

Bertolt Brecht (ca. 1970)

To collaborate with Brecht was the dream of a lifetime for me. When I got to know *Flight of the Lindberghs* and *The Yes-Man* by Weill and other things while in Berlin in the late twenties—not to mention *The Three-Penny Opera*—I was fascinated.

I became casually acquainted with Brecht in Baden-Baden at the time of *Little Mahagonny*. He was sitting on a bar stool wearing a white suit and smoking a cigar; we said good evening to each other and I met a friendly young man. And there the matter rested, for I knew exactly what I was doing by not wanting to push for a meeting with him. A friend of mine, an Austrian and a student of Webern, had told me that he had once gone to see Brecht to do something together with him—and Brecht had told him: "At the moment I'm very busy for the next two years." It was a polite refusal, and I kept my thoughts to myself.

I knew quite well that I didn't yet possess the necessary maturity to meet with the man and ask him to work with me. I sensed this on the basis of my entire output at that time. I wasn't that far along yet—politically, artistically; I still had a lot to learn. At that time

I was writing my own texts, for example the *Children's Cantata.* I would surely have been turned away, just like my Austrian friend, and that certainly would have harmed the prospects for our later collaboration. It would have been easy for me to go to Brecht, right? He would have said: "Sir, that doesn't interest me," since he was busy with Eisler and Weill at the time. I added all this up and said to myself: not now. And then, when I met him in New York in 1942, I was prepared. I had composed the "Song of Joan" from *St. Joan of the Stockyards,* and finished the music for *99%,* later known as the *Fear and Misery of the Third Reich.* That's eight songs, after all—and that was a basis for speaking with the man. . . .

I was not only a violinist, rehearsal pianist, and conductor while in exile; I also sang publicly, my own chansons and songs.

Then a man came to me—Alexan was his name—and said: "Dessau, Brecht is coming to New York next week and is doing a performance. He'll need some music for it; what things by Brecht have you composed?" To this I replied: "I have this and that; I don't like the one too much, but I have here this song from *St. Joan.*" Whereupon he promised to arrange a rendezvous with Brecht. He did so, and three days later I met Brecht on the bank of the Hudson. I sang the song for him, and he approved. I then suggested a female vocalist to him; Brecht rehearsed it with her, and two days before the performance she backed out. Whereupon Brecht said: "Splendid! She's no good anyway, so sing it yourself! Eisler always does it that way too." He knew this would get me— I really do like to sing!

Translated by Michael Gilbert

Models (ca. 1970)

I like people who are courageous. I don't like people who keep their opinions to themselves. I like people who are open, who take risks. I am a Communist. That means that I know our weltanschauung won't advance at all unless we have courageous people at work. And we have wonderful models—take Pablo Neruda. Unfortunately, I've only set four of his poems to music, but these include one of his finest works, "To My Party." Or think of Karl Liebknecht and Rosa Luxemburg, or Ernst Thälmann, not to mention Lenin. These are people you can rely on.

For the hundredth anniversary of Lenin's birth, I tried to arrange his favorite piece, the *Appassionata,* for orchestra. It ends very softly. Does he need me to celebrate this occasion with trumpets and drums? My audience can surely follow the thoughts much better if the music is soft than if I pound it into their ears. I think our music contains too few *piano* passages and far too few rests, which would provide time for thought. Heroism does not always have to be loud. It can also be very quiet. Loudness usually expresses a guilty conscience. I once called it the technique of the Brandenburg Gate or of the Victory Avenue, which has fortunately been destroyed.

I like courageous people, and I like talented people. I don't like those who are only semitalented. Perhaps I myself am only semitalented, and that's why sometimes I don't like myself. But then you just have to work on yourself enough to get closer to yourself. That's what interests me. And that's what moves me to go back to my desk, again and again. I know what my great predecessors have done better than I. Actually, if one really grasped this, one wouldn't be able to work at all. But that won't do. In my experience, composing can steadily improve somewhat from day to day, and it is an enormously enriching activity. If one's conception of the world is right—and the notes.

Translated by Carol Poore

Paul Hindemith

To Gertrud Hindemith (1939)

[Los Angeles] March 27, 1939

My dearest Pushu,

. . . When I was here last month, everything I heard about the music industry seemed more or less funny to me. I've laughed myself to tears again about many things—especially Toch's detailed stories. But all of this is more than just disgraceful. The whole thing is a nightmare—gold-digger's madness. Anybody you see and talk to is trying to find one of the gold nuggets lying around. Whoever gets to the golden trough for just one minute, whether through agents, friends, racketeering, or just coincidence, stuffs himself full— since he will perhaps (or even probably) wait for years and years for another lucky break. Some, who together with directors and momentarily shining stars have made it to the top via the well-known route of the bar or bed, are earning a fortune. Almost all of them are totally worthless; many of the brilliant composers (people swear to me) have given up trying to learn what a sixth chord is—they can't get it into their heads. Small-time orchestral musicians who crowd around the huge cadaver of this artistic carcass like little dung beetles beneath a dead donkey are earning up to $1,000 a week; one orchestral bassoonist here has two black servants and a cook all to himself. Nowhere are ability and quality taken into consideration—everything depends on whether you hit upon the current taste of the masses, or what is thought to be current. Others get money but write nothing; most of them sit there and wait in vain for the golden blessing. The whole enterprise is very similar to the way herrings spawn. Hundreds of thousands of tiny, worthless little eggs swim around in the big pool, and each one waits for the glorious moment when the producer sprays his invigorating piss all over them. A few are then fertilized, while the rest can drop dead. And what comes out in the end is really not worth much more than herring. Even Disney, who clearly towers over the others with his aims and type of work, is despondent. I was together with Fischinger one evening, and what he had to say was so discouraging that I was happy when the enclosed letter from Disney arrived (I had written him from New York). Even if everything here were splendid and promising, the question would still arise as to whether one could work with a man who is such an exacting craftsman. I think I've been cured of the idea of doing something with film here (an idea based on the completely crazy notion of producing something of artistic value). You can't do that seriously here. The only question left open is whether one should accept an offer at some point for purely financial reasons. But the likelihood of getting such an offer is so slight that you'd be better off directing your efforts towards another goal.

In this huge city, there is no musical life worth speaking of apart from the movie business. There isn't even a real music school. Klemperer is conducting the orchestra, but that's as isolated a case as the legendary tree in the Odenwald. There isn't any educated musical society or even an interested or sustaining organization in the background here, unless you consider the usual crowd of fat old ladies, the board of trustees of whatever. I always get slightly ill when—as I have repeatedly witnessed—such a gussied-up meat patty goes before the orchestra and negotiates with it about hours, salaries, and artistic questions. A music director has no say at all in such matters. Still, for the training of future patron-cows there is a Junior League, consisting of not yet overripe ladies who are assigned the task of raising money to cover this year's deficit of $150,000, partly out of their own pocketbooks and partly through fund-raising appeals. On Friday morning I had to do the usual question-and-answer gibberish for half an hour at their meeting. It wasn't as abysmally ridiculous as usual in that there were clearly a few pretty figures beneath the furs of every imaginable bi- and quadruped, under those dried plums, the mousetraps, breakfast croissants, dumplings, and clumps of licorice (and whatever else they wore as hats, with brightly colored thirty-inch long feathers), and behind the plastered-on lipstick, the reddish-blue fingernails, the flushed red cheeks, and eyelashes rolled together like the tips of Mikosch's mustache. [Richard] Lert, at any rate a name, and for years the music director of the Berlin State Opera, even if he wasn't first-rate, is conducting something like an orchestra of half-dilettantes in Pasadena, while Schönberg is teaching beginning harmony at the university (which serves him right). All of the once great minds are fumbling around this way, like the municipal music director of the well-known town Kyritz on the Knatter, with the one difference that the Knatter, when compared to the Los Angeles River, surpasses the Castilian well in terms of fecundity about like the Main does the Königsbrünnche. . . .

Farewell, dear!
Your Y.

Translated by Michael Gilbert

Preface to *Elementary Training for Musicians* (1946)

The music student entering a class in harmony is in general insufficiently prepared with respect to basic principles—governing Rhythm, Meter, Intervals, Scales, Notation—and their correct application. In all phases of his teaching, the harmony teacher has to face the fact that his students have no solid foundation to build upon. There is little doubt that, save in a few exceptional cases, the methods by which those basic principles are taught are deplorable. Most musicians pick up what they know of these things at random, along with their accumulating knowledge of more "practical" musical matters. Others do go through courses in Elementary Training, but in general these courses provide hardly more than a certain amount of casual information, and even if in some subsequent courses in Dictation a weak attempt is made to fill the gaps left open in the beginning, no real fundamental knowledge can be gained by so defective a method.

This book seeks to provide exercises which—if applied in the right way—must infallibly supply such fundamental theoretical knowledge. It is by no means the first comprehensive attempt to discuss elementary material. It does not even pretend to present this material in an original form. Its content has been set forth and explained countless times before, and there are some excellent books on the subject in various languages. But in order to understand the best works in this field and to make the proper use of them, one must already be a fairly advanced musician. Such a musician will find in them a remarkably good survey of the basic material, but a beginner will hardly be in a position to digest the overwhelming mass and variety of facts and procedures, or to select what is useful for him. Moreover, the exercises given in such books (when any are given) are insufficient.

There is, on the other hand, no lack of less comprehensive, more specialized works, full of exercises for the beginner. But here the difficulty is that those books that try to give general theoretical instruction are either antiquated, in opinion and approach, or insufficient for a professional's education; and in most cases their exercises seem to be made for the author's satisfaction and self-assertion rather than for the student's profit, or they are so dry that even the most docile user cannot see their relationship to living music.

There are numerous highly specialized text-books on Dictation, Sight-Singing and Sight-Reading, Ear-Training, Clef-Reading, and other subdivisions of our subject. But anyone who wished to collect his knowledge by picking it grain by grain out of comparatively elaborate books on comparatively minor subjects would have to spend years on that part of his musical education—which, after all, is but a preparation for more important things to come.

A musician brought up on the method of Solfège, as practised in countries under the influence of French or Italian musical culture, will probably deny that there could be any better method. And if one knows the comparatively high standard in sight-reading of melodic and rhythmic patterns (even higher in the rapid pronounciation of the solmisation syllables!) reached by students of this method, one is tempted to agree. But the disadvantages of this method show up later in the musician's course of study: it is extremely difficult to introduce students so trained to a higher conception of harmony and melody, and to bring them to a certain independence in their own creative work. They either cannot take the step out of their narrow concept of tonality (which by the uniform nomenclature for a tone *and* all its derivations is distorted almost to the point where reason turns into nonsense!), or they plunge more easily than others into what is assumed to be a new freedom: tonal disorder and incoherence.

There are still other methods which try to remedy the weakness of Solfège by expressing through all kinds of symbols (in writing, speech, and gesture) the meanings of the scale tones. These range from primitive information for amateurs to most consistently developed "functional" systems. The first category is negligible for the professional musician—unless he wants to specialize in the teaching of amateurs—since it leads him no further than the first steps in the spatial and temporal conception of music. The second category erects in addition to (or instead of) our normal everyday elementary training other systems of theory, the assimilation of which takes more effort and time than the musician not specializing in theory can well afford.

No textbook, whatever the honest intentions of its author, and whatever the quality of its plan and contents, will remain uncriticized. I can easily foresee what the objections to the present book will be.

It will be said that the book is too comprehensive to be used by everyone. The student seeking only some superficial information does not want to digest too many uninteresting things. The highly specialized musician of today, knowing thoroughly the facts and procedures in his particular field of activity, cannot be expected to know everything. Helpful as it may be for a future conductor to have some experience in reading the various clefs, it would be a waste of time for a pianist to bother with such special problems. To sing the right tones at the right time may prove valuable for a singer, but when will a violinist ever be asked to do so? The violinist, in turn, must learn to be fluent in reading high notes, with many ledger lines, while such fluency can be of no value to a timpanist. Essential prerequisites for a player in an orchestra may be utterly unimportant for a virtuoso; increased knowledge of theoretical facts will not instantly improve a cellist's playing; practical experience in music is not necessarily a criterion for the quality of a composer's or theorist's ideas.

There is only one answer to these objections: they are unfounded. The exercises in this book are, in the first place, not written for the amateur's superficial information (although this kind of work will do him no harm, if he is interested). The words "for musicians" in the book's title define clearly its purpose. On the other hand, objections to all-round elementary training for musicians—such as is attempted in this book—can be voiced only by those who acquiesce in the present wide-spread deterioration in musical education.

Apparently the times are gone when no one was considered a good musician who did not possess, beyond his specialized instrumental or vocal achievements, a thorough knowledge of the subtle mechanism of music. Can the majority of to-day's great virtuosi stand a comparison of their theoretical knowledge with Liszt's, Rubinstein's, or Joachim's? Do not many of them bitterly complain that in their youth they were trained excessively in their special craft and not sufficiently in general musical subjects? Theoretical knowledge certainly will not directly improve a violinist's finger-technique; but is it not likely to broaden his musical horizon and influence his ability to interpret a composition? If our performers—players, singers, and conductors alike—had a better insight into the essentials of musical scores, we would not be faced with what seems to have become almost a rule in the superficially over-polished performances of today: either the rattling through of a piece without any reasonable articulation, without any deeper penetration into its character, tempo, expression, meaning, and effect—or the hyper-individualistic distortion of the ideas expressed in a composer's score.

As for singers, nobody denies that most of them are launched on their careers not because they show any extraordinary musical talents, but because they happen to have good voices. On account of this advantage a singer is usually excused from any but the most primitive musical knowledge—knowledge such as could be acquired by any normal mind in a few weeks of intelligent effort. Rare indeed is the singer nowadays who can do what you would expect to be the most normal of all the activities of a singing musician: hit a tone at any interval, even if it is not part of a simple stepwise progression or an easily understandable broken-chord melody, and even if it is not directly supported by its accompaniment. Would a singer not profit by being led through a severe course of general musical training? It certainly would not hurt his voice to gain some additional knowledge, which, although it will not immediately further his vocal aims, amounts after all to no more than that minimum of basic facts that a professional musician is supposed to know.

Admittedly, a composer can have wonderful ideas without a background of highly developed practical experience. But is it really imaginable that without such experience he should be able to present his ideas in their strongest form, and exploit them to the fullest extent? Owing to the general decline of such experience, the composer, once venerated as a super-musician, nowadays occupies almost the lowest ranks of musicianship as far as handicraft is concerned. How few are the composers of today whose achievements are based on their activities as players or singers—in bygone times considered the only sound and stable basis for creative work! All too often we see it happen that a fellow who is not good enough—physically or intellectually—for any instrumental or vocal work still finds a comfortable and uncontested place in the field of composition. The decision to become a composer is in many cases based on no better musical talent than that of listening to records and turning them at the right time (when a mechanical record-changer doesn't eliminate even this last remainder of musical "activity"). Is it strange then, that any tootling, key-pounding, or merely victrola- and radio-active high-school boy who has not written his first symphony before he is through his first year of harmony is already looked on with scorn by his classmates?

I should think that in this situation any method would be welcomed that aimed at keeping our noble guild of composers free of the nitwits and the ungifted. No composer-to-be or future theory teacher who after some practising is not able to do the exercises in the present book easily and thoroughly should be admitted to more advanced theoretical work. In a higher sense he ought to be regarded as unfit for any professional musical activity—which process of reckless weeding out could only be advantageous to our entire musical culture.

For those, however, who by their natural musical gift and intelligence are eligible for any of the branches of musical activity, such a method will be the sound basis for their further musical development. They will find in the present book all a musician needs as a preparation for higher theoretical and practical studies, offered without detours and evasions. The book does not use solmisation syllables, since they are misleading. It avoids special names and fancy symbols, since they distract attention from the main object: the knowledge of all the basic conventions and facts of musical theory and their traditional representation in written form. This knowledge is presented through the most intensive kind of work: exercises. The great number of exercises compels the student to practise seriously. Thus it will be demonstrated that Elementary Theory cannot be learned by simply having superficial information handed out for one or two semesters, or without incessant exertion of the student's intellectual capacities. In his very first steps he must be converted from an attentive listener into a working musician. This can be accomplished only by making him articulate. The familiar type of theory class, in which one never hears a tone of music, sung or played, except for the chords pounded out on the piano by the teacher, must disappear! Such classes are as silly as is the usual splitting up of Elementary Training into separate courses of Instruction and Dictation, or of Harmony into "Written" and "Keyboard" courses. It certainly makes more demands upon a teacher to lead a class through an all-round course of theory or harmony, with its constant cross-references to the different sections of the student's activities, than to follow the comfortable, unimaginative path of a split-up course.

A lazy teacher will always present this excuse: How can a beginners' class be articulate if the students can neither sing nor play decently? The answer is that the teacher himself must make them sing and play—not like singers or advanced players, but so that they can open their mouths (willingly!) and produce tones just as any singer in a chorus does. It is quite common to find excellent instrumentalists (not to mention composers) who have gone through six or more years of practical and theoretical studies without ever having opened their mouths for the most natural of all musical utterances! What is true for singing is true for playing, too: every student can strike the keys of the piano enough to play primitive exercises, and if he is not constantly obliged to follow rules of fingering, hand position, and other technical directions, and if we give him time to practise those exercises, he may even develop a kind of unprejudiced, preliminary skill of playing, which can easily be used as a favorable preparation for future regular piano instruction. The same is true for all other instruments, on which, of course, many of the exercises can be played.

After these observations the aim of this book ought to be clear: it is *activity*. Activity for the teacher as well as for the student. Our point of departure is this advice to the teacher: Never teach anything without demonstrating it by writing and singing, or playing; check each exercise by a counter-exercise that uses other means of expression. And for the student: Don't believe any statement unless you see it demonstrated and proved; and don't start writing or singing or playing any exercise before you understand perfectly its theoretical purpose. To produce this kind of compelling activation demands some additional work from the teacher: the *statements* in this book are reduced to their shortest, most condensed form, which in most cases will be too difficult for the average student to understand. Hence the teacher is obliged to dilute and predigest this material, he must find his own way to a more detailed demonstration. The *exercises,* on the other hand, are to be used in the form presented; but, even so, ample opportunity is given for further activities. Frequently enough the teacher will face the necessity of inventing additional exercises, and the student's imagination is constantly spurred by the recurring remark "Invent similar examples." Particularly eager students will find supplementary tests for their wits and their zeal in certain sections of exercises, marked "More difficult." . . .

The book grew out of the demands of my classes in theory, and was written for the benefit of my students. Needless to say, then: all the examples have been tested thoroughly, and only those have been included that have proved their usefulness—this as an answer to the fears of the doubtful and the short-sighted.

New Haven, Conn.   Paul Hindemith
Yale University
Spring 1946

Written in English

Hanns Eisler

Ludwig van Beethoven (1927)

He was not a composer of the proletariat, but his music never-theless belongs to us, the ascending working class, not to the bourgeoisie.

He lived at a time when the bourgeois revolution had first to be accomplished, not the proletarian. But the powerful momentum of the great French Revolution, the resounding "Ça ira!" of the rev-olutionary song of the Parisian sansculottes, the victorious ad-vance of the French revolutionary armies against the united pow-ers of European monarchist reaction—the momentum of the young, strong, confident revolution—this Ludwig van Beethoven knew, understood, greeted, and captured in sound.

Beethoven came from the western part of Germany, from Bonn, along the Rhine. Far from the desolate, crude burden of decaying Prussian feudalism, far from the medieval, provincial obtuseness of central Germany, and free of the yoke of the corrupt and archreactionary Hapsburg monarchy, the Rhineland lay immedi-ately on *the border with France,* which at that time became the heart of Europe, the heart of civilized peoples: the France of the great Revolution.

Beethoven was born in 1770. His early manhood coincided with the period of revolutionary struggle. The effect this had upon the people born an entire generation later, but who still felt their af-tershocks in that fertile Rhineland, impregnated by the Revolu-tion—all this can be seen so well from the *Book Le Grand* of the young Heine. The revolutionary hymn, the Marseillaise, still resounds in his emphatic glorification of Napoleon—outwardly soft, to be sure, but in reality all-determining—and the Napoleonic pièce de résistance is called: the Red Guillotine March. To the young Heine, Napoleon was the general of the Revolution.

To the mature Beethoven in the prime of his life, the Emperor Napoleon was the *traitor of the Revolution*. It is not merely of anecdotal value, but rather of deeper significance for the man and artist Beethoven, that he furiously tore up the dedication of his Third Symphony when he learned that the Consul Napoleon had made himself Emperor. It had been dedicated to the Consul Bonaparte, the general of the victorious Revolution, the victorious enemy of reactionary Austria. It was called the *heroic symphony, "Eroica,"* and it retained this name, even after the author had struck out any reference to the hero Napoleon. Napoleon had been a hero to him not merely as a military commander, but rather as the commander of the Revolution, as leader of the war against the same Austria in whose capital Beethoven lived.

This is the kind of man he was: Even if he outwardly seemed to be on good terms with the artistically appreciative nobility, dignitaries, and the Hapsburg monarchy, he didn't hesitate in the least to dedicate his most recent work *to the mortal enemy of this monarchy in the midst of the war;* and he withdrew the dedication with equal decisiveness when his hero proved to be a traitor to the idea which alone had made him a hero to the composer. He ceased to be a hero, a hero of the Revolution when he became a hero of the new monarchy, self-made hero, a hero of the counterrevolution.

But the *Eroica* remained the work of a man who time and again celebrated in song the struggle and victory over the powers of darkness.

Such was the nature of the man the philistine bourgeoisie claimed to love. In every respect unlike another alleged darling of the philistines, Herr Privy Councillor Goethe, who sought in absurd farces to slur the Revolution, who submissively placed his most humble servitude at the feet of the *Emperor* Napoleon, who was a servant of princes and never comprehended that those wretched despots who ruled "by the grace of God" and before whom he fawningly bowed weren't worthy of cleaning the shoes of a man of the spirit. Again, it is of more than merely anecdotal value to know that Beethoven once promenaded in Karlsbad with Goethe, who bowed and scraped like a lackey before some princely personages, and reprimanded him with the observation that not these simpletons were princes, but rather those who had actually accomplished something.

Obstinate and independent, taciturn and strong, yet not introverted and egocentric.

The Third Symphony of the mature, *as yet young Beethoven* is called the *Eroica*. It glorifies the hero of the Revolution, and this hero is not an individual person but rather *the revolutionary people*.

The motto of his *last symphony*, however, *the Ninth*, the great work of the man on the threshold of old age, of the deaf composer left to all appearances to his own resources, is: "*Be embraced, O millions*, this kiss to the entire world!"

The Ninth Symphony concludes with the Schillerian ode "To Joy," and in the age of reaction one had to say joy if one meant freedom (as it also stood in the original text by Schiller). This greatest work by Beethoven concludes powerfully, certain of victory, rejoicingly, confidently, masculinely.

His music is strong, masculine music. For that reason we can say with complete justice that his music today, one hundred years after his death, also speaks to the proletariat, can convey energies to it.

His music is masculine, even at those points where it is tender, where it is intimate, where it is gentle. His tenderness is never without shape, formless, decadent. His musical thoughts are firmly rounded and clearly structured. Often, very often, the great simplicity of these thoughts is startling. Often they are borrowed from a *folksong*, or approximate a folksong in rhythm, melody, and form. And where peculiarities are evident that many would like to call romantic, it is precisely there that his music, in spite of all this, maintains firm, angular contours. Precisely at such moments (as for example in the great fugue of one of his last piano sonatas) it for the most part expresses a strong, forward-directed will.

Because his music is *life-affirming*, confident, strong, for that reason Beethoven, even a hundred years after his death, is a musician the proletariat can claim for itself.

Among the large number of his works, three groups stand out. He wrote works for piano solo, chamber music—in particular string quartets—and orchestral works. In addition, he wrote an opera, *Fidelio*.

This opera is a most unusual work, certainly for the time of its composition, and even today. The artistic genre of opera was always oriented toward courtly pomp and splendor, or else it dealt with some inconsequential love intrigues. Greek mythological matters were highly favored (Gluck)—subjects which didn't matter to the spectator in the least. The exceptions to this were few, for example Mozart's *Magic Flute* or also *Don Giovanni*. In later times as well—right up until our own time—one imposed upon the opera listener as texts mostly incredible nonsense; and the Wagnerian mythological texts also move in the direction of the nonsensically colossal.

Fidelio has often been referred to as the "Song of Songs of Conjugal Love." Such a designation, however, touches upon only one side of its content. The other shows us the struggle against tyranny and arbitrary despotism, and this is the actual content of Beethoven's only opera.

Of his chamber works only little is known to the workers, since chamber music is falsely regarded as an "aristocratic" art form. Once the chamber music organizations have taken up the task of playing Beethoven string quartets for the workers, it will quickly become evident that these works are understood by the workers. The same can be said of his numerous piano works, which need only be performed without virtuosic nonsense but with complete technical mastery to make a deep impression upon every music listener.

Of his orchestral works, the greatest, the Ninth Symphony, would perhaps be most readily and easily appreciated by the workers, as being close to them. Here, after three long, purely orchestral sections a large chorus is added in the final movement, just as if the composer had wanted to clothe his feelings and thoughts in readily graspable words and conceptually articulated thoughts. And when this tremendous hymn "To Joy" swells up, builds, and concludes rejoicingly, every class-conscious worker, filled with strength and confidence, can and must say to himself: These sounds, which already convey energies to us, the yet struggling workers, will properly belong to us once we have triumphed over the ruling class and jubilantly proclaim to the heretofore oppressed masses with Beethoven's song of victory: "Be embraced, O millions!"

Translated by Michael Gilbert

On Modern Music (1927)

The patient's death rattle is so boring that those dutifully assembled are falling asleep.

But their snoring also sounds like a death rattle, so it is difficult to say who's actually dying. That is the relationship of bourgeois society to modern music.

If you're wondering, however, who is actually dying, there's really only one answer: both of them.

Music has always been a decidedly communal art. It arose out of shared labor (work songs, providing for an even work rhythm), from festivals, rituals of religious cults, and dances.

At a time when the other arts—poetry and sculpture—were already highly developed and utilized very refined artistic means, as for example in Greco-Roman culture, music was still very simple and made use of quite primitive resources. For the development of music requires a high level of general technology, allowing for the construction of ever better instruments, which then make possible the presentation of richer, more complex sounds and tonal combinations.

The great blossoming of music as a communal art took place in the sixteenth, seventeenth, and eighteenth centuries. At that time music really did serve a community, as an important part of church services. The crisis of feudalism and finally the bourgeois revolution brought about a tremendous transformation in music as well; and in the nineteenth century, in Beethoven's time, music became more and more the expression of the personal feelings of the individual.

If the revolutionary individual was still expressing himself in Beethoven's music, in the following period it was really just as Heine said: "From my great pain I make my little songs." The purpose of music in the era of Romanticism was to express one's own personal experience or one's own most private weltanschauung. Examples of this: Schumann's lyric songs, Wagner's philosophical operas, and the symphonic music of Strauss and Mahler.

With the crisis of the bourgeoisie and the general crisis of capitalism, a new crisis of music sets in. The chapter Modern Music begins.

The most characteristic feature of modern music is this: In the postwar years, a number of truly revolutionary artists emerged in almost all of the arts. In their works these artists drew genuine consequences from the social situation. *In music this was and is not the case.* To this day there are no truly revolutionary musicians—no composers who have created genuinely revolutionary works. Among musicians, a mushy petty-bourgeois mentality or an urbane nihilism is becoming all-pervasive.

What, for example, did Richard Strauss, the greatest bourgeois musician, write following the war? A ballet: *Whipped Cream.* Content: breakfast rolls, etc. stage a revolt, led by matzos. Then a keg of Munich beer appears in a cloud and pours down its contents upon the agitated breakfast rolls. Result: all is bliss, and everyone dances the Munich heavy-beer roundelay. Or: Arnold Schönberg, this truly ingenious, so courageously forward-thrusting composer writes *Jacob's Ladder,* an oratorio. Escape into mysticism.

From 1918 to 1923, at the time of the great inflation, the Spartakus struggles, the Soviet Republics of Munich and Budapest, the Red Army at the gates of Warsaw, musicians only scuffled over purely technical matters. There wasn't one among them who felt so much as a touch of the spirit of these times.

The consequence of this "timelessness" and narrow-mindedness in music is that modern music has no public; no one wants it. As the private concern of well-bred people, it is a matter of indifference to the proletariat. The bourgeoisie is looking for stronger stimulants and forms of entertainment.

Hardly any other form of art leads the phantom existence that modern music does—one that can only be sustained by artificial means.

Of all of the arts, it is music which most emphatically expresses the dissolution of bourgeois culture. In spite of all technical refinements, it is becoming empty, for it is devoid of ideas and community. An art which loses its community loses itself.

The proletariat will simply have to create a new music for itself, using the experience and artistic resources of the bourgeoisie.

Translated by Michael Gilbert

Theses (ca. 1931)

1. Music is the organization of tones.
2. The organization of tones reflects the social situation. Changes in the methods of production and changes in class structure also bring about changes in the methods of organizing tones.
3. On the analysis of bourgeois music:
   i. The formalistic, reactionary tendencies correspond to petty-bourgeois ideology under the leadership of industrial capital. This ideology does not want to alter methods of organizing music from the end of the nineteenth century.
   ii. The new fascism in music. This extremely interesting trend rejects all music after Bach as the music of civilization. It also continues to oppose the bourgeois manner of consuming art. Just as fascism goes back politically to a social system organized around the estates, this direction falls back primarily on religious and folk music from the sixteenth to the eighteenth centuries. Its struggle is also directed against the social nature of bourgeois music, namely, the concert scene. This trend in music arrives at a clear political formulation. It aims at depoliticizing youth by means of the spirit of true German folk and art music.
   iii. The petty-bourgeois aesthetic trend (led politically by democrats, that is, by commercial capital). This trend is antagonistic to trend i. It opposes formalistic, reactionary tendencies and strives toward refining the techniques of bourgeois music. This leads as a matter of course to *l'art pour l'art*.
   iv. Left bourgeois music unites all the progressive tendencies of i, ii, and iii. It opposes the concert scene like no. ii, and it strives toward a new collectivity. For the most part, this

trend is eclectic and should be viewed as a kind of extreme liberalism. However, it includes some very interesting formal directions.

v. The workers' music movement is led politically by reformists and the petty bourgeoisie, by democrats, and it indiscriminately accepts all the musical opinions and products of each of the four trends described above. Its tendentious art is petty-bourgeois, red-tinged musical material. Formally more reactionary than progressive, and politically reformist, its condition can be best described as "confused." Its left opposition led by the Communist Party has not been able to develop a theoretical position yet, in spite of its political clarity.

4. Art music is the privilege of the ruling class. The economic situation of the proletariat invests music with a specific task. Music *qua* music demands the ownership of the musical means of production. The music of the proletariat can be only an applied art. It will utilize primarily the musical means of production that the working class possesses, namely, the human voice. The organized upswing in the German Workers' Singing Federation is indicative of this.

5. The first task, which must be undertaken most energetically, is the liquidation of tendentious music as a superstructure over outdated methods of the class struggle. Such music no longer corresponds to the latest developments in scientific socialism. This task is historically necessary and conditioned, but we cannot rely on the dialectical course of history to accomplish it. The liquidation of tendentious art is a very difficult cultural, political, and organizational task. Since tendentious music was always the front against the petty-bourgeois singing society, this struggle can be carried out only by demonstrating the petty-bourgeois component of tendentious music itself. The danger lies in furthering reactionary trends among the singing workers through incorrect tactics.

6. The dependence of changing musical style on history must be clarified—that is, the changing organization of tones.

7. The relationship between text and tone must be investigated.

8. The next debate and the next critical analysis must be directed against fascism in music and against left bourgeois music. This

polemic and this analysis can exploit the confusion in the workers' music movement. Therefore, it will be necessary to carry this discussion into the organizations of the workers' music movement.

Translated by Carol Poore

Statement (1947)

For the past five months I have found myself attacked and publicized to a very unusual degree. The reason for this campaign against me is clear. I am accused of being the brother of Gerhart Eisler. And I have stood by him. I shall continue to do so.

What are the facts? I arrived in Hollywood in 1942. My activities have been artistic activities. In addition to the chamber music, piano and orchestral works I composed in Hollywood, I wrote the musical score for nine motion pictures, including *Hangmen Also Die, Spanish Main,* and *None But the Lonely Heart.*

My knowledge of American politics is limited, and I have never dabbled in them. That does not mean that I am not interested in world affairs, or that I advocate the old theory that an artist should remain isolated in his ivory tower, for which it is becoming increasingly difficult to pay the rent anyway.

It is not surprising to me that due to the accident of my geographical situation—I am living in Hollywood—and the coincidence of my family ties, the House Un-American Activities Committee should find me a most convenient target for attack. But what does infuriate me, and what is most unfair in the announced investigation of my "Hollywood activities," is the attempt to intimidate and smear my friends and the artists with whom I have had professional contacts.

In Germany it had been necessary for an artist who wished to remain a living and an eating one (though not a corrupted one) to participate in this struggle as a musician, and my contribution was a modest one. My contact with politics and political parties has always been casual. But on all my concert tours, professional trips which took me whether to Amsterdam, Brussels, Copenhagen, Zurich, London, Madrid, Paris, New York, Prague, or

Moscow, I was received not only as a composer, but also as a co-fighter against the Nazis and their collaborators.

In my travels I met antifascists of every description: Communists, Social Democrats, Liberals, Monarchists and Confusionists—of all social strata. I saw mistakes and confusion, setbacks and defeats. It was a bitter time. What could I contribute? I was a musician, so I contributed music: songs, stage music, cantatas, and oratorios. I did my best to inspire all those who fought against the Nazi criminals. Among these were Communists, reliable fighters with good discipline, who fought heroically under the most complicated conditions, where mercy was not expected and mercy was not given. Neither the syndicated hysteria of a certain press with its smear campaigns, nor a House Committee on Un-American Activities will be able to intimidate me or prevent me from saying this.

And nobody can prevent me from stating my sympathy for labor. In my earliest childhood already I had heard my father speak with respect of labor. He was a distinguished philosopher, whose book, *The Encyclopedia of Philosophical Terminology,* is still considered a classic. My mother was the daughter of a worker. My father's philosophic attachment to labor was based on the works of Kant and Hegel, which he masterfully interpreted.

I was raised in the tradition of German classical music: Bach, Mozart, Beethoven. I realized how susceptible the greatest musicians have been to the spiritual trends of their times. Johann Sebastian Bach, in his B Minor Mass, in the *Passion According to St. John,* and in the *Passion According to St. Matthew,* gave voice to the incredible sufferings of the German people after the Thirty Years War. His musical style was a great progress from the cold, empty musical routine of his contemporaries. Mozart, for one of his most beautiful operas, chose a play by the radical playwright Beaumarchais. In his chamber music and symphonies he developed a new sensitivity and differentiation of musical language which was clearly a response to the ideas of his age, the "Age of Reason and Enlightenment."

In my student days, modern music had to fight hard battles against reaction, both cultural and political. When the Nazis came to power, they outlawed modern music, and if the great master,

Arnold Schoenberg, my teacher, had not succeeded in leaving Germany, he would have ended in the gas chambers of Auschwitz. Of course I wrote many compositions of concert character; symphonies, chamber music, orchestral suites, cantatas, oratorios, and piano pieces. But I am proud of those of my works which have been used in the great struggle against the threat of barbarism and destruction. And I am very grateful to my many friends in Hollywood who have stood by me in the present-day continuation of this same struggle.

(If the House Committee of Un-American Activities is interested in other facts of my life or my professional activities, it can find them in most standard music encyclopedias, or in *Who's News and Why 1942*, and without attempting to create a public hysteria.)

Written in English

Statement on Leaving the U.S.A. (1948)

I leave this country not without bitterness and infuriation. I could well understand it when in 1933 the Hitler bandits put a price on my head and drove me out. They were the evil of the period; I was proud of being driven out. But I feel heartbroken over being driven out of this beautiful country in this ridiculous way.

What am I accused of?

Of participating in the fight of the American people for the honest and lost causes?

Unfortunately not.

I am not accused of having fought against reaction and fascism in this country. I have not fought against those who want to involve the world in a new war.

I have not fought against the shamelessness and corruption and commercialism of a certain press and magazines which create a paper curtain separating the American people from political and economic realities.

I have not fought for the rights of veterans to get decent housing.

I have not fought against the impudence of profiteers who make the living of simple men unbearable. I have not fought for the classic tradition of this great country of upholding decency and freedom for the common man.

I have not fought against the shamelessness of the Taft-Hartley Bill.

I have not fought against the monopoly imposed on art: music, films, literature, radio.

I have not fought against corrupt political machines.

I have not fought against the radical discrimination oppressing my colored brothers.

I have not fought against anti-Semitism.

No, I am not accused of being a fighter.

My trouble started when I was subpoenaed a witness before the House Committee on Un-American Activities. I listened to the talk and the questions of these men and I saw their faces. As an old antifascist it became plain to me that these men represent fascism in its most direct form. That they represent the ignorance and barbarism which could lead to a new war. I was against them. There is a limit to the patience of an artist.

I saw these evil men trying to take over the affairs of this great country at a time really complicated and indeed dangerous for all of us. And I had to stand up against these men, regardless of consequences.

A composer knows that music is written by human beings for human beings and that music is a continuation of life, not something separated from it. And I had to defend music.

Now I am forced to leave. But I take with me the image of the real American people whom I love.

Written in English

Bertolt Brecht and Music (1957)

Brecht's rejection of certain sorts of music was so extreme that he invented another variety of music-making, which he called "misuc." Misuc he regarded as a way of music-making basically differing from music, since it is misuc and not music.

Brecht's efforts in this field were really based upon his dislike of

Beethoven's symphonies (though he loved the music of Bach and Mozart). For thirty years I tried to prove to him that Beethoven was a great master. He often admitted as much to me; but after doing so he was ill-tempered and looked at me distrustfully. "His music always reminds one of paintings of battles," he said. By this Brecht meant that Beethoven had fought Napoleon's battles once again on music paper. And since he did not admire the originals—Brecht had not much symphathy for battles—he did not like the imitations either. For this reason, and for other reasons too, he invented what he called misuc.

For a musician it is difficult to describe misuc. Above all it is not decadent and formalist, but extremely close to the people. It recalls, perhaps, the singing of working women in a back courtyard on Sunday afternoons. Brecht's dislike of music ceremoniously produced in large concert halls by painstaking gentlemen in tails also forms a constituent of misuc. In misuc nobody may wear tails and nothing may be ceremonious. I hope I am interpreting Brecht correctly when I add that misuc aims at being a branch of the arts which avoids something frequently produced by symphony concerts and operas—emotional confusion. Brecht was never ready to hand in his brain at the cloakroom. He regarded the use of reason as one of the best recreations.

Brecht's strivings for reason in music are a heavy blow for us musicians. For in the case of music, where is reason? I have friends who would not go through fire in the cause of reason in music.

Writing these lines, I recall that Brecht accused me of having a skeptical and condescending attitude towards misuc, his invention. Unfortunately he was right.

Translated by John Peet

Kurt Weill

Radio and the Restructuring of Musical Life (1926)

Within a remarkably short period of time, radio has become one of the most essential elements of public life. Today, it is one of the most frequently discussed topics among all segments of the population and in all organs of public opinion. In particular, however, for certain groups immediately involved in entertainment radio, this new institution presents a totally unexpected problem, whose solution is being urgently sought. For this type of radio, as an "art industry," has already taken on a significance not previously possessed by any other institution. And, for better or worse, those organizations of artists who until now have attempted to negate the artistic and economic significance of radio must take a stand on this important question of artistic life. The Universal German Music Society, that important association of creative and performing artists, which since its founding by Liszt has gathered annually for a music festival to present recent musical production and discuss important questions—this group met most recently in Chemnitz, and it was clear from the outset that this strong organization of musicians would have to deal publicly and at length with the problem of radio. Unfortunately, the speaker who dealt with this topic at an extraordinary session appeared from the start to approach the questions about radio with the kind of negative attitude that is still considered good form in certain musical circles. It isn't clear to us why radio should be viewed as such a dangerous enemy of creative or performing artists. First, as far as the artistic "dangers" are concerned, we do have to admit that radio is still in need of some improvements in the areas of technology and organization. But we shouldn't be impatient. The entire movement of radio is just beginning. Only long years of experience will reveal entertainment radio's true mission. A special technique of singing and playing for radio purposes will develop; and sooner or later we will begin to find special instrumentations and new orchestral combinations suited to the acoustic requirements of the broadcast studio. And we can't yet foresee what new types of instruments and sound-producing devices may develop on this foundation. In later times, people will probably look back upon everything we are doing today as mere experiment. Still, a number of goals have already been reached in satisfactorily reproducing certain artistic presentations, and there can no longer be any doubt that the preconditions for the development of an independent artistic genre of equal stature are present here—one which will go far beyond a more or less perfect "reproduction" of earlier artistic achievements. The artistic significance of radio can be glimpsed only in the development toward this special type of radio art, and by no means in a continuation of the prevailing concert system. For the most important and weightiest argument of radio's enemies is the lack of the personal give-and-take between artist and listener. In the radio art of the future, this personal interaction between podium and auditorium, which, of course, is indispensable in the concert hall, would have to be consciously and intentionally eliminated in its entirety. At that point nothing would stand in the way of a purely artistic development of radio.

Even less sound are the reasons advanced against the economic significance of radio. Today there is only a handful of very prominent artists who have not placed themselves at the disposal of radio. They emphasize (with some justification) that for the full development of their talent they need the personal relationship with the public lacking in the broadcast studio. All the others—droves of actors, singers, and instrumentalists of all kinds—are eager to get involved in broadcast studio work. Many of them earn their living entirely from radio work; and for many others this work provides an indispensable supplement to their theater and concert income. One frequently hears complaints about insufficient pay, and it appears urgently necessary to establish new ground rules for the remuneration of performers as well as for types of engagements.

The offers being made to performers are, however, steadily increasing in value, and cases are not infrequent in which artists of high stature are willing to make dangerous artistic concessions in order not to pass up the income associated with radio work.

The strongest prejudice of artists against radio, however, stems from a view of radio as the strongest enemy of the art of the podium, from a notion that it is responsible for the decline in concert attendance. This completely ignores the fact that empty seats in concert halls are only a symptom of the tremendous restructuring of artistic-economic relationships currently underway. That intellectual class of society, from which the concert public was drawn, is by now hardly in a position to fill the concert halls, and seems satisfied to observe the further development of music in a couple of important winter concerts. The process of separation has in part already been completed; truly valuable concerts have again begun to show better attendance. But that type of concert which only served as a pretense for a social occasion is dying out. The socially formative power of music is beginning to have an effect among the masses. Concerts are no longer to be "meeting places for the elegant world," but rather uplifting, festive hours for the broad mass of a people that is musically inclined. To be sure, this is the point at which radio is most directly and strongly involved in the restructuring process. For only radio can replace those ostentatious gala concerts, which have become superfluous, with a truly valuable and productive mass art form. Only radio can guarantee the broadest general public—the people who will make up the concertgoing public of the future—the participation of first-rate performers and outstanding performances. (Indeed, that is the reason why we demand repeatedly that radio station directors let themselves be guided only by the highest and most serious artistic principles—precisely because the radio concert should form the new, more beautiful replacement for the earlier "elite concert.") As for the practice of music in the concert hall, there remains plenty to do: the cultivation of good tradition and conveyance of greatest individual achievements; the most serene and intensive artistic activity, needed to maintain and recreate the foundation of musical culture; and, above all, the enormous area of new music. We must not allow radio to become a competitor with public musical life, but rather a valuable part of it. Participating in this should be the preeminent task of the important artistic organizations.

Translated by Michael Gilbert

A Note on Jazz (1929)

Today we undoubtedly stand at the end of the era in which one can speak of an influence of jazz on art music. The essential elements of jazz have already been utilized by art music. In the case of those composers who haven't openly resisted this influence, these jazz elements form firm, integral components of musical structure, although they no longer appear as jazz or dance music, but rather in modified form. Some critics have tried to reproach modern music for being more strongly influenced by jazz than the art music of earlier times was by its corresponding dance music forms. This overlooks the fact that jazz is more than just a social dance, that it contains elements which go far beyond the influential possibilities of a waltz. In the midst of a time of heightened artistic abstraction, jazz appeared as a piece of nature, as the healthiest, most powerful kind of artistic expression, which because of its popular origins immediately became an international folk music of broadest consequence. Why should art music have sought to close itself off to such an influence? Whether they withstood that influence depended upon the strength of the individual talents who exposed themselves to jazz; and it was inconceivable that the serious European musician would seek to imitate or in any sense "refine" this American dance music. It is unmistakable, however, that jazz played an essential role in the rhythmic, harmonic, and formal relaxation we have achieved today, and above all in the steadily increasing simplicity and comprehensibility of our music.

More important to me today than the influence of jazz on the production of music is that the performance practice of jazz is finally breaking through the rigid system of musical practice in our concerts and theaters. Anyone who has ever worked with a good jazz band will have been pleasantly surprised by an eagerness, a devotion, a lust for work that one seeks in vain in many concert and theater orchestras. A good jazz musician has complete command of three or four instruments; he plays by memory, and is accustomed to a type of ensemble performance in which each individual collaborates on the overall sound. But above all: he can improvise, he cultivates a free, unrestrained type of musical performance in which the interpreter accomplishes productive work to the broadest extent. The extent to which all of this can be applied to art music depends very much, of course, upon the nature of the musical product, which, to be sure, does not always permit such freedom of interpretation. Economic considerations play a role here as well: the jazz musician is not a civil servant; he is subject to competition, and his artistic ambition is greater because better performance brings him more money. But it is entirely possible that we will experience from this point on an artistic and economic reorganization of interpretive practice.

Translated by Michael Gilbert

On the Composition of *The Three-Penny Opera* (1929)

Actually, the success of our piece proves not only that, artistically speaking, we chose the proper moment for the creation and promulgation of the new genre, but also that the public seemed to expect a rejuvenation of this popular type of theater. I do not know whether our genre is going to replace that of the operetta. After all, there is no reason why, after Goethe's return to earth in the form of an operetta tenor, other historical characters or, at least, members of the nobility should not also have their tragic moment at the end of the second act. This matter will take care of itself, and I don't believe that there will be a gap that is worth filling. More important for all of us is the fact that, for the first time, an inroad has been made into the entertainment industry, which was hitherto reserved for a completely different type of writer and composer. With *The Three-Penny Opera* we reach a public which either did not know us at all or thought us incapable of captivating listeners whose number far exceeds the size of concert hall and operatic audiences.

Seen from this point of view, *The Three-Penny Opera* is part of a movement which affects almost all of our young musicians. The renunciation of the *l'art pour l'art* principle, the rejection of individualism in matters artistic, the present concern with music for the cinema, the newly established connection with the movement sponsoring music for young people, and the simplification of the musical means of expression which results from all this, are all steps in one direction.

Opera alone persists in its splendid isolation. The operatic audience still constitutes a coherent group of people who seem to exist apart from the average theater fans. *Opera* and *theater* are still regarded as two completely different phenomena. Dramaturgically as well as in the use of language and choice of subject matter, modern opera remains totally anachronistic. How frequently one hears it said: "This may be possible in the theater, but not in opera." Opera was founded as an aristocratic form of art, and all operatic conventions serve to emphasize the sociological nature of the genre. But no other such genre is now in existence; and the theater in particular is bent on reshaping society. If the framework of opera is unable to withstand the impact of the age, then this framework must be destroyed.

The above reasons cogently explain why, basically, the nature of all recent operatic experiments was destructive. In *The Three-Penny Opera,* reconstruction was possible insofar as here we had a chance of starting from scratch. We wanted, most of all, to restore the primitive form of opera. Every new work for the musical stage raises the question: how is it possible that music and, especially, song can be used in the theater? We solved the problem in the most primitive manner possible. I was faced with a realistic action and had to use music in opposition to it, since I do not think that music can achieve realistic effects. Thus we either interrupted the action in order to introduce music or deliberately led it to a point where singing became necessary. Add to this that the piece gave us an opportunity to treat opera as the principal theme of a dramatic presentation. At the very beginning of the play, the audience is told: "Tonight you will see an opera for beggars. Since this opera was to be as sumptuous as beggars alone can imagine, and since it was to be cheap enough for beggars to afford, it is called *The Three-Penny Opera.*" The last finale, accordingly, is by no means a parody, since here the concept of opera forms an inherent part of the action and had to be dealt with in the purest and simplest manner.

This return to a primitive form of opera entailed a drastic simplification of the musical language. I had to write music that could be sung by actors, i.e., laymen. But what originally seemed to be a limitation, soon turned out to be a real blessing. For the creation of a new type of musical theater, such as we have in *The Three-Penny Opera,* became possible only through the use of easily grasped and identifiable melodies.

Translated by Ulrich Weisstein

Ernst Krenek

That Noise Called Music (1945)

Radio takes the musical work out of its original context. Music was for the most part never intended to be heard in the living room. The simple but significant result of this change is that music is constantly being heard at a much reduced level of aural volume. Composers of symphonic works may not always have included the size of concert halls and of audiences in their calculations, but they certainly never foresaw that their works would be listened to by an infinite number of individuals, each in his own separate room. If symphonic music exerts any social influence at all, if it is capable of transforming a motley crowd into a community of beings with a more or less similar spiritual outlook, this power is severely handicapped by reduced tonal volume and the isolation of its listeners.

The musician who wishes to concentrate on the quality of a composition or performance naturally welcomes the objectivity inherent in radio reproduction. As long as everything remains in proportion, the reduction of volume does not worry him. He can arrange the lights in his room just as he wishes them to be, can follow the score at will, can smoke, drink, or do whatever he thinks necessary to put him into a suitable frame of mind.

Most of our concert halls are, in any case, too large and acoustically of doubtful quality, so that even in those places which appear to be designed for it, the music, coming to the ear from a distant corner, sounds indistinct and distorted. I can think of a very fine-looking concert hall in the Midwest which gives nobody any reason to complain that he is not getting his money's worth: every note is lovingly echoed three times. And in another hall of my experience, many a symphony sounds like a piece for solo tuba with orchestral interludes: whenever the softest grunt emerges from that towering brass funnel nothing else can be heard. Radio engineers are, as a rule, able to avoid such crudities.

Radio broadcasts therefore, by removing the distractions implicit in a "live" performance, are an aid to wise and serious concentration. Yet nonetheless several disturbing factors have emerged in the routine of radio presentation. Stuck fast in memories of early stages of their development, radio companies persist in putting music across as if it were a novelty. As many of us can still recall, it was the sense of sharing instantaneously in something happening many miles away that made our first experiences of radio appear so sensational. Since then twenty years have passed, but in the studio the feeling of wonder still lingers. The fact that one can listen to the Ninth Symphony at home is considered much less important than the fact that this same Ninth Symphony is being played some two thousand miles away. "We are now taking you to Carnegie Hall," the announcer says, and the illusion of a visit is at once emphasized by the sound of tuning instruments. However, when this procedure is repeated week after week, one begins to suspect that the sound comes from a specially prepared gramophone record: it seems unlikely that every Sunday at exactly the same time the identical tuning noises are to be heard in Carnegie Hall.

In radio circles, reality itself is considered to be less reliable than a concoction of the typical manifestations of reality. One radio manager used to tell, not without an undertone of cynicism, a story of the raw early days of broadcasting. It had been advertised that on Christmas Eve there would be a relay of the great bell of a cathedral. Just before the broadcast was due to begin a cable broke: the damage was irreparable. In the depths of despair the radio company sent for the timpanist of the local opera house. He reached the studio with his instruments in the nick of time. And as he manipulated his cymbals and his gongs the announcer, his voice throbbing with emotion, told of the hallowed bell sending its message out into the Holy Night. Not a single listener noticed that he was being tricked.

Some years ago another radio station went to the other extreme

with a "live" broadcast. A reporter was sent complete with microphone into some swampy forest to pick up the trills of the nightingales who were thought to live there. A rash enterprise, for who
could say whether the stars would be willing to cooperate? The
main burden fell on the man with the microphone: he and not the
nightingale had the job of evoking the magic of that mild May night.
Surely it would have been easier to have put on a record of a
nightingale singing in the zoo and to have read over it a stunning
description of a May night as it should be, penned by a resource-
ful scriptwriter in the middle of January; or—even better still—to
have dropped the whole bag of tricks in favor of a sensible program.

All this goes to show that events, to be thought worthy of radio
presentation, must be pressed into the mold of reporting. When it
is music that has to be put over, the process becomes perhaps a
bit more complicated. So long as the performance takes place in a
studio, things are relatively easy. But even then there is a noticeable tendency to give the impression of a "live" performance. An
imaginary audience is encouraged to inspire the artists by strenuous applause; or the announcer, after dutifully mentioning that
the ensuing program is recorded, will proclaim, "The artists appearing today are . . ." so as to make us believe that Lily Pons is
really there.

One might feel that in a studio concert it would be quite enough
just to give the names of the works played and the people playing
them. But the announcer takes another view. He presents the music as if it were part of some unique experience occurring in the
studio. Musical tidbits scattered about in a non-musical program
serve the opposite purpose: they give the factual material a background of fantasy.

Everybody knows that motor manufacturing companies have a
habit of sponsoring entire symphony orchestras together with expensive conductors and soloists. Why do they do it? I am still
looking for the man who in the act of buying a car exclaims, "A
Ford of course: no one conducts better than Ormandy!" Nor have
I yet heard anybody who, having decided on a Chrysler, has been
suddenly smitten by pangs of conscience and has said, "No, I can't
do this to General Motors, which puts on those splendid Toscanini concerts." It seems that some of the industrial giants enjoy

being associated with artistic greatness. Not that they expect bigger sales from it, but it gives them the appearance of being educators when they get Toscanini to conduct Beethoven.

Music lovers might feel that in matters of this sort more respect was shown in feudal times. They picture the king entering a richly and elegantly decorated Baroque hall, where beautiful ladies and imposing gentlemen are gathered to hear the symphony commissioned by His Majesty: a picture apparently far more in accord with the sublime spirit of music than that of a hard-bargaining, check-flourishing publicity agent. Yet quite a few of the kings and bishops who paid for the exquisite musical blossoms of their own day had no higher conception of "public service" than our modern businessmen. They too sponsored music for the sake of a vaguely defined publicity. If the price we have to pay for an hour of good music is five minutes of attention to a poem about the virtues of rubber tires and chassis, are we any worse off than Mozart's contemporaries, who had to make their bows to the royal box before they could settle down to enjoy the music? And if we cannot conceive what General Motors gets from engaging the NBC Orchestra, should we not equally ask ourselves how the lavishness of those Baroque princes repaid itself? It is, of course, possible that some of them loved music. But that possibility is not ruled out among capitalists either. Between the old days and now there is, as far as I can see, only one very great difference: in those times it was fashionable to sponsor contemporary music; today that is certainly not the case.

A sponsor of public performances hopes that people will be led by the pleasure of their experience to think of him, and he is confident that this will eventually bring its reward. It is taken for granted that entertainment leaves behind pleasant impressions. But if entertainment does mean enjoyment, everyone who listens to music will want to get enjoyment from it. And opinions differ widely about what constitutes enjoyment. Some people enjoy playing chess, others like smashing lampposts.

Since the people who subsidize radio music are manufacturers of articles for mass consumption, they go for works which will give enjoyment to as many listeners as possible. Now the most popular form of enjoyment is, without a doubt, love. The musical experience of the "ordinary man" is frequently connected with affairs of the heart: he takes his girl friend to a dance for instance, thus paving the way for a less formal approach. So it is felt that the music which serves such ends must possess an absolute enjoyment value. And for that reason, the radio with devastating logicality pumps out dance music at all times of day. In consequence the state of bliss engendered by music becomes associated irrevocably with the idea of the noisy consumption of expensive drinks.

Disgruntled highbrows are brushed aside with the excuse that this is exactly what the majority wants, and it is not only expedient but also democratic to provide it. Unfortunate, but very true. Complex characters who, though not immune to the joys of love or even of cocktail bars, have a wider conception of "enjoyment," are free to switch off and await those problematic broadcast programs which the industrial tycoons project.

But the purveyors of dance music are mistaken if they imagine that highbrows have no time at all for their wares. In fact, there is scarcely one among the hundreds of serious musicians I have known who does not find some enjoyment in jazz. Most of them, I suspect, have found even more enjoyment in it than the "ordinary man" for the reason that they know more about the way it works: their enjoyment is based on informed judgment. It is certainly both possible and indeed desirable to take pleasure equally in the *Eroica* and in *Caldonia*. Everything in its proper time and place.

Radio, which supplies both sorts, is not organized to sharpen critical wits into the bargain. That, and not the prejudiced attitude of the highbrows, is the real trouble.

Throughout the day the radio set delivers its acoustic stimulants with no discernible shades of contrast. We are taken at one time to the tabernacle at Salt Lake City, at another to the center of Chicago's night life, now to the "Palladium" of Hollywood, at other times to Carnegie Hall or into a studio or a cathedral or a fairground. And it all sounds exactly the same, rather mushy, rather treacly, an unceasing ghostly gloss, diminished as a rule to form a tolerable background noise for the accomplishment of household tasks. The average listener (the one who makes a habit of keeping his set switched permanently on) is never given any hint that it might be worth his while to readjust his listening apparatus when a Beethoven symphony is being played. All that in the nature of things he is aware of on such occasions, is that the background noise has assumed a somewhat unusual flavor, and if the strangeness is pushed beyond a certain point he will, thrown off his mental balance, put an abrupt end to the specter.

This climactic moment, more feared by radio people than damnation itself, is reached most frequently when new music is put on the air. Though Beethoven and Schubert may have nothing to do with jazz, one tends to accept the vocabulary they use as a harmless prototype of later discoveries. A listener who is used to the simple structure and the strong stimulants of jazz music will probably be bored by passages in classical works in which relatively simple sound patterns are marked by all the greater intensity of expression. But he will only be bored, whereas contemporary music with its hard sounds, jagged contours, startling turns, and its many complex relationships, really antagonizes him. It contains nothing that "gets" him. Accessibility is, however, the most important component of that animal sense of well-being which the big boys of radio are out to convey. Music, whose job it is to beautify our homes like a sort of acoustical wallpaper, must be music that is familiar to everyone or at any rate sounds familiar. Revelations, confessions, problems—manifestations of struggle and defeat—would ruin the wallpaper.

The music that is put out on the radio nowadays gets swallowed up in effect in a thick fog of noise from which only trumpet players, bandleaders, virtuoso conductors, and wailing heart-throb experts, trained in the art of putting themselves across, emerge: the friendly household gods of the "ordinary man," putting in their appearance at set hours. They go along together with those other Lares and Penates of modern man, the heroes of the comic strips. The housewife is soon held in thrall to the friendly spirit, and she becomes a fan: a Sinatra fan, a Toscanini fan, or whatever it may be. Yet I have never heard of any lady who through the medium of radio has become a Beethoven fan. Not even Brahms (who for some unexplained reason is the only serious composer permitted to measure his strength against the ubiquitous Russians) is as familiar to listeners as any of the stick-waggers who keep the musical tapeworm going.

Who can say exactly what this unending stream of radio music has done to the millions of people who are subjected to it? Yet one thing should at any rate have become clear by now: the idea that by pumping masses of music into their homes, people are transformed into connoisseurs, is a mistaken one.

Whatever music might do, it does only when one approaches it with an open heart and shares actively in its being. All these millions have been absorbing music in a way that is highly dangerous: they simply cannot live without a habitual background noise. Perhaps they will have developed a superficial sense of discrimination. Whoever stares for years at the wallpaper in his room is bound one day to notice that the second leaf of the seventh rose to the left of the wardrobe is darker than the other leaves, but he will still know nothing at all about the art of painting.

Of course there is always the chance that a few of those who have ears to hear will be affected (though they will certainly have to use some other means than radio to get their ears in training). And perhaps that rumored innkeeper out in the wilds who but for radio would never have discovered the glories of symphonic music does really exist somewhere. Nevertheless the question remains whether such a result justifies the enormous waste and the terrifying drop in values inherent in such musical inflation.

There are some hypocrites who have spread the idea that by jazzing up the classics one can bring "good music to the masses." However, no one has yet succeeded in demonstrating that a person ignorant of classical music has been won over to Mozart through hearing those eight bars of the C Major Piano Sonata which tinkle through a popular swing number bearing the classical title "In an Eighteenth Century Drawing Room." Still, daylight robbery of this sort is not worth the indignation which it has aroused among self-appointed guardians of the Grail. It is true that Botticelli's Venus should not be made to serve as a pin-up girl; but if it is, the painting remains what it always was. The delicate and subtle music of Mozart is made of sterner stuff than those who have abused it: many masterpieces have survived long periods of silence in which scarcely an ear was turned toward them; they will also survive the period in which far too many ears are turned to them far too often and far too idly.

What happens to music on its way through the ether confirms the opinion held by some that mankind lets its power of invention run away with it. We are dissipating our musical heritage for the sake of one ingenious machine and are heading for a musical famine. True progress will be possible only when listeners alter their ideas about what they expect from music. But it is unlikely that the radio will make them do that.

Translated by Margaret Shonfield and Geoffrey Skelton

America's Influence on Its Émigré Composers (1959)

In the wake of the political turmoil of the early 1930s, composers began to emigrate from Europe to the United States. The wave of migration reached its peak when Germany, ruled by the National Socialist Party, set out to absorb neighboring territories; it reached its conclusion with the collapse of France. Even while these events were in process, an interest arose in their bearing on the creative work of the composers affected by them. The question was raised to what extent this work was influenced by their more or less forcible, unplanned departure from customary surroundings and by their new living conditions. It might be worthwhile to take up this question once again, for the answers to it today are likely to be different from those of some thirty or more years ago.

The very composers in question have been inclined to consider the influence of these events as insignificant. One might explain this as revealing a defensive attitude on their part, a kind of psychological mechanism that comes into play to protect the self-confidence of the émigré. He seeks shelter, it would seem, in convincing himself that the shock of uprooting did not encroach upon his innermost life substance. Guided by this point of view, the emigrant is likely to maintain that he would have composed whatever he *did* compose after settling in his new milieu even without this change. He is likely to maintain that all deviations from his earlier modes of writing, in the event that such can be observed, are the result of an inner development that has nothing to do with outer circumstances. As a matter of fact, this view is hard to invalidate, for there is no way of setting up an experiment that would demonstrate what a man would have created had he not emigrated. Yet from the present vantage point, the matter seems to take on a somewhat different appearance.

The emigration of a group of renowned composers, and a string of lesser-known men, hit America at a time when the appeal for an autonomous musical production became increasingly loud in its formulation. The generation of seventy-year-old composers of today had reached full maturity, coming forth with the demand to be acknowledged as creators of the first original American music. These composers were vehement in their protest against conductors of the larger American orchestras who seemed to prefer European music to American works. Up until today, as a matter of fact, the well-known American symphony orchestras have had Europeans as their directors. (The appointment of Leonard Bernstein to head the New York Philharmonic represented the first quite notable exception to the rule.) Yet these European conductors were, for the most part, not political refugees, but had been imported to America because it did not have adequate conductors of its own.

American composers may well have been justified in their grievances. Still, their colleagues who emigrated from Europe were scarcely able to convince them that conductors were disposed not so much against modern American music as against modern music in general. In place of Piston and Harris it was not Schönberg or Bartók who got played, but Brahms and Tschaikovsky. Yet the prevailing mood of the time darkened the facts of the case, and one tended to look upon the European exodus with more scruples than it deserved. Though slight in numbers when compared with the mass migrations of the nineteenth century, the immigration of the thirties aroused these scruples primarily because it brought to the country a large number of publicly conspicuous intellectuals who were qualified for high, prominent positions. In keeping with the American tradition, the emigrant composers, as victims of oppression, were received with open arms and given warm assurances of readiness to help. But even without their being told so directly, they could feel that in regard to the professional situation people would have been happier had they not been forced to come. Thus the immigrant was pushed, from the outset, into a certain defensive attitude that was hardly conducive to a far-ranging, adventurous creative spirit.

Other factors operating similarly were the necessity to assure oneself of survival in a new environment and the desire to communicate, as far as possible, with this environment. During their years in America, almost all European composers held teaching positions. For men like Hindemith and Schönberg there was nothing new about this experience. For many others, among them the present writer, a teaching position meant a way of living that was still untried. In general, the teaching composer was left to determine aesthetic principles. Yet more often than not, he was made to realize that his pedagogical effectiveness was viewed with distrust if the teaching was overly "progressive," that is, if it extended to atonality and, especially, to twelve-note technique. For this reason I myself lost my first teaching post in America at Vassar College. The only time I was able to carry on instruction with full independence and free of importunity was when I was given the chance to build up my own music department at Hamline College (Minnesota), a more remote and, in many respects, more limited institution, to be sure.

Wherever one goes, the academic mentality is, by nature, prejudiced; it takes up a defensive attitude toward the new. In America during the critical years of the early forties this attitude was even more strongly emphasized by the traces of xenophobia described above. What was new and fraught with hazards seemed, in fact, to have been brought to the country by the strangers who sought its shores. At the time of America's entrance into World War II, I chanced upon a pamphlet (in manuscript form) that was written by a very influential schoolmaster. The author demonstrated to his own satisfaction that twelve-note technique was the purest expression of fascist and Nazi philosophy, conveniently overlooking the contradiction that this technique was so hated by both fascists and Nazis that they forced the twelve-noters into exile. He was led to declare that with the expulsion of the dodecaphonists Hitler killed two birds with one stone: on the one hand, he got rid of the corrupting composers of new sounds; on the other, he made them the agents, against their own knowledge and will, of his striving for world dominion, for in the countries where he drove them—above all, naturally, in America—they now would lead the younger generation to ruin with their abominable doctrine. In the defense of American journalism, it should be said that no one was prepared to print as stupid and vicious a denunciation as this.

Still, it would be wrong to pretend that the constant inhalation of an atmosphere that contained such noxious gases was not without its effects on those people whom certain circles had aimed at poisoning. Much time and energy was spent by the European composers demonstrating that the radically new—that is, atonality and twelve-note technique—was a legitimate and logical further development of traditional values. Schönberg, in whose nature conservative traits had always been very strong and became even more prominent with old age, served as a model in this respect.

It so happens that pedagogical activity as such favors this kind of thinking, since the presentation of the substance of art as something that grows organically in the course of history not only is advantageous as a method but also offers the aesthetic satisfaction experienced in so organizing the subject matter. Virgil Thomson once remarked that it was to the composer's detriment to take up teaching as a sideline. For as a teacher, he can use to illustrate his remarks only the best music of all periods, and he must have answers ready for all questions. Both things would make him blasé and presumptuous; they would oversimplify his artistic conception of the world. Thomson's observation is rather astute, although the really good pedagogue may be distinguished by the courage he has now and then to let a question go unanswered, rather than having to deny in the end statements he made, yet should have known better than to make.

Another factor which worked inhibitively upon the pursuit of the creative adventures begun in Europe is the public mentality of pragmatism which consequently tends toward conformity. In line with this, the idea that an artistic utterance as such can awaken purposeless interest and need not convey to man useful information, spiritual uplifting, or, at the very least, entertainment is not directly intelligible to the American consciousness. It has made its way most clearly in painting where for years abstraction has been acknowledged as the leading principle of stylistic formation. Thinking about music has remained behind the development of progressive thinking in other artistic domains, and in America still further behind than in Europe. From this it follows that in Europe the seemingly absurd has a good chance of gaining an audience on the basis of its very absurdity, for it appeals to the receptive organs of a whole class of men who are only too willing to be affected by the esoteric. Not so in America, where the extraordinary meets with uncomprehending indifference, because it does not allow a classification into the categories of the useful, the practical, and the simply functional. That the composer who by nature feels the urge to communicate is influenced by such conditions of the mental climate seems quite evident.

There were composers who even before their emigration leaned to the moderate center and conformed to the line of tradition. Hence one might hardly notice that those pieces of theirs written in America had for their authors men who had been transplanted to an entirely different environment. Composers like Hindemith and Martinů belong to this group. Hindemith's music, above all, exhibits an attitude of busy-ness, firm structures based on traditional learning, thus easily perceivable, obviousness of form and content, and practicality of execution as well. These traits bring it within reach of a public which is far less inclined to contemplation than to being busily occupied, a public that does not fancy speculation, but wants to know what the matter is. As a result of its Puritan heritage, it is inclined to consider those things that are less entertaining as serious and weighty.

Composers whose American works point up new characteristics unknown in their earlier works should not for that reason be automatically accused of having struck an unethical compromise. That is, they should not be reproached for having taken great pains, against their better judgment, to cultivate modes of writing conditioned by their surroundings. If Kurt Weill in America seemed to exchange the aggressive, bald, and sarcastic style of his Brecht period for the sumptuousness, the mundane sentimentality, and the, if at all, circumspect irony of the Broadway manner, he was probably hardly aware of the fact that in so doing he descended in our eyes below the level of his tradition and his earlier works. Rather he did, as he himself told me, what seemed necessary to comply with that natural, invincible urge of his to communicate via the musical theater: he adapted this communication to the only vehicle at his disposal, namely, the Broadway stage.

Less conspicuous, but all the more interesting are such modifications as may be ascribed to the change of continents in the creative work of a different variety of musicians—those whose European works, to start with, were not essentially motivated by the urge to communicate. In the case of Béla Bartók how nice it would be to secure some evidence to the effect that the character of his last works is to be attributed to an inner reorientation, a reorientation which must be respected, however much one tends to disavow its results. Without such evidence one is misled into considering the possibility of concessions on the part of the Hungarian master whose name won respect for his unbending integrity.

Arnold Schönberg's American works, to be sure, leave no room for upsetting conjecture. The fact that in America he wrote a series of "old-fashioned" tonal works carries little weight. These are works set in a rather unattractive landscape overgrown with a post-Regerian thicket; nevertheless, they are clearly recognizable as occasional products conditioned by external circumstances. Schönberg's central creative work, on the other hand, shows that the previously described atmospheric influences of America did not pass him by without leaving their traces. In his writings one meets time and again with the concept of "comprehensibility." He tended to regard its achievement as one of the most important incentives in the formation of his style and technique, in particular, the twelve-note method. Schönberg may have been deluding himself. Yet his holding fast to the basic ideas of classical construction, i.e., unfolding and development (which the composer called "progressive variation") and to standard classical structures (sonata, rondo) was clearly bound to increase the comprehensibility of his music for a public favorably disposed to such forms. It seems to be on equal footing with that urge to conform with the surrounding environment. Although no proof may be adduced to the fact, yet one might well imagine that Schönberg, even without the influence of his pragmatic surroundings, would have come by himself to some of the technical and stylistic conclusions he arrived at in his works, and that some of a younger generation developed further in theirs. The simplified writing of his Piano Concerto and, above all, the musical idiom of the *Ode to Napoleon* which crystallizes about a tonal center are, to be sure, characteristics of an expressive urge whose aim is greater comprehensibility.

It is clear to me today that certain decisive changes in my own development did not come about when they were near at hand. I am inclined to ascribe their failure to do so to the influence of the mental climate of America, for these changes did come about when I renewed my contact with Europe. As far back as my Viennese lectures "On New Music" of 1937, I pleaded for the notion that one of the main concerns of dodecaphonic thinking ought be the working out of new forms obtained from the conditions of serially ordered tonal material. In my *Lamentatio Jeremiae prophetae* which I sketched out in 1941, that is, some three years after my arrival in America, I applied the principle of "rotation" for the first time on a systematic basis. By "rotation" I mean a mutual and sectional permutation of serial elements which proceeds according to a determined order. The principle proved to be of decisive significance for me when, more than ten years later, I turned to totally serialized composition. It is indicative that, at that time, I considered the *Lamentatio* unfeasible in practice and laid it aside after its completion. I did not pursue further the line of development begun then, as I did not believe I was personally or practically able to afford spending my energies on works that possessed no powers of communication. In the future I was to use rotation technique in some later works, but did so more with the intention of loosening up twelve-note technique than of imparting to the serial principle a more far-ranging validity. Here I followed Schönberg's precept by attempting to keep alive classical ideas of form in an idiom (atonality) of an essentially different orientation. The exploration of new structures was temporarily shelved. Only in the later fifties did it become clear, of course, that far greater powers of communication were possessed by works in the *Lamentatio* category than by my other relatively conservative pieces.

Yet it is typical of the "echolessness" of the vast American expanses that as far back as the early forties, when I pointed time and again to the significance of Anton Webern—which became clearer to me as time went on—I seemed to be delivering a monolog that went unanswered. Note, too, that it was in the later fifties that I became cognizant of the fact that Milton Babbitt had, in the year 1945, already begun to operate with the extension of the serial idea of twelve-note technique to the dimension of time. How indicative that this undertaking was acknowledged as a revolution shaking the foundations of Western music only when several years later it was launched in the works of a group of younger European composers!

There is little doubt that America has sharpened the sense of reality of the European composers who came to its shores. Yet at the same time it seems to have made them neglect what Robert

Musil cleverly set up as a contrasting sense, the "sense of possibility." A development in a contrary direction might be pointed to only in the works of Stravinsky. Some of his later neo-classical pieces composed in America show the increase of a fairly unconciliatory mode of writing that makes them less appealing than his earlier popular oeuvre. These pieces prepare the change to the introvert serial style of his most recent works. However, the latter could not have come about, to be sure, were it not for the discovery of Webern's music following the renewal of contacts with Europe after the war. Yes, the land of unlimited possibilities taught us to be more attentive to reality. Yet it was reserved for the old continent of limited reality to awaken in us anew the desire for the impossible.

Translated by Don Harran

Werner Egk

On My *Irish Legend* (1955)

Dear Reinhold Kreile,

. . . The thing which fascinates me about this story is the conception that an individual, conscious of his own responsibility and against all odds, undertakes an escape from hopelessness in an apparently hopeless situation. It may perhaps interest you that this thought already moved me some time ago (1937) when I wrote the cantata *Nature-Love-Death* using poetry by the Göttingen Grove poet L. C. H. Hölty. For me, the first of the three poems became a lyric symbol of the idea that even that which is tender and apparently weak can assert itself against force.

"Veiled in silver sheaths" lies the wintry garden; "where most recently glowed the ripe gold of the fruit tree now hangs ice which no sun can melt."—"Only you, my little box-tree, put forth your green head against the frost and mock winter's power." Perhaps you can still remember the libretto for my oratorio *Fearlessness and Goodwill* (1931), the first larger-scale musical work I wrote. The text owes its genesis to an Indian saga which treats a related problem in a simple, uncomplicated form. Through fateful circumstances the peasant Gamani is unjustly accused three times of major crimes and has no witnesses to prove his innocence. He is therefore sentenced by the royal court to be trampled to death by state elephants. His only defense is a fearlessness rooted in the efficacy of truth and the goodwill toward all men which emanates from this consciousness—including goodwill toward those who accused and want to kill him, and even toward the creatures designated to carry out the sentence. "They brought Gamani into the middle of the square, removed his clothes and ordered him to lie on the ground. The elephants shook the ground with their steps and turned toward him. Suddenly, however, they stopped in their tracks and returned quietly to their stalls."

You must admit that Gamani's faith in the power of truth and the unconditional altruism in the *Irish Legend* evoke similar effects, and that both stories stand next to each other like sisters. *On revient toujours à ses premiers amours.* Also, the inner connection of *Magic Fiddle, Peer Gynt, Joan von Zarissa,* and *Abraxas* with the *Irish Legend* is basically easy to recognize, even if each of these works deals with a different theme. The subject matter for each of them comes from folk sagas, for the most part from those which represent the rootstock of European literature and a pure crystallization of the European spirit. Most contain images of vivid expressiveness and take their underlying thought to the ultimate extreme. There is hardly any difference here between the story of Gamani, the saga of Don Juan, and the legend of Countess Cathleen. They all deal with the "most extreme case" and point with extreme consistency to the absolute.

Time and again it has been mythical subjects that have attracted me more than anything else—beautiful symbols of a great order whose deciphering has occupied saints, poets, and rulers for millennia. Even the light-hearted, burlesque *Magic Fiddle* is still illuminated by a lost reflection of the light that filled the myths of Orpheus. To be sure, it is possible that the superficial expectations of a certain public which understands neither the *Magic Fiddle* nor *Peer Gynt,* and in no case *Abraxas,* will not profit by the *Irish Legend.* Do you find that so tragic? Perhaps, however, a larger public will be more than richly compensated by the profuse imagery of the legend, which allows the essential things to be grasped from immediate observation, and which—totally apart from the music—can have an effect deep down, where no analytical effort is involved. The tiger, the snake, the owls, the vulture, the condemned Faust, the angelic Cathleen, the poet, the nurse—all of these figures stand so eloquently upon the foundation of the saga like the king, the queen, the rook, the knight, and the pawn upon the chessboard, ready and eager to play their great game.

On the other hand, what does the fashionable concept of "conformity to the line" mean? Don't you also believe that an old truth is worth more than a "new hat"? Or do you find that Bert Brecht was indeed right when he sang thirty years ago: "Everything new is better than everything old"? Don't you also believe that the proud and unapproachable Carl Hofer acted properly in "always saying what he thought; finding many ways to say it, and only saying that which he had to say"—to paraphrase Hilaire Belloc's comment about Hans Christian Andersen? Or would it have been better if he had left us an "Inventaire des techniques rédactionelles" of the art of painting instead of his pictures? I don't think so.

This is not to argue against the development and application of new techniques and the institution of *laboratoires sonores*. An alert analyst can also discover in the score of *Irish Legend* a series of modern techniques, which, however, are never used as ends in themselves. For example, in a presto section the method of "change-ringing" (a widely practiced art of bell-ringing in England, done according to arithmetic rules) has been used for the resolution of an eight-voice chord. This technique produces an intellectually organized, pattering sequence of sound at the climax of an exciting scene. The dynamic tension of polytonal counterpoint; the cold shift between complementary chords; the lyric flow of new scales, from which interesting chordal mixtures are obtained; the lively monotone character derived from the systematic decomposition of "indestructable rhythms" through the simple shifting of accents; the long-range harmonic disposition based on certain groups of chords; the stylistically important definition of the characteristic chord c-d♯-f♯-a-f-a♭-b: I mention all of this by way of example.

You ask what is closer to the public: analytic cynicism and the hopelessness which has already become traditional since Kafka, or the escape from hopelessness in the *Irish Legend*? This question cannot be dealt with theoretically. My piece is a symbol, not an object of literary or philosophical speculation. I find that one can't argue with pictures, and if you draw my attention to the fact that at the end of *Abraxas* there is a descent into hell while in the legend there's an ascent into heaven, I'd like to respond: "Light and darkness are mutually exclusive," and at the same time add: "But they condition each other."

With best wishes,
Your
Werner Egk

Translated by Michael Gilbert

Karl Amadeus Hartmann

My Yes to Luigi Nono (1963)

On the Performance of Nono's *Canti di vita e d'amore*

Must it be emphasized?—It must! Why this piece, people will ask me, why *this* Nono, one would have to ask. Because these songs are Nono himself, in form and content the deepest artistic confession of the human being Luigi Nono, of the young person who is politically involved, who rises up in anger, who fights against the threat to life posed by the power of war, who sides with all living creatures in the battle against the inhumane.

Nono accuses, and his language is fire. In fighting against the bomb, the greatest threat to humanity, he combats want and pain, hunger and sickness, destruction and war. He is unrelenting and hard, for the threat is enormous and directed at humankind, the one and only purpose of creative work to Nono, the artist and human being.

To Nono, Hiroshima is this world's great wound. It will never heal; the world will remain marked. But the wound will form a scar when the singer of Hiroshima can step down, when the bomb is banned. Then the day will also not be far off on which the night of blood will be engulfed.

Then, however, there will be life and human beings who will live without fear, who will really live, for the skies will be clear—without the shadow of the billowing mushroom cloud.

Could I, who witnessed the terror, who know the horror, could I say no, no to the person, the artist Nono?

Translated by Michael Gilbert

Hans Werner Henze

Music as an Act of Desperation (1968)

Our society is prosperous. Fast cars, smoothly functioning kitchens and economic relationships, jet set and the tabloid *Bild-Zeitung* to do its thinking for it—these make every expression of doubt about this situation seem irrational, criminal, or incited "by the East."

People's conversations about life's difficulties, even when intimate, are still caught up in consuming prefabricated means of production, including the consumption of art as brand-name articles. Everything seems to be in order. Thank God nothing is in flux. Vietnam, Newark, and Bolivia are far away. We are surrounded by friendly people concerned about calmness and regularity, increasing domestic comfort, and improving their job performance in newly built cities and the secure surroundings achieved through hard work. It is hard to explain to these friendly people that they do not comprehend the real extent of their misery, the extent to which they are manipulated and cheated in their valid claims to happiness. Their friendliness ceases only when other members of their society try to direct their attention toward these facts in the name of love and freedom.

It will not do for "minorities" to say these things using modes of expression that can be manipulated. Rather, they must select means of expression that cannot be coopted and are therefore profoundly democratic. People tend to call these means of expression fascist, and they respond to them fascistically with water cannons, billyclubs, and tear gas. They lump together all those who do not succumb to the hypnosis of prosperity (not a genuine prosperity at all), who have no pragmatic alternative, and who imagine the "impossible."

I see myself entangled in an insoluble contradiction that can no longer be reflected adequately in works of art. Under existing conditions, music can only be an act of desperation, a negation. Possibly, it can still vaguely suggest a utopia of freedom, but the freedom we mean is greater than its surrogate, the work of art. Wherever art still assumes a positivistic pose, it functions as a counterfeit likeness of culture.

New museums, opera houses, and premieres are unnecessary. What is necessary is to begin fulfilling dreams. It is necessary to abolish totally the rule of man by man. It is necessary to transform the human being, and that means: what is necessary is the creation of the greatest artwork of humanity, the world revolution.

Translated by Carol Poore

Opera Belongs to Everyone (1974)

[On the plans to dissolve the Opera and Philharmonic Orchestra of Dortmund]

The Germans are envied the world over for their opera theaters. In the United States, England, and France, increased efforts are being made to establish new music theaters or new orchestras in the provinces. In such places this is considered to be culturally progressive.

For the civilization of a modern city, the closing of an opera house signifies a decisive step in the direction of alienation. For centuries it has been important for the internal cultural life of a city that musicians belonged to the citizenry. We owe it to them that musicality has spread and that musical thinking and feeling is so deeply ingrained in our people. All of this would come to an end, all of this cannot be replaced by guest performances (which would certainly have more of a token character than resident opera company productions).

The most outdated, boring, and musty of all perspectives, however, is that opera is "bourgeois" and an obsolete form of art. To be sure, there are obsolete styles of presentation, outdated and boring productions, and an old, worn-out routine which makes it hard for many theater lovers and comrades to grasp the content of the works performed. (Is that the case in Dortmund? I don't know, but I can't imagine that it is.) Objectively, however, this form of art contains riches which number among the most beautiful inventions of the human spirit. They belong to all people; they were not written for the ruling class, but in a fraternal way, for all brothers. Anyone who has ever seen, for example, how young workers and farmers in Havana have appropriated symphonic music and opera, how they fill the opera house, *their* opera house to hear *their* composers, Mozart, Verdi, Beethoven, will no longer be able to harbor any doubts about the direction progressive cultural work must take. Certainly not that of doing away with one of the most elemental components of our culture.

It is not opera that is reactionary, but rather a linear (nondialectical) concept of progress, typical of the bourgeoisie, which is turned on by trendy ideas, is frustrated and elitist, and calls for different forms of music and music-making. In order to escape reality, to by-pass it, the bourgeoisie also calls for forms which could not exist at all because they lack a basis (in the political and philosophical sense). Progress in art and artistic life is conceivable only in connection with social progress. That means starting deep down, at the root of things.

One more thing about Dortmund. The Dortmund Philharmonic Orchestra is one of the best orchestras in the Federal Republic. A so-called "top-notch" orchestra. Doing away with it would only mean that this new and peculiar form of "progress" in the artistic life of our country has already progressed further than most of us had suspected or feared.

Translated by Michael Gilbert

Paul Dessau (1979)

I got to know Paul in the winter of 1948. The writer, Grete Weil, who later wrote the libretto for my first opera, *Boulevard Soli-*

tude, brought us together in Berlin. I often visited him in his study in the Deutsches Theater; I was permitted to inspect the still unfinished score of *Lucullus,* and I did so gratefully, with a great deal of curiosity and a strong desire to make up for lost time. In this room, filled with mountains of books, piles of music, photographs of productions, and an old piano, there was also a little corner for me; it was there that I worked on the final copy of my Third Symphony. Sometimes Paul took me with him to the neighboring Theater am Schiffbauerdamm, so that I could watch Brecht rehearsing his adaptation of Lenz's *The Private Tutor,* and later also attend the premiere, full of vigor and presented with many fresh ideas that still prove fruitful today. I was even once introduced to Brecht, in the Seagull restaurant, and I can still vividly recall his handshake, his friendly grin, his lively eyes, his clothes, and his cigar.

During that time Dessau was working closely and continuously with Brecht, whose spirit was, as it were, present at our discussions; and I had the opportunity of seeing Brecht at work during the closing stages of the rehearsals for his production. These encounters had a special impact on me, and the production style of *The Private Tutor* was of direct and lasting influence on my own work for and in the theatre. It was Dessau who introduced me to Brecht's theory of art, for at that time nothing had yet been published.

I remember how excited I was that such a busy and famous man as Dessau could give so much of his time to a young unknown musician like me. No one has ever spoken to me of Mozart with more understanding and more love than Paul, and in everything that he said his aesthetic was revealed, which I liked a great deal, and which made me reflect for the first time on the role of the artist in society. For him the task of the composer consisted and consists in a constant dialectical rapport with everyday life, in interrelationships, and in an altogether feverishly combative existence. I was perhaps too young then, and still too caught up in the cold war climate of the West, to understand fully everything that Paul said about political things. For this very reason he tried to open my eyes and enlarge my view of the world, and I did in fact learn, and attained a better understanding of certain things; Paul made them concrete and tangible. I grasped how he was deeply concerned to see and shape music as a living component of the world;

as speech and reply; as an instrument of the class struggle, in which process he strived also to incorporate inherited means of expression that had been brought to the latest stage of their technical development. I learned from him how a composer can develop possibilities of realizing this concern, how tradition can intervene and help to mediate expression, how history can remain living and contemporary, even in the context of the latest achievements. I can think of no one else today who has so much grace in his thought and writing, so much humor—real, knowing humor—so much wit, and yet is never ironic or hurtful. The brio that dominates a score like *Puntila,* determining the sound of the whole, and can be detected in the smallest nuances of the instrumentation, is firmly in the tradition of comic opera from Mozart to Rossini to *Falstaff;* a frenetic, unremitting realism—what a delight, what intelligence, what fine workmanship! This score is a summation of the whole of Dessau; it can also be found in his filigree chamber music, his songs, both tender and hard, and his austere polyphonic symphonic music. I believe that many of these works are not yet sufficiently known internationally, and that their potential has not yet been realized; but this will come, for this is music that belongs to the future, and whose humanistic seriousness and historical decisiveness will urgently be required.

Dessau didn't influence my music; at any rate, not technically. We talked mainly about the classics, and not very much about contemporary music. We did sometimes show one another our latest pieces—and were astonished by the patience with which we read the scores, down to the most minute detail.

My friendship with Paul endured, and even when I went far away from Berlin and started to live in southern Italy, from 1953, our exchange of letters and ideas never ceased. We met as often as we could, in Berlin and Italy. Paul and his wife, Ruth Berghaus, were there when the Hamburg 1968 premiere of *The Raft of the Medusa* was broken up, and we saw one another often during the time of the West Berlin Vietnam congress. I attended many of his premieres and concerts, just as he took an interest in my work in a spirit of critical friendship and friendly criticism. I am therefore indebted to him for many valuable pieces of advice, and without a doubt many of his suggestions have gone into my work and made it richer and more solid. This was not just during the last ten years—

during which we also came much closer to one another in political matters—but much earlier, indeed right from the start. My friendship for him was always mingled with a certain admiration, as if for an elder brother of whom I could be proud, because of his sincerity, his courage, his energy, and his refusal to compromise. Paul expects everyone to be as strong and intelligent and talented as he is, and he is quite right to do so: this is a program. I myself am no longer going to achieve it, but I know that one day the whole world will be inhabited by *uomini sociali,* and they will be as pure and healthy and inventive, and as full of love and brotherhood, as my marvelous old friend Paul.

Translated by Peter Labanyi

German Music in the 1940s and 1950s (1982)

The Darmstadt summer courses were extremely important in promoting knowledge of modern music, at any rate during the first few years. It was the idea of the chief cultural administrator there, Wolfgang Steinecke, to bring congresses and conferences to the blitzed city of Darmstadt. The first summer course was in 1946. We put on Brecht's *Didactic Play on Acquiescence* (I conducted it), and there was a great deal of discussion about the text and its meaning, but nobody discussed Hindemith's music. At the beginning none of the composers who were later to become famous was there. I was the only young composer among instrumentalists and singers of my age. There were also a few senior composers who had more or less collaborated during the Third Reich—I've forgotten their names—but nobody wanted to know about them; their music was no good, and they quickly vanished from the scene.

Darmstadt's development was dynamic; decisions were swiftly made and guidelines laid down. As early as 1947 René Leibowitz gave a class analyzing Schönberg. He was a marvelous teacher and, what is more, a delightful man; he taught me a great deal. We wanted to know in more detail what twelve-note composition was all about. But there were hardly any scores or recordings, let alone theoretical works, and my teacher, Fortner, had informed me in Heidelberg in 1946 and 1947 that twelve-note music had gone out long before 1930. That was his verdict. And then suddenly one heard Bartók's Violin Concerto, which contains some disconcerting twelve-note passages. Was the dragon not slain after all? So we very quickly realized that dodecaphony and serialism were the only viable new techniques: fresh, and able to generate new musical patterns.

When I say that decisions were made and guidelines laid down in Darmstadt, I have in mind the technocratic conception of art, dodecaphony's mechanistic heresy, which became official doctrine there at the beginning of the 1950s, and which for many years dominated radio networks and composers. In so far as it is at all possible to speak of a market for modern music, dictatorial control over it was exercised from Darmstadt, and also from Donaueschingen. The radio stations were behind this, as their producers scrambled for new works—in other words, for the prestige of a first performance. Along came Karlheinz Stockhausen, amid much pomp and circumstance, with claims that were immediately acknowledged. He said out loud what he thought: there was nobody around who knew anything about music apart from him. This marked the end of the solidarity that had previously existed among young composers. At the beginning it had looked as though we were all working together on a humanistic project, as if we were all brothers, comrades, allies. That was now gone. Slowly but surely we became, or were made into, competitors in the same market.

As a small boy Karlheinz must already have possessed a boundless sense of mission; at any rate his behavior always indicated something of the sort. He was always in a fever, on cloud nine. I remember a music festival in Vienna at the beginning of the 1950s. We were driving back to the city with publishers from Universal Edition after an evening's drinking in Grinzing, when Stockhausen said, on seeing the still somewhat sparsely lit city: "Look, down there you can see the ocean of light that is Vienna. In a few years' time I will have progressed so far that, with a single electronic bang, I'll be able to blow the whole city sky-high!" I pointed out that there were already perfectly adequate explosives for such purposes, and that musicians might therefore do better to turn their attention to other matters. . . .

On reflection, I can begin to understand my differences with the Darmstadt School. It may seem a bit far-fetched, but I have often thought that their attempt to make music non-communicative had something to do with the ruling class's belief that art is a thing apart from life, better kept that way, and without any social dimension. The reason why this 'non-communicative' tendency, which possessed a mystical, indeed an expressly Catholic element, was so vigorously promoted was, I think, the desire to prevent people from seeing music as simple, concrete, and comprehensible communication between human beings. The former Bauhaus painter, Werner Gilles, whom I often used to visit in Munich and also saw in Italy, was an acute observer of the times. As is often the case with painters, he was deeply familiar with the reality of the natural world. He took a negative view of the development of the arts in postwar Germany. The worst thing, in his eyes, was the kind of pressure that made young artists dependent on the official line in modern art, thus preventing them from discovering their own way.

But this was only one phenomenon. The period of political reconstruction around and after 1950 was also that leading up to the banning of the KPD [German Communist Party]; old comrades, who had been imprisoned by the Nazis, were locked up again. I have never heard anyone mention this in musical circles. Music is, after all, unpolitical! The ban, incidentally, also killed off workers' music and the democratic tradition of folk song. The poet Enzensberger was one of the first intellectuals in the Federal Republic who spoke out publicly against these arrests. The newspapers began to resurrect the idea of the 'German soldier.' People asked themselves: "Are we going to have an army again?" The answer was: "And what if we are?" I remember effusive articles that appeared—it may have been in the magazine *Stern*—proclaiming: "It was wonderful to be a German soldier" and suchlike, everyone conveniently forgetting that the war had cost 50 million lives. The result was a rehabilitation of German militarism. All this was extremely skillfully engineered, and one day there it was: this new army for peacetime and defense, the Bundeswehr—something which in 1945 no one would have thought possible. It looked to me like a gradual return to the recent past, under which its appalling conditions once again became conceivable.

In addition there was my social isolation as a homosexual. For it was then socially impossible to be a homosexual as this was considered a pathological state, an affront to "healthy popular sentiment" and to that of the concert-going public. For instance, according to a West Berlin lady who telephoned me the following day, I really shouldn't have taken Fernando, my friend from Calabria, to the party for Stravinsky in Blacher's house—even though he was much better looking than everyone else there, apart from Stravinsky! Or, at six o'clock one morning the police arrived to haul off my friend and myself. We were questioned separately, and in those days (when the law still took an inflexible stance on the subject) there was no alternative but to deny one's orientation if one wanted to avoid a trial and imprisonment; one had to behave like a criminal trying to slip through the net of justice. For this elevating patriotic experience, granted me in the winter of 1948–49 in Constance, I have to thank an informer, a landlady. Small wonder that I was already thinking of emigration as early as that.

Such experiences were part and parcel of the climate of the 1950s, as was the constant pressure to achieve, to attain status. One also had to learn how to survive the scrutiny of the press, and to win its favor. This meant that one always had to have a new idea to sell. A composer in the late-capitalist world is more or less a small industrialist, an entrepreneur, a self-employed producer whose products can't afford to be forgotten. During those years I was on more than one occasion 'out.' One had the unmistakable impression that one was always expected to produce something sensational—like a tightrope-walker, professional boxer, or magician.

These pressures prevented you from articulating your own hopes and point of view, and from seeing what was really going wrong in the world, from getting to the bottom of social questions. So it happened more and more often that I would switch off the news on the radio and stop reading the newspapers, for together with all these other 'obligations,' such things didn't really seem to concern one that much. We were repeatedly told: "Create, artist, and hold your tongue!" Or: "Music has nothing to do with politics!" I think that the most important thing for someone in my position was, and is, to arrange matters in such a way that he does not constantly have to meet these obligations. That is the only luxury that an artist under this system can earn for himself.

When I crossed the Alps to Italy in early 1953 in my car, which I had bought on installments out of my earnings in the Federal Republic, and which was loaded with a couple of suitcases, some music paper, and a few classical scores (I'd had to sell everything else, even my books), I felt a bit like someone who had been rescued from a disaster. In order to start afresh, I was now turning my back on postwar Germany, where the old guard again, or still, had a considerable share of the say. I felt I had the chance to do something real, to forget what I had suffered, and to listen to what was around me; to study people's interests in a revolutionary country with a classical culture.

Translated by Peter Labanyi

ACKNOWLEDGMENTS

Every reasonable effort has been made to locate the parties who hold rights to previously published translations reprinted here. We gratefully acknowledge permission to reprint the following:

CARL PHILIPP EMANUEL BACH: Autobiography, translated for this volume by James Steakley.

JOHANN SEBASTIAN BACH: Dedication of the Brandenburg Concertos, Contract with the Thomasschule, and letter to George Erdmann from *The Bach Reader: A Life of Johann Sebastian Bach in Letters and Documents,* revised edition, edited by Hans T. David and Arthur Mendel. Copyright © 1966, 1945 by W. W. Norton & Company, Inc. Copyright renewed 1972 by Mrs. Hans T. David and Arthur Mendel. Reprinted by permission of W. W. Norton & Company, Inc. Dedication of *A Musical Offering* from J. S. Bach, *A Musical Offering,* edited by Hans T. David. New York: G. Schirmer, 1945.

LUDWIG VAN BEETHOVEN: Excerpts from Ludwig van Beethoven, *Letters, Journals and Conversations,* edited and translated by Michael Hamburger. London: Jonathan Cape Ltd., 1966. Reprinted by permission of Michael Hamburger.

ALBAN BERG: "Postscript Concerning *Wozzeck*" from *Musical Quarterly* 38, no. 1 (January 1952): 20–21, translated by Willi Reich. New York: G. Schirmer. Reprinted by permission of League of Composers—International Society for Contemporary Music, U.S. Section, Inc. "The Teacher," "On the Hundredth Anniversary of Franz Schubert's Death," and "On Mahler's Ninth Symphony" were translated for this volume by Michael Gilbert with the permission of the Alban Berg Stiftung, Vienna.

JOHANNES BRAHMS: Letters to Clara Schumann from *Letters of Clara Schumann and Johannes Brahms, 1853–1896,* edited by Berthold Litzman. 2 vols. New York: Longmans, Green; London: Edward Arnold, 1927. Letter to Marie Lipsius translated for this volume by Michael Gilbert.

ANTON BRUCKNER: Letter to Baron Hans von Wolzogen from *Letters of Composers: An Anthology, 1603–1945,* edited by Gertrude Norman and Miriam Lubell Shrifte. New York: Alfred A. Knopf, 1946.

FERRUCCIO BUSONI: "Rules for Practicing the Piano" and "Mozart" from Ferruccio Busoni, *The Essence of Music,* translated by Rosamund Ley. London: Barrie & Rockliff, 1957. New York: Dover Publications, 1965. Reprinted by permission of Hutchinson Publishing Group Ltd. and Dover Publications, Inc. Translation in the English language appears with the sanction of Max Hesses-Verlag, Berlin-Wunsiedel.

CARL CZERNY: Excerpt from *Reminiscences from My Life,* translated for this volume by Michael Gilbert.

PAUL DESSAU: Excerpts from *Paul Dessau: Aus Gesprächen,* ed. Dieter Boeck et al. Leipzig: VEB Deutscher Verlag für Musik, 1974, translated for this volume by Michael Gilbert and Carol Poore with the permission of VEB Deutscher Verlag für Müsik.

KARL DITTERS VON DITTERSDORF: Excerpt from *Autobiography of Carl von Dittersdorf*, translated by A. D. Coleridge. London: Richard Bentley, 1896.

WERNER EGK: "On My *Irish Legend*," translated for this volume by Michael Gilbert from Werner Egk, *Musik-Wort-Bild*. Munich: Albert Langen/Georg Müller, 1970. Translated by permission of Müller Verlag.

HANNS EISLER: "Bertolt Brecht and Music" from *Hanns Eisler, A Rebel in Music*, edited by Manfred Grabs. New York: International Publishers Co., 1978. Reprinted by permission of International Publishers Co., Inc. Other material (some of it translated for this volume by Michael Gilbert and Carol Poore) from Hanns Eisler, *Musik und Politik: Schriften, 1924–1928*, edited by Günter Mayer. Munich: Rogner & Bernhard, 1973. Translated and reprinted by permission of VEB Deutscher Verlag für Musik, Leipzig.

CHRISTOPH WILLIBALD GLUCK: Excerpts from *The Collected Correspondence and Papers of Christoph Willibald Gluck*, edited by E. H. and Hedwig Mueller von Asow and translated by Stewart Thomas. London: Rockliff, 1962. Reprinted by permission of Hutchinson Publishing Group Ltd.

GEORG FRIEDRICH HÄNDEL: Letters to Johann Mattheson and Georg Philipp Telemann from Otto Erich Deutsch, *Handel: A Documentary Biography*. London: A. & C. Black (Publishers) Ltd., 1955. Reprinted by permission of A. & C. Black (Publishers) Ltd. Letters to King George I and Charles Jennens, Jr., from Herbert Weinstock, *Handel*, 2nd edition, revised. New York: Alfred A. knopf, 1959. Reprinted by permission of Alfred A. Knopf, Inc.

FRANZ JOSEPH HAYDN: Excerpts from *The Collected Correspondence and London Notebooks of Joseph Haydn*, edited and translated by H. C. Robbins Landon. London: Rockliff, 1959. Reprinted by permission of Hutchinson Publishing Group Ltd.

KARL AMADEUS HARTMANN: "My Yes to Luigi Nono," translated for this volume by Michael Gilbert from Luigi Nono, *Texte: Studien zu seiner Musik*, edited by Jürg Stenzel. Zurich: Atlantis Musikbuch-Verlag, 1975. Translated by permission of Atlantis Musikbuch-Verlag AG.

JOHANN ADOLF HASSE: Letter to the Abbé Giovanni Maria Ortes from *Letters of Composers: An Anthology, 1603–1945*, edited by Gertrude Norman and Miriam Lubell Shrifte. New York: Alfred A. Knopf, 1946.

HANS WERNER HENZE, "Music as an Act of Desperation" and "Opera Belongs to Everyone," translated for this volume by Carol Poore and Michael Gilbert from Hans Werner Henze, *Musik und Politik: Schriften und Gespräche, 1955–1975*, edited by Jens Brockmeier. Copyright 1976 Deutscher Taschenbuch Verlag GmbH & Co. KG, Munich. Translated by permission of Deutscher Taschenbuch Verlag. "Paul Dessau" and "German Music in the 1940s and 1950s" from Hans Werner Henze, *Music and Politics: Collected Writings, 1953–1981*, translated by Peter Labanyi.

© 1982 by Hans Werner Henze. English translation © 1982 by Faber and Faber Ltd. Reprinted by permission of Faber and Faber and Cornell University Press.

PAUL HINDEMITH: Letter to Gertrude Hindemith, translated for this volume by Michael Gilbert from Paul Hindemith, *Briefe,* edited by Dieter Rexroth. Frankfurt am Main: Fischer Taschenbuch Verlag, 1980. Translated by permission of the Hindemith-Stiftung, Blonay/Vevey. Preface to *Elementary Training for Musicians* by Paul Hindemith. New York: Associated Music Publishers, 1946.

ERNST THEODOR AMADEUS HOFFMANN: "Beethoven's Instrumental Music" from *Source Readings in Music History,* compiled and edited by Oliver Strunk. Copyright 1950 by W. W. Norton & Company, Inc. Copyright renewed 1978 by Oliver Strunk. Reprinted by permission of W. W. Norton & Company, Inc.

ERNST KRENEK: "That Noise Called Music" from *Exploring Music: Essays by Ernst Krenek,* translated by Margaret Shonfield and Geoffrey Skelton. Copyright © this translation Calder and Boyars 1966. Reprinted by permission of John Calder (Publishers) Ltd., London, and Riverrun Press, Inc., New York. "America's Influence on Its Émigré Composers," *Perspective of New Music* 8, no. 7 (1970): 112–17.

FRANZ LISZT: Letter to Robert Schumann from *Letters of Franz Liszt,* edited by La Mara (i.e., Ida Marie Lipsius) and translated by Constance Bache. Vol. 1. London: H. Grevel, 1894. Letter to Countess Marie d'Agoult from *Letters of Composers: An Anthology, 1603–1945,* edited by Gertrude Norman and Miriam Lubell Shrifte. New York: Alfred A. Knopf, 1946. "Visit to Beethoven" from Ludwig van Beethoven, *Letters, Journals and Conversations,* edited and translated by Michael Hamburger. London: Jonathan Cape Ltd., 1966. Reprinted by permission of Michael Hamburger.

GUSTAV MAHLER: Letters to the Members of the Budapest Opera House, to Arthur Seidl, and to the Members of the Court Opera House from *Selected Letters of Gustav Mahler,* edited with an introduction by Knud Martner, translated by Eithne Wilkens and Ernst Kaiser and Bill Hopkins. This revised edition and translation copyright © 1979 by Faber and Faber. Reprinted by permission of Faber and Faber Ltd. and Farrar, Straus & Giroux, Inc. Letter to Alma Mahler, from *Gustav Mahler: Memories and Letters* by Alma Mahler, translated by Basil Creighton. Copyright 1946 by Alma Mahler Werfel. Copyright 1968, 1969 by John Murray (Publishers) Ltd. Reprinted by permission of John Murray Ltd.

FELIX MENDELSSOHN BARTHOLDY: Letters to Carl Friedrich Zelter and to Marc-André Souchay from *Felix Mendelssohn: Letters,* translated and edited by G. Selden-Goth. New York: Pantheon, 1945. Reprinted by permission of Pantheon Books. Letter to the Committee of the Lower Rhine Music Festival from *Letters of Felix Mendelssohn Bartholdy,* edited by Paul Mendelssohn Bartholdy and Carl Mendelssohn Bartholdy, translated by Lady Wallace. London: Longman, Green, Longman, Roberts & Green, 1863.

WOLFGANG AMADEUS MOZART: Excerpts from *The Letters of Mozart and His Family,* volumes 1–3, translated and edited by Emily Anderson. London: Macmillan, 1938. Reprinted by permission of Macmillan, London and Basingstoke.

CHRISTIAN GOTTLOB NEEFE: Excerpt from the *Autobiography*, translated for this volume by Felix Potter.

OTTO NICOLAI: "Some Reflections on Italian Opera in Comparison to German," translated for this volume by Michael Gilbert.

HANS PFITZNER: Letter to Bruno Walter, translated for this volume by James Steakley from *Harmonie und Chaos: Musik der Gegenwart*, edited by Hans Schnoor. Munich: J. F. Lehmanns Verlag, 1962. Translated by permission of Otto Spatz-Buchhandlung, Munich and Hamburg.

JOHANN JOACHIM QUANTZ: "How a Performer and a Piece of Music Ought to Be Judged" from *Source Readings in Music History*, compiled and edited by Oliver Strunk. Copyright 1950 by W. W. Norton & Company, Inc. Copyright renewed 1978 by Oliver Strunk. Reprinted by permission of W. W. Norton & Company, Inc.

SAMUEL SCHEIDT: Letters to Duke August of Brunswick and Heinrich Baryphonus from *Letters of Composers: An Anthology, 1603–1945*, edited by Gertrude Norman and Miriam Lubell Shrifte. New York: Alfred A. Knopf, 1946.

ARNOLD SCHÖNBERG: "New Music," "My Public," and "My Attitude toward Politics" from *Style and Idea: Selected Writings of Arnold Schoenberg*, edited by Leonard Stein and translated by Leo Black. London: Faber and Faber, 1975. Reprinted by permission of Faber and Faber Ltd. Letters to William S. Schlamm and Josef Rufer from *Letters of Arnold Schoenberg*, edited by Erwin Stein and translated by Eithne Wilkins and Ernst Kaiser. London: Faber and Faber, 1958. Reprinted by permission of Faber and Faber Ltd.

FRANZ SCHUBERT: Excerpts from *Franz Schubert's Letters and Other Writings*, edited by Otto Erich Deutsch and translated by Venetia Savile, with a foreword by Ernest Newman. New York: Alfred A. Knopf, 1928. Reprinted by permission of Alfred A. Knopf, Inc.

HEINRICH SCHÜTZ: Letter to Elector Johann Georg I of Saxony from *Letters of Composers: An Anthology, 1603–1945*, edited by Gertrude Norman and Miriam Lubell Shrifte. New York: Alfred A. Knopf, 1946. Dedication of *Symphoniae sacrae* II from *Source Readings in Music History*, compiled and edited by Oliver Strunk. Copyright 1950 by W. W. Norton & Company, Inc. Copyright renewed 1978 by Oliver Strunk. Reprinted by permission of W. W. Norton & Company, Inc.

ROBERT SCHUMANN: "Rage Over the Lost Penny," "Chopin's Piano Concertos," and "Schubert's Symphony in C" from *The Musical World of Robert Schumann: A Selection from His Own Writings*, translated, edited and annotated by Henry Pleasants. London: Victor Gollancz Ltd., 1965. Reprinted by permission of John Farquharson Ltd. Letter to Felix Mendelssohn Bartholdy from *The Letters of Robert Schumann*, edited by Karl Storck and translated by Hannah Bryant. London: John Murray, 1907. Letters to Friedrich Wieck and to Clara Wieck from *Early Letters of Robert Schumann*, translated and edited by May Herbert. London: George Bell & Sons, 1888.

LOUIS SPOHR: Excerpt from *Louis Spohr's Autobiography*. London, 1865.

KARL STAMITZ: Letter to King Friedrich Wilhelm II of Prussia from *Letters of Composers: An Anthology, 1603–1945*, edited by Gertrude Norman and Miriam Lubell Shrifte. New York: Alfred A. Knopf, 1946.

RICHARD STRAUSS: "Is There an Avant-Garde in Music?" and "On Inspiration in Music" from Richard Strauss, *Recollections and Reflections*, edited by Willi Schuh. Copyright 1949 Atlantis-Verlag, Zurich. English translation copyright 1953 by Boosey & Hawkes Ltd., London. Reprinted by permission. Letter to Hugo von Hofmannsthal from *Correspondence between Richard Strauss and Hugo von Hoffmannsthal*, translated by Paul England. London: Martin Secker & Warburg Ltd., 1927.

RICHARD WAGNER: "The Artist and the Public" and excerpts from "A Pilgrimage to Beethoven" from *Wagner Writes from Paris: Stories, Essays and Articles by the Young Composer*, edited and translated by Robert L. Jacobs and Geoffrey Skelton. London: George Allen & Unwin Ltd., 1973. Reprinted by permission of David Higham Associates Ltd. Excerpt from *The Diary of Richard Wagner, 1865–1882: The Brown Book*, edited by Joachim Bergfeld and translated by George Bird. New York: Cambridge University Press, 1980. Reprinted by permission. Letter to Friedrich Nietzsche from *The Nietzsche-Wagner Correspondence*, edited by Elizabeth Foerster-Nietzsche and translated by Caroline V. Kerr. Copyright 1921 by Bobi & Liveright, Inc. Copyright renewed 1949 by Liveright Publishing Corporation. Reprinted by permission of Liveright Publishing Corporation. Excerpt from "Opera and Drama" from *The Essence of Opera*, edited and translated by Ulrich Weisstein. Copyright © 1964 by The Free Press, a Division of Macmillan Publishing Co., Inc. Reprinted by permission of Macmillan Publishing Co., Inc. Letter to Karl Gaillard from *Letters of Richard Wagner, The Burrell Collection*, edited by John N. Burk. Copyright 1950, and renewed 1978, by Macmillan Publishing Co., Inc. Used by permission.

JOHANN WALTHER: Foreword to the Revised Edition of the *Wittenberg Hymnal* from *Source Readings in Music History*, compiled and edited by Oliver Strunk. Copyright 1950 by W. W. Norton & Company, Inc. Copyright renewed 1978 by Oliver Strunk. Reprinted by permission of W. W. Norton & Company, Inc.

CARL MARIA VON WEBER: "On the Opera *Undine* by E. T. A. Hoffmann" from *The Essence of Opera*, edited and translated by Ulrich Weisstein. Copyright © 1964 by The Free Press, a Division of Macmillan Publishing Co., Inc. Reprinted by permission of Macmillan Publishing Co., Inc. "Autobiography" and "Essay on Johann Sebastian Bach" from *Writings on Music*, edited by John Warrack and translated by Martin Cooper. New York: Cambridge University Press, 1981. Reprinted by permission.

ANTON WEBERN: "The Path to Twelve-Note Composition" from Anton Webern, *The Path to New Music*, edited by Willi Reich and translated by Leo Black. Bryn Mawr: Theodore Presser, 1963.

KURT WEILL: "Radio and the Restructuring of Musical Life" and "A Note on Jazz," translated for this volume by Michael Gilbert from Kurt Weill, *Ausgewählte Schrif-*

ten, edited by David Drew. Frankfurt/Main: Suhrkamp-Insel Verlag, 1975. Translated by permission of David Drew. "On the Composition of *The Three Penny Opera*" from *The Essence of Opera,* edited and translated by Ulrich Weisstein. Copyright © 1964 by The Free Press, a Division of Macmillan Publishing Co., Inc. Reprinted by permission of Macmillan Publishing Co., Inc.

HUGO WOLF: Excerpts from *The Music Criticism of Hugo Wolf,* edited and translated by Henry Pleasants. Copyright 1978 by Holmes and Meier Publishers, Inc., New York. Reprinted by permission of Holmes and Meier, Publishers.